Transforming Formative Assessment in Lifelong Learning

Transforming Formative Assessment in Lifelong Learning

Kathryn Ecclestone

with *Jennie Davies, Jay Derrick* and *Judith Gawn*

Open University Press

Open University Press
McGraw-Hill Education
McGraw-Hill House
Shoppenhangers Road
Maidenhead
Berkshire
England
SL6 2QL

email: enquiries@openup.co.uk
world wide web: www.openup.co.uk

and Two Penn Plaza, New York, NY 10121-2289, USA

First published 2010

A catalogue record of this book is available from the British Library

ISBN-13: 978-0-33-523654-1 (pb)   978-0-33-523655-8 (hb)
ISBN-10: 0-33-523654-5 (pb)   0-33-523655-3 (hb)

Library of Congress Cataloging-in-Publication Data
CIP data has been applied for

Typeset by Aptara® Inc., India
Printed in the UK by Bell and Bain Ltd, Glasgow

Mixed Sources
Product group from well-managed forests and other controlled sources
www.fsc.org Cert no. TT-COC-002769
© 1996 Forest Stewardship Council

The McGraw-Hill Companies

Contents

Acknowledgements

The book is authored by Kathryn Ecclestone, with Jennie Davies (University of Exeter), Jay Derrick (National Research and Development Centre for Adult Literacy, Language and Numeracy (NRDC) and Jude Gawn National Institute of Adult and Continuing Education (NIACE).

We are very grateful to Irena Andrews, Principal Lecturer in Post-Compulsory Education at the University of Brighton, and Carol Collins, Research Manager at the Learning and Skills Research Network for carrying out extensive fieldwork and working with us on interpreting the findings of the project.

The book owes a very great deal to the insights and enthusiasm of the project directors: John Vorhaus, deputy director at the NRDC during the research project, Maggie Greenwood, director of research at the Learning and Skills Research Network during the project, Jan Eldred, research director at NIACE during the project, and Joanna Swann, Reader in Education at the University of Brighton. We also benefited enormously from the constructive criticism and expertise of the project's Advisory Group (Harry Torrance, Ann Hodgson, Paul Black, Paul Newton, Gordon Stobart and Richard Daugherty, Alison Rowlands and Charlie Hendry).

Crucially, the book has depended on the enthusiasm, inputs and insights from the project's participating teachers, Debbie Watson at the University of Bristol who worked with us on the project in its first year, and the managers of all the institutions which took part in the project. We thank them wholeheartedly for their involvement.

Finally, the development of ideas and insights in the book would not have been possible without the collective expertise and wisdom of the Assessment Report Group (Paul Black, Jo-Ann Baird, Richard Daugherty, John Gardner, Wynne Harlen, Louise Hayward, Pail Newten, Gordon Stobert).

Introduction

The rise of rampant instrumentalism

> The students...said to me, 'We want it crystal clear. Pass criteria
> [*sic*], number P5, you need to do this, this and this. You've missed
> this, you haven't done that.' Crystal clear, short comment, each
> criteria, not a holistic comment. Because, they said, 'The holistic
> comment can be misinterpreted and what I'm thinking might not
> be what the criteria's asking me to do.' So they want it crystal clear.
> (David, lecturer, BTEC National Diploma in Public
> Services, Oldminster College)

Over the past twenty years or so, three significant shifts in assessment have
led to the Holy Grail of 'crystal clarity', a phenomenon now embedded
throughout the various sectors that comprise 'lifelong learning'. The first
is a move from using homogeneous assessment methods to test and confirm students' knowledge, skills and understanding, to a much wider range
of methods, and the idea of accumulating 'evidence of achievement'. The
second is to use assessment diagnostically and formatively, to identify students' starting points, goals, targets, interests and difficulties in learning,
and then to provide detailed feedback that helps students to recognize
their strengths and weaknesses, take an active role in their learning, and
motivate and engage them in assessment processes. The third shift is to
regard assessment methods as instruments in their own right, as the centre of attention and effort during the whole of a course. This emphasis has
increased significantly with the rise of interest in diagnostic and formative
assessment.

In some parts of the education system, most notably in vocational education, these changes have produced endemic instrumentalism, where instruments of assessment once used to confirm achievement or to diagnose
strengths and weaknesses in learning and provide feedback, have become
ends in themselves. We therefore use the notion of 'instrumentalism'
throughout the book to mean the dominance of assessment instruments
over the content, process and outcomes of education, and teachers' and
students' compliance with those instruments. Both a cause and effect of
instrumentalism has been an almost total merger between summative assignment specifications, teaching methods, and diagnostic and formative

assessment activities into one blurred 'pedagogy'. Oral and written feed-back that coaches students to improve their summative grades, with very detailed direction against each grade criterion, and a large proportion of class teaching time devoted to working on summative assignments, now characterize general vocational education courses. In adult literacy, lan-guage and numeracy (ALLN) programmes, the introduction of Skills for Life (SfL) national qualifications with summative multiple choice tests has also led to forms of close coaching, where repeated opportunities for students to pass the tests raise questions about their much-proclaimed validity in confirming more adults as literate and numerate.

In an earlier study of the impact of different assessment systems on achievements and attitudes to learning in post-compulsory education, the authors noted that traditional definitions of summative assessment as 'assessment *of* learning' and formative as 'assessment *for* learning' were pretty much irrelevant: instead, the merging of summative and formative assessment activities with teaching meant that much practice had become 'assessment *as* learning.'[1] While this undoubtedly increases levels of par-ticipation, retention and achievement, it raises important questions about the quality and content of that achievement, and therefore about its edu-cational value. Indeed, a new development since fieldwork for that study between 2003 and 2004, or perhaps one that was simply more noticeable in our project fieldwork between 2006 and 2008, is that participation in, and a positive attitude towards, formative and summative assessment pro-cesses have become an end in themselves, depicted as a 'life skill'. Teachers and students in our project regarded this as useful for future employment. For young people in programmes such as Entry to Employment (e2e), par-ticipation as a 'life skill' comprising appropriate dispositions and attitudes is used to change and manage behaviour through close personal mon-itoring and emotional support. In some contexts, most notably in e2e, *assessment as learning* has, in many ways, become a curriculum in its own right, with the self and its dispositions, attitudes and behaviours as the focus. The situation is different in adult literacy, language and numeracy programmes for reasons we explore later in the book.

The prognosis for assessment that is educationally worthwhile

This book is based on an extensive, three-year, in-depth study of the ways in which small teams of teachers in 12 vocational education courses (two in one school and the others across three further education colleges) and 18 Skills for Life programmes for adults in literacy, language and numer-acy introduced changes to their formative assessment practices, and then evaluated these changes with a team of researchers. The courses were based in three further education colleges and four adult and community learning centres run by local authorities in three very different locations, and the project involved 49 teachers and 58 students. Researchers worked with a small team from each course over a year, focusing their evaluation of formative assessment practices and their effects on teaching and learning through the perspectives of one teacher and two students. Teachers took part in three development days, three observation and post-observation interviews and detailed discussion of emerging findings, and completed a questionnaire. Students took part in three post-observation interviews and completed a questionnaire.[2] Six case studies are presented in Section Two, exploring the purposes and effects of teachers' strategies for formative assessment in GCSE Applied Business and Health and Social Care, Advanced Vocational Science, BTEC National Diploma in Public Services, Entry to Employment programmes, literacy, numeracy and English for Speakers of Other Languages.

This research illuminates what has happened to optimism among many qualification and course designers, teachers and researchers during the 1980s and into the early 1990s that outcome-based and competence-based assessment systems would transform teaching and learning, improve motivation and engagement, widen access to formal qualifications and raise achievement. Much was made of the idea that these forms of assessment would broaden the range of methods and 'evidence' that students can use to show their achievement, accredit prior learning and motivate and engage young people and adults alienated from, or unsuccessful in, traditional approaches. These goals are embedded in the official policy texts for assessment systems, in the inspection and professional development that supports them, and in teachers' own espoused theories about learning, teaching and assessment. As our case studies show, they have had very profound effects on beliefs about the purposes, processes and outcomes of education, and on teachers' and students' expectations of assessment.

In some ways, the picture of rampant instrumentalism presented in this book is very negative, confirming findings from the few earlier studies of formative assessment in post-compulsory education carried out in the late 1990s/early 2000s (see Chapter 1, for discussion). These showed how and why instrumentalism, and an accompanying narrowing of teaching and learning around tightly defined assessment targets, have grown over the past ten years.

Our case studies extend this earlier work to show the profound effects of intensification. This has changed teaching and assessment methods and eroded subject content, made the relationship between students and teachers increasingly conditional, and changed teachers' educational values and beliefs. Some of our examples indicate that teachers have surrendered some of their previous confidence about the purpose of their professional role and about teaching and assessment, to become more compliant, and to have lower expectations of students than they might once have had. Other cases show that a minority of teachers in our project were highly instrumental and while aware of tensions, largely accepted a target-driven ethos that dominated their practice.

However, three of our cases offer a more positive picture. They show that, in some contexts, instrumentalism can either be a springboard to deeper, more meaningful learning or can be resisted in quite robust and empowered ways. These cases illustrate what we regard as exemplary formative assessment, embedded into everyday teaching and underpinned by teachers' strong confidence and enthusiasm for their subject, clear beliefs about educational purposes, and positive rather than diminished images of students and their potential. One was in Advanced Vocational Science (Derek Armstrong at Moorview College, a community school) and two were in English for Speakers of Other Languages (Ruth Merchant and Allan Thompson at Westhampton College). Another case study of adult literacy and numeracy at Larkshire Adult and Community Education Centre, while demonstrating instrumentalism, shows the rich potential for something deeper and more educationally worthwhile.

Contrasting themes of instrumentalism, compliance and deeper educational goals enable us to draw out the ways in which political, institutional, social and educational factors can produce very different effects from the same method between courses and institutions. Implementation of a better, more 'effective' method should not, therefore, be the point of professional development. Instead, understanding the 'learning culture', and those features in it that teachers can influence, enables us to evaluate whether a method is educationally worthwhile or narrow and instrumental. Drawing on earlier work in further education,[3] the concept of 'learning culture' enables us to show how the progressive rhetoric of formative assessment can become distorted to little more than coaching to the summative targets, while, in other contexts, the same assessment is embedded in everyday teaching activities in a sound and positive way. Understanding why these differences occur offers a strong basis for challenging the worst excesses of instrumentalism and for enabling teachers to identify which factors they can and cannot influence in order to transform their formative assessment for the better.

Resisting instrumentalism

Doing their presentations, the students ask 'Is it part of the assessment criteria?' I say, 'Well, no, but it is good for you because it's good that you can actually stand up there and it's good for your team work because you actually plan and develop and the more you do it the better you'll get.' 'Oh no, but it's not part of the criteria, so *why* do we have to do it? Does that mean we can be rubbish at it?'

(Neil, BTEC National Diploma lecturer, Oldminster College, his emphasis)

There's no point in jumping through hoops for the sake of jumping through hoops and there's no point in getting grades for the sake of getting grades. I know that's not the answer, the answer is . . . 'we should be getting them to get grades'. But that's never as I've seen it and it never will be.

(Derek Armstrong, teacher Advanced Vocational Science, Moorview Community College)

The quote about transparency that begins this Introduction, and Neil's quote above, reflect widespread acceptance of a demand that teachers must respond to what students expect from formative and summative assessment. In contrast, Derek's strong beliefs and confidence about his role as a teacher and assessor were unique among our project sample: we discuss them and their effect on his students in Section Two. We use it here to signal that we take a strongly normative position on what we regard as good formative assessment practice. By 'normative', we mean that we make our educational values and beliefs explicit as part of depictions throughout the book of what we believe comprises 'good' or 'effective' practice.

A decision to place a normative view at the heart of this book was highly contested in our project team, where there were very different perspectives about how far instrumentalism was 'realistic' given the 'types' of students and conditions that prevail in colleges and in adult education. There was also scepticism about making explicit the contrast between what we and some of our teachers saw as 'good' and 'poor' practice. For a while, the project team adopted the term 'sustainable' learning as a contrast to 'instrumental' or 'superficial' learning in order to avoid value judgements about 'educationally worthwhile' content and practice. Dissemination of our research findings to audiences of teachers, staff developers and researchers, together with our own uses of findings to inform teaching on teacher education and professional development courses, show that an underlying unwillingness to make educational value judgements is widespread.

Despite general reluctance to cast instrumentalism as 'poor educational practice' or to contrast it with notions such as 'deep' or 'meaningful' learning, this book presents instrumentalism as highly problematic, unless it is a conscious springboard to something better. By 'better', we mean educationally worthwhile and genuinely engaging rather than compliant, and, crucially, rooted in acquiring subject knowledge and related practical skills. As we show in the book, this goal can no longer be taken for granted in vocational and adult education.

Adopting a normative view at the outset should not suggest that we overlook the huge pressures on teachers and students that shape practice in particular ways, some of which they can influence and some of which they cannot. Nor are we unsympathetic to the daunting pressures that many teachers in FE colleges now experience and the challenges that some of their students present. Indeed, we take an equally normative stance to criticize oppressive conditions of service, including cuts in course hours and overloaded, unrealistic and prescriptive assessment systems. We also criticize the way in which definitions of formative assessment come directly from highly misleading policy guidance and far too brief (and sometimes plain wrong) advice on initial teacher education and professional development courses.

In a context of target-led institutional and funding regimes, it is not surprising that most of our teachers equated formative assessment, summative targets and teaching with feedback for improving achievement, often in very mechanistic ways. None of this is surprising when professional autonomy and confidence to influence curriculum content and purpose and then to design teaching and assessment activities around them have been almost completely erased by officially specified, prescriptive and increasingly homogenized assessment requirements. These findings, if not our interpretations of their implications, concur with those in other recent studies of teaching, learning and assessment in further and adult education.[4]

Reasserting the subject

Our project revealed another powerful factor that exacerbates instrumentalism but which, with the exception of the Nuffield Review of 14–19 Education, has not been discussed in other recent studies of teaching and policy in lifelong learning. The meaning of 'vocational' has become extremely diluted through an ever-expanding range of broader social purposes for vocational education courses. Unless teachers have a very strong sense of, and enthusiasm for, a recognized vocational subject with a clear body of knowledge and related practical skills, prescriptive assessment criteria and punitive targets for participation, retention and achievement make teaching to assignment tasks based on the summative assessment criteria entirely rational. As we show in some of our case studies, assessment itself has become a life-related, employment-related goal, running the risk of eroding subject knowledge, concepts and cognitive skills even further.

In contrast, and despite similar pressures for target-driven assessment in Skills for Life programmes, two important factors can counter these pressures. First, literacy, numeracy and language have a recognizable subject-base that teachers need to acquire in order to teach them well, and, second, many adult education teachers, despite being part-time and often untrained, appear to be less beleaguered than their vocational education colleagues and to retain strong expectations of their students' potential for achievement and motivation. The latter characteristic is far from the case in vocational education.

Finally, reasserting the subject as an educational goal and resisting in strumentalism and low expectations, require attention to the nature and content of professional development. Our project showed that focused professional development needs to be based on identifying problems that teachers themselves highlight as meaningful, where they can design and implement their own approach or method and then evaluate it with experienced researchers. In the case of formative assessment, this creates an educational and motivating process where teachers learn for themselves what formative assessment is and is not and evaluate why their practice takes a particular form.

We cannot make strong claims about the lasting effects of the project on participants' understanding and practice because we have not been able to follow up our work with them. Nevertheless, the problem-based approach we adopted in the project does seem to be both cost-effective, engaging and genuinely developmental. In our discussion of it in the final chapter, we recommend that it be used more widely.

Our research questions

The chapters that follow address these research questions:

- Which factors in the broader political and social context of change to assessment systems and practices in vocational education and adult literacy, language and numeracy programmes lead teachers to change and justify their formative assessment practices in particular ways, and to judge them as 'good' or 'effective'?
- Why do ostensibly similar assessment practices have different effects in different 'learning cultures' of further and adult education courses?

- What forms of motivation and autonomy are evident as outcomes from the formative assessment strategies that our teachers adopted in the project?
- When does formative assessment lead to instrumental compliance and when does it lead to learning that we might regard as educationally worthwhile, and what factors make it likely to be one or the other?
- When are teachers' formative assessment practices a springboard for educationally worthwhile learning, and when do they act as a straitjacket on the purposes and content of learning?
- What advice can we offer about ways in which teachers in different contexts might improve their formative assessment?
- How can teachers and those responsible for teacher education and continuing professional development improve formative assessment?

Using this book

The book is divided into three sections. The first section comprises three chapters that set the scene for analysis of assessment practices in the six case studies of Section Two. Chapter 1 explores the changing face of assessment in vocational education and adult literacy, language and numeracy over the past 30 years, and highlights the significance of changes in goals, expectations of students and teaching and assessment methods. Chapter 2 aims to clarify what formative assessment is, and, crucially in the light of widespread misunderstandings, what it is not. The third chapter outlines our use of the concept of 'learning culture' and aims to show its potential usefulness in understanding why ostensibly similar assessment practices can take such different forms in different contexts.

In Section Two, we present six case studies, four from vocational education, two from adult literacy, language and numeracy. Each is chosen to reflect a particular trend or characteristic of formative assessment and to show how and why it takes the form it does in a particular 'learning culture'.

In the first of two chapters in Section Three, we draw out implications of our findings for changing teachers' assessment practices in lifelong learning. In the final chapter, we highlight drawbacks to how particular formative assessment approaches are used, focusing on tutorials and reviews of progress, questioning and feedback, and self- and peer assessment. We also evaluate how more nuanced understandings of students' motivation and autonomy can challenge low expectations of what students will and will not put up with, before evaluating the prognosis for transforming formative assessment in lifelong learning.

Our selection and interpretations of data

Any in-depth project generates volumes of fascinating data and far more than a book can accommodate! We have therefore selected case studies to explore specific examples of formative assessment which enable us to develop a line of argument and to draw out implications for improving practice. This means we have left out at least three other case studies. Even within the ones we have included, we have had to omit data that illuminate our arguments further. To add insult to the injury of leaving out valuable and important data, we have also judged and interpreted our data in ways that not all our participating teachers would agree with. We are also aware that we have interpreted data from observations, group and individual interviews and questionnaires which can only be a snapshot in time.

Despite these caveats, we reiterate here, as we do in each case study, that pressures in different learning cultures can affect values, beliefs and practices in different ways. We have tested out our emerging findings and, in some cases, the final drafts of each case study, with some of our participating teachers and with other audiences over the past two years through conferences, seminars and professional development sessions. We therefore believe that our interpretations resonate strongly with the day-to-day reality of many teachers in vocational and adult education.

Terminology

A word on our use of terms for the various sectors and courses that comprise what we have called in the title of this book 'lifelong learning'. Although the term 'further education' has disappeared from policy, to be replaced with the 'learning and skills sector', we use 'further education colleges' to describe some of the sites because that is how they are still known, and 'adult and community education centres' for others because, again, that is how they are known!

While the term 'lifelong learning' is familiar as a marketing tool for publishers trying to appeal to as wide an audience as possible, we are aware that two of our case studies include 14–16-year-olds doing Applied GCSE courses and so, technically, are part of compulsory education. Teachers in this part of the system tend not to regard themselves as part of 'lifelong learning'. More specifically, we focus on, and refer to, 'general vocational education' and 'adult literacy, language and numeracy' since these are the subject of our research.

We also use 'teachers', 'tutors' and 'lecturers', depending on how our participants described themselves and to reflect broader understandings in different parts of the vocational and adult education systems. However,

although we have used 'students', 'participants' and 'learners' inter-
changeably in places, we have tended to prefer 'students' even though
the term currently in vogue everywhere is 'learners'! We come back to our
reasons for this in discussion of 'learning' in the final section of the book.

Notes

1. Torrance et al. (2005). This and other studies referred to in the Introduction are discussed in Chapter 1.
2. For a summary of the project, see Chapter 11.
3. James and Biesta (2007), discussed in Chapter 2.
4. See James and Biesta (2007); Coffield et al. (2008); Ivanic et al. (2009);
   Journal of Vocational Education and Training 2004, discussed in Chapter 1.

Section 1

Formative assessment in lifelong learning

1 All change: pedagogy and assessment in lifelong learning

Introduction

Political influence over post-school curriculum content, teaching methods and assessment during the past 30 years has been effected through the growing prescription and regulation of assessment systems in work-based training, general vocational education 14–16 and 16–19, language, literacy and numeracy programmes, Access to Higher Education courses, and Foundation degrees in further education colleges. Assessment and associated accountability measures have intensified managerialism, performativity and the regulation of qualifications and teaching practices through inspection, awarding body quality assurance and funding targets. These have had profound effects on professional autonomy and teachers' sense of professionalism and on teaching and assessment practices.[1]

Despite the huge importance of assessment systems in driving change in the different sectors that comprise the 'lifelong learning' system, research has had relatively little to say about the impact of formative and summative assessment on teaching in these areas.[2] More importantly, in the light of our concerns about instrumentalism, outlined in the Introduction to this book, research has had even less to say about what assessment systems have done to the fundamental goals and content of further and adult education. More specifically, there has been no analysis of what happened to the profound and heartfelt enthusiasm of the 1980s and 1990s that major changes to formal, summative assessment and certification would transform participation, motivation and achievement, and thereby democratize education and training.[3] Understanding the impact of these goals and subsequent political regulation on teaching methods, curriculum content and underlying educational goals and purposes is crucial for challenging a now-endemic tendency to teach to the assessment criteria.

Locating contemporary assessment practices in a recent historical and political context is essential, not least because developments across vocational and adult education are so complicated, and have changed so often over the past 30 years, that attempts to unravel them are not for the faint-hearted. We take 1976 as our starting point, because of its highly symbolic beginning with the Ruskin College speech by the-then Labour

Government's Prime Minister, James Callaghan. This was a watershed in the history of both compulsory and post-compulsory education, marking the beginning of a huge political shift in both intention and attitudes towards organizing the education system as a whole. More significantly perhaps, it sparked powerful changes in ideas about the purpose of education. It began the inexorable rise of employers' influence on the goals, processes and outcomes of general education, vocational preparation and work-based training, and justified the beginning of 30 years of political regulation of content and practice.

This chapter summarizes some implications for content, pedagogy and assessment methods arising from key historical shifts around these themes, between 1976 and 2009, focusing on language, literacy and numeracy programmes targeted specifically at adults (ALLN), and for general vocational education qualifications taken by young people at school or further education college between the ages of 14–16 (Level 2 qualifications) and 16–19 (Level 3). While there are strong similarities and some overlaps in developments in both areas, the history of each also shows important differences: these affect, for example, teachers' conditions of service and experiences of professional development, and their perceptions about room for manoeuvre within prescriptive assessment systems.

In the first section, we outline the rise of political intervention and its professed goals of making assessment systems both more transparent and more relevant across the two areas covered by this book. In the second section, we show how the introduction of Skills for Life affected traditions of adult education, and how the drive for 'parity of esteem' affected the goals of vocational education. In the third section, we focus on two highly influential texts, one published in 1979, the other in 1991, and their impact on ideas about progressive pedagogy and assessment and appropriate subject content. In the fourth section, we evaluate how the growing dominance of regulated summative assessment systems has led to particular methods and approaches. Finally, in the fifth section, we explore how changes to assessment, subject content and teaching have accompanied, and been fuelled by, changes in images of 'typical' students and the view that they need particular forms of 'support'.

1. Democratic transparency and relevance

The rise and rise of political intervention

Following the Ruskin speech, policy-makers began to take a much closer interest in curriculum content, teaching and assessment methods in schools and further education colleges. Between 1976 and 1989, the first wave of mass unemployment, first among young people leaving school with no qualifications, and later among skilled and unskilled adults, began with the oil crisis of 1973. Responses to unemployment changed irrevocably the purpose, methods and content of post-compulsory education and training. As our case studies in Section Two show, these changes now extend to provision for vocational education in schools.

During this period, the Manpower Services Commission (MSC), a powerful and influential agency of the then-Department of Employment, expanded its training provision for the unemployed on a large scale, overlapping and competing with mainstream educational provision.[4]

From 1978, programmes for the unemployed run by the generously-funded MSC expanded significantly, encompassing training for school leavers and adults. It also, through the Technical Vocational Education Initiative (TVEI) introduced in 1984, had a very strong influence on 14–19 education in schools and colleges. Building upon Mode 3 Certificates of Secondary Education, introduced to motivate young people who had to stay on in formal education after the raising of the school-leaving age in 1972, the TVEI and its parallel, the Certificate of Pre-Vocational Education (CPVE), introduced by the then-Department for Education and Science in 1985, encouraged schools and colleges to develop more active, pupil/student-centred teaching methods and more variety in assessment methods.

As we show in more detail below in this chapter, two highly influential texts have shaped assumptions about students' attitudes and dispositions, and about desirable forms of teaching and assessment methods for particular 'types' of student. The first, published in 1979 by a curriculum development organization, the Further Education Unit, *A Basis for Choice* (ABC), changed the face of pre-vocational and general vocational education courses. The second, published in 1991, *Outcomes: NVQs, GNVQs and the Future of Education* was written by the then-head of National Council for Vocational Qualifications, formed in 1989. In very different ways, both presented outcome-/competence-based assessment as profoundly democratic, thereby changing the format, methods and purposes of assessment, first in work-based training through the competence-based regime of National Vocational Qualifications (NVQs), introduced in 1989, and in general vocational education through General National Vocational Qualifications (GNVQs), introduced in 1991. The former was almost universally regarded as progressive, the latter was lauded and lambasted in equal measure.[5]

Taken together, both texts fundamentally changed the goals, processes and outcomes of vocational education, adult education and work-based training. As we show below, they were also introduced for certain 'types' of students and were seen as radical and controversial alternatives to existing modes of teaching and assessment. They also embedded certain claims and beliefs about appropriate pedagogy into courses for all students in schools and colleges, particularly for those deemed to be 'disaffected' or 'disengaged'.

In adult education, programmes funded by the MSC were a testing ground for later policies which focused public funding ever more narrowly on adult education for employment. A centrally-controlled curriculum framework, supported by quantitative performance measurement systems, eroded the part played by local authorities as democratic bodies. Although a key element of many of the MSC's programmes was adult basic education, there was much greater emphasis on narrow employment outcomes and a radically different approach to pedagogy and curriculum. This was based on the traditions of industrial training rather than the liberal humanist ideas or a commitment to social justice which had characterized adult education before these developments.

Another effect of a greater focus on employment outcomes was growing interest in the development of qualifications for literacy and numeracy, which, apart from GCSEs in English and Mathematics, were almost non-existent. Initially, the lead on designing appropriate qualifications was taken by the Open College network, which pioneered and widely tested a system in which students and teachers used 'off-the-shelf', peer-designed, peer-approved learning outcomes accumulated into recognized qualifications at levels below GCSE English and Mathematics. The role of teachers in designing and quality assuring these qualifications was paramount. In most programmes during this period, however, working towards these or other qualifications was, at most, an option, and almost never a requirement.

During this period, work also began on rationalizing vocational qualifications into one national framework. This project involved agreement across all vocational sectors of a set of 'standards' for each level of the new framework which were broadly equivalent, and the consequent streamlining of thousands of vocational qualifications by the relevant sector bodies. The aim was to make the whole vocational training system more flexible and accessible in an increasingly complex, continually changing world of work. It can now be seen as a key element of a key innovation in the next period of policy, a national funding system. The emerging qualifications for ALLN learning were designed to fit comfortably within the developing national framework for vocational training as a whole.

2. The rise of standardization and regulation

Statutory provision of ALLN

With the introduction of Skills for Life in 1999, ALNN gained statutory status for the first time in the history of adult education. Provision leading to qualifications that were part of the national framework was guaranteed to be funded, and this enabled providers to take a longer-term strategic approach to provision. This opened the door to increased professionalization of the teaching workforce through increased numbers of permanent teaching posts across the sector. Some colleges converted part-time contracts into permanent employment for some staff. However, at the same time, unit funding was forced down: although the number of participants increased dramatically, funding increased only slightly. In general, all teachers had to become much more 'productive' than hitherto, measured in terms of students enrolled, retained on programmes, and achieving qualifications.

Over the period encompassed by our summary, changing political views about the aims and purposes of ALLN, about the best way to organize programmes about appropriate curricula, quality assurance and quality control, and indeed, the role of policy itself, have interacted with the views of practitioners and researchers, with influence flowing in both directions between each. There has been a huge shift from policy playing a very minor role from the 1970s through to the late 1990s, to the current situation where policy-makers play a much more dominant role. As Hamilton and Hillier (2006) point out, the statutory status of ALLN made it a discernible and discrete area of vocational study within further education. While it was free for all participants, its funding regime required progression, summative assessment and accountability. It was therefore no longer primarily open-ended and community-focused.[6]

Predictably perhaps, provision that did not fit the funding methodology rapidly became much less secure. Along with other programmes outside the specific part of the national framework known as 'non-Schedule 2 provision', most of which was formally designated by default as 'non-vocational' or 'leisure', ALLN's continued existence depended on the decisions of ever-more cash-strapped local authorities and voluntary organizations, or on managers' success in chasing short-term development funding.

The profile of the ALLN provider institutions during this period was complex and changing too. Depending on the decisions of individual local authorities and newly-incorporated colleges, some ALLN teachers and managers were transferred to further education colleges, others were retained as local authority staff, and in other cases, colleges carried out both Schedule 2 and 'non-Schedule 2' ALLN provision under contract from the local authority. In some places, these arrangements were changed repeatedly in response to changed political and financial circumstances.

However, whichever provider or partnership led ALLN in a particular area, this phase saw immense pressure for all institutions on funding. This created bigger classes, consolidated programmes in multiple community-based sites into large, centralized sites relatively remote from the communities they served, and encouraged the sale or re-allocation of buildings that had been used for community-based adult education including ALLN. It has also led to the gradual disappearance in many areas of generalist community education workers who had previously helped set up and promote new provision tailored to community needs.

For ALLN teachers during this phase of political intervention, changes were felt in contradictory ways. On the one hand, ALLN work within Schedule 2 gained statutory status, allowing providers and funding agencies to invest in it. This led to increasing professionalization of what had, until this time, been a highly diverse, often voluntary area of work, characterized by relatively untrained staff on temporary and part-time contracts of employment. On the other hand, a field which had been politically marginal and poorly funded but in which teachers, for better or worse, were almost completely autonomous, was now a key part of a newly-standardized, co-ordinated and, above all, regulated sector. In this new world, corporate strategic and financial considerations about the provision of ALLN took precedence over the professional judgements of teachers and curriculum managers.

The search for 'parity of esteem' in vocational education

The UK's general vocational education system has evolved after 30 years of repeated attempts to create a coherent, high status alternative to general academic education into a clear pathway. This runs alongside general academic education, workplace training, and vocational education and training courses that prepare people for different roles within a broad occupational area. General vocational education is now (since 2008) an option for young people at age 14 before leaving compulsory education, or after compulsory schooling at age 16 as an alternative to general academic education or a work-based apprenticeship.

The general vocational education pathway, seen in our project through Advanced Vocational Certificates of Vocational Education (AVCEs) and Applied General Certificates of Secondary Education (GCSEs), is now found in Diplomas introduced in 2009.[23] Its roots are in earlier programmes for *pre*-vocational education, such as the CPVE mentioned above. The pathway enables young people deemed to be unsuitable or unwilling to do general education based on traditional subject disciplines to explore very broadly defined areas such as Leisure and Tourism, Health and Social Care, or Business Studies. At the ages of 16 and 18, a general vocational education qualification enables young people to progress to more focused vocational education and training courses in post-compulsory education, such as further education colleges and universities that prepare them for occupational roles in a clearly defined area, such as Media and Performing Arts, Catering, Nursery Nursing and Engineering (among others).

The introduction of Diplomas in 2009 was the latest of repeated attempts to persuade all young people to consider vocational education alongside general 'academic' education. Yet, despite dropping the term 'vocational' from 'Diploma', and despite attempts to make the assessment regime of general vocational qualifications as rigorous as academic ones are perceived to be, choices remain stubbornly segregated.[7] Confusion created by 30 years of reform and changes to the vocational routes available, and to their assessment systems and methods have not created stable assessment systems for vocational education that are well understood by teachers, students, parents, admissions tutors in universities and employers.

The situation is different in other Western European countries. While parity of esteem between 'general/academic' and 'vocational' education is an unresolved problem in many if not all countries, good levels of resourcing, including highly qualified teachers, together with stability and continuity in policy, have enabled countries like Finland to have clearly differentiated, well-respected pathways for vocational education and training courses run in partnerships between vocational colleges and local workplaces. Many countries have managed to create a coherent, long-standing vocational education and training pathway that prepares young people for occupational roles at different levels, from leaving compulsory schooling at 16, to workplace apprenticeships and/or to higher level qualifications in polytechnics.

In Britain, repeated attempts to define outcomes, standards and curriculum content for vocational education, to create parity and to create a unified system, have been dogged by the need to open up opportunities for young people to participate in education they will find engaging and useful, which will enable them to progress to workplace learning or further and higher education and to show credible 'standards' of achievement in comparison to academic courses. Assessment in vocational education is therefore more complex in both its roots and contemporary characteristics than in workplace training or general education, or ALNN.[8]

Changing employment patterns, the decline of unskilled jobs (or home populations unwilling to do them), social change where growing numbers of young people are disaffected from compulsory schooling, and political instability over assessment systems have led to competing aims:

- motivating learners who would otherwise not stay on in post-compulsory education or who are disaffected at school, by responding to, and rewarding, learners' expressed interests and notions of relevance;

- expanding routes into higher education while also making sure that expansion does not lead to over-subscription for limited places;
- preparing students for progression into work and job-related training and assessment;
- encouraging young people to carry on gaining qualifications;
- convincing young people, parents, teachers, admissions tutors and employers that vocational education has parity of esteem with academic qualifications;
- ameliorating poor levels of achievement in numeracy and literacy through 'key/basic/functional skills';
- satisfying demands from different constituencies, such as employers, subject and professional associations, etc., to include 'essential' content and skills;
- having credibility in compulsory schooling where there is less vocational expertise among teachers than there is in further education colleges.

3. Changing the subject of vocational and adult education

A Basis for Choice

Amidst the many reports and initiatives that have come and gone in further education over the past 30 years, a number of researchers have analysed the impact of a report by the then-Further Education Unit, *A Basis for Choice*, published in 1979.[9] This report, regarded favourably as radical and progressive by many teachers, researchers and qualification designers at the time, challenged 'traditional' forms of teaching and assessment. These were seen as not only old-fashioned but also elitist, excluding and irrelevant for the vast numbers of young people displaced by mass unemployment into colleges and government-run employment schemes from the late 1970s onwards.

The important point here in understanding profound changes to pedagogy and assessment for what we call the 'learning cultures'[10] of further education generally, and of vocational education, pre-vocational courses like e2e and ALLN programmes in particular, is that *A Basis for Choice* proselytized notions of 'student-centred learning', 'ownership of learning', 'experiential' and 'practical' learning realized through democratic and informal relationships between teachers and students. More 'personalized' ways of working were based on collaborative, negotiated projects with opportunities to collect diverse evidence of outcomes and achievement.

A Basis for Choice also paved the way for a growing array of personal, social and work-related dispositions, attitudes and behaviours to be characterized as 'skills', characterizing these as 'learning outcomes' that had to be assessed. This opened up young people's own perceptions of their attributes and behaviours to diagnostic, formative and summative assessment, and to teaching activities.

Another enduring influence of *A Basis for Choice* was its call to move away from 'general and liberal studies' which had been part of FE courses during the 1970s, offering day-release and full-time vocational students access to topics such as law, politics, sports, film and arts studies. The first erosion of this educational goal was to recast liberal studies first as 'communication studies' in the mid-1980s, and then to focus on 'transferable skills' and dispositions, attributes and behaviours.

This shift was paralleled and reinforced by the growth of programmes in 'life and social skills' in the unemployment schemes introduced by the MSC in 1978, and discussed above. These moved the self and its attitudes to learning, work and relationships to the heart of teaching and assessment, encouraging the idea of training people to develop the dispositions and attitudes deemed to comprise social and work-related personal skills. Taken together, *A Basis for Choice* and these programmes initiated a long series of attempts to define personal, functional and social skills and to assess them formatively and summatively through records of achievement, introduced in 1985, and portfolios.

Not only did these developments erode a particular meaning of general education, they also began to undermine the core goal of acquiring a body of vocational knowledge and skills. Instead, the study of certain topics became instruments or vehicles to assess and develop broader personal 'skills'. In the CPVE, for example, introduced in 1985 and a precursor to General National Vocational Qualifications, introduced in 1991, assignments on vocational topics were designed to develop and assess self-awareness, team working and reflecting on one's learning. These attributes were as important as knowledge about the topic. In AVCE and applied GCSEs, discussed in Section Two of this book, grading criteria encompass these skills as well as those of understanding and using knowledge.

Competence-based assessment

The second major influence on pedagogy and assessment across further and adult education, and also in parts of higher education, was the introduction in 1989 of competence-based qualifications in the workplace, and the parallel introduction of outcome-based assessment throughout adult education and in general vocational education through the introduction of GNVQs two years later.

In the influential text *Outcomes*, published in 1991, Gilbert Jessup, the architect of NVQs, outlined the rationale for deriving 'standards' of competence from authentic analysis of work roles and other activities. This contrasted older, norm-referenced notions of standards with claims that improving the 'standards' of occupational performance or competence comes from adhering to well-defined specifications. More valid, authentic measures of performance and 'coverage' or 'mastery' of performance can be specified in the criteria. 'Ownership' of the criteria and formative assessment, feedback, setting and reviewing targets based upon them not only enable more students to reach the required standard but are seen also to be inherently democratic, inclusive and motivating processes in their own right.

Promotion of competence-based standards laid down a gauntlet to old beliefs that any cohort contains a limited pool of innate ability that can be measured reliably as the basis for selection through competitive examinations and norm-referenced grading. The idea that failure is an inevitable adjunct to success is removed by offering a more transparent basis for teaching and assessment. Competence-based systems are therefore seen as more democratic, accessible and relevant, both to the individual's own sense of self and to real-world activities. A particular focus for Jessup's challenge was the 'elitist', 'irrelevant' and time-consuming place of theory and knowledge in vocational training courses.

Strong counter-arguments to this attack on the place of knowledge, and the introduction of competence-based assessment did not prevent a radical shift in the balance of power from educational institutions and awarding and professional bodies, to groups of representatives from different occupational sectors who defined standards of competence.[11] The ideas behind competence-based assessment were taken up enthusiastically in parts of adult education and used also to change assessment systems for adults progressing to higher education.[12]

Of course, strong forms of norm-referencing still operate in contexts where assessment must select people for licences in professional practice or where it has to restrict access to certain jobs and over-subscribed parts of higher education. Outside these areas, the expansion of work-based assessment and general vocational education has moved all assessment systems, including academic ones at all levels of the system towards a hybrid model, with varying degrees of strong or weak criterion-referencing.

In general vocational education and adult education, the aims and technical features of competence-based assessment can be seen in the following characteristics:

- competences and outcomes can and should be defined in detail to encourage higher achievement by enabling better formative assessment, 'transparency' of assessment demands for students, shared understanding of the criteria and standardization of assessment decisions;

- strong emphasis on teacher and workplace assessment and locally-designed assessments against pre-defined outcomes, with a focus on initial diagnostic assessment, individual target-setting based on the criteria, recording achievement and portfolio-building;

- external assessment and moderation by an external authority such as an awarding body, or other national/state agency, and standardization of grading which combines criterion-referencing and loose notions of rank-ordering;

- overt presentation of the contrast between the demotivation of assessment that compares students with each other, and an upbeat focus on achievement and opportunities to succeed.

4. The dominance of summative assessment, 1998–2009

Skills for Life (SfL)

The third period of policy intervention saw fundamental institutional and organizational change. ALNN was incorporated into a standardized, quality-assured, and regulated sector, known as 'further education' until 2001 and then re-designated the 'Learning and Skills sector' in 2007. This encompassed all government-funded post-school education outside higher education. A key difference from earlier periods was that policy intervention extended to the ALLN classroom.

Skills for Life (SfL) has provided well-produced, and, in some contexts, badly-needed, resources for teachers, and a more coherent, consistent model of their work. The SfL policy has also brought adult literacy, numeracy and language teaching more closely into line with other parts of the national system of funding, quality assurance, and accountability put in place for all parts of the post-school education and training system outside higher education during the 1990s. This enables the policy to be more easily managed by provider organizations, whether they are large general purpose colleges of further education, voluntary community-based organizations, or commercial work-based training companies.

ALLN provision, now tightly-packaged into SfL qualifications, fits smoothly into this system. Intervention over the past 30 years has led to the enforcement of more consistent practice towards controlled outcomes. It also enables a wholly quantitative approach to performance measurement, through comparison of 'success rates' at regional, institutional, departmental, and individual teacher levels.

The national tests play a central role in SfL. They are used to accredit participants in ALNN, as a key tool for performance measurement of both provision and teachers, to determine significant amounts of 'achievement funding' for each qualification gained, and finally as the key currency for measuring progress toward the national targets. The tests (practice examples are available at http://www.edexcel.org.uk/sfc/onscreen/alan-test/) are available at two levels, the higher of which is notionally equivalent in level of difficulty, though not in breadth of content, to the GCSE in English Language or in Mathematics. At each level and subject, the tests consist of a timed series of 40 multiple choice questions. One hour is allowed to complete the literacy tests, and one and a quarter hours for the numeracy tests. The tests can be taken on paper or online and are marked using a computer. The questions come from a specially developed question bank and are intended to cover the full range of national standards.

The qualifications and standards required for ALLN teachers have been systematized and significantly raised as part of the Skills for Life initiative, with teachers now having to achieve degree-level qualifications in both generic teaching and subject specific domains.

The Skills for Life initiative also developed the research base for Adult Literacy, Numeracy and ESOL. It sponsored a national survey of literacy, numeracy and language skills and led to the establishment of the National Research and Development Centre for adult literacy and numeracy (NRDC) in 2003.[13]

Vocational education: a hybrid assessment model

In schools and further education colleges, educational and social purposes of assessment have broadened significantly to encourage wider access and participation and to motivate and engage those disaffected from schooling and traditional academic assessment methods. A corresponding impetus is to recognize and certificate a much broader range of life and personal skills than in the past, and to engage people actively with the processes of learning and assessment. A key goal here is to encourage the attitudes, dispositions and habits of 'lifelong learning'.[14]

Such goals have shifted the strong norm-referenced systems developed in the 1950s to select people for limited, or rationed places in education, work and training, to strong and weak forms of criterion-referencing. In theory, criterion-referenced systems can measure a wider range of real-life skills and attributes while enabling people to get the grade they deserve, providing they meet the publicly-defined criteria. As we showed above in our summary of claims made for competence-based assessment, these aims dominated developments during the 1980s and 1990s of competence-based, workplace qualifications.

In the Advanced Vocational Certificates of Education and Applied GCSEs of our case studies, methods of assessment combined approaches used in academic education, practical subjects, and workplace training, based broadly on three types of assessment tasks:

- summative 'tests' such as an end of unit/module multiple choice test on 'underpinning theory or knowledge' or a written examination paper requiring short answers;
- compilation of a portfolio of evidence that enables students to accumulate different pieces of work in order to show competence or achievement against a set of pre-defined outcomes (depending on the course, subject area and local opportunities, these might include testimonials from work experience, evidence of tasks carried out during work experience, photographs, audio and film recordings and written work);
- coursework summative assessment based on discrete modules or units, where students complete group and/or individual projects or 'assignments' that have practical and written elements and come in a variety of sizes in terms of credit value. For example, students on a health and social care course might plan and run a 'health awareness day' for fellow students or for a school that involves research into different topics, presentations through posters, talks and written work, interviews with local health practitioners and a written evaluation of how well they did in the project, and of the personal and social skills they gained.

Some assignments are locally-devised and teacher-assessed, providing they work to the specifications of outcomes and criteria. Others are set by national awarding or bodies, marked by teachers locally and standardized or moderated regionally or nationally. Grading criteria and detailed descriptors of achievement within grade bands are based on skills in 'learning to learn', teamwork, self-assessment and communication as well as on evidence of subject understanding. A final summative qualification mark is usually derived from a grade point average from the modules completed during the course, with some weighting given to a final project.

Earlier developments such as CPVE and GNVQs had goals for imaginative, personalized and flexible assessment tasks. In the GCSEs and AVCE explored in our case studies, the move towards written, standardized formats that are amenable to moderation and standardization is very evident. In AVCE Science, the teacher, Derek Armstrong, refers to the tedium and impoverishment of having to assess what he calls 'assignment clones'.

5. Changing images of adults and young people

Second chances

Changes to assessment systems and the various aims that have justified them also reflect, and are fuelled by, particular images of students and their 'typical' dispositions, 'needs' and 'barriers to learning'. These reflect subtle but significant changes in expectations over the past 30 years.

Some teachers in our case studies, as well as some of the students, viewed young people and adults on their courses as 'second chance learners'. In part, this reflects a long-standing and very positive ethos in further and adult education. Yet, while maintaining this ethos, *A Basis for Choice*, discussed above, also offered new images of 'types' of young people coming into FE in the late 1970s. Although well-meaning and perhaps often realistic, *A Basis for Choice* presented young people displaced by unemployment as 'reluctant' and 'non-traditional' students; they were not in colleges to follow day-release craft qualifications from work, to repeat failed examinations at the end of secondary schooling or to do academic Advanced levels in a different environment to school, as colleges had catered for through the 1960s and 1970s.

Instead, being a 'pre-vocational' student depicted uncertainty about what occupation to follow and a need for functional (literacy, numeracy and ICT) skills as well as personal and social skills. Psychologically or emotionally-based images also appeared, through lack of confidence and low self-esteem, being failed by the school system, being demotivated and disengaged and therefore unable and unwilling to 'cope with' particular forms of teaching and assessment. More recently, as some of our case studies in Section Two show, stereotyped expectations, particularly in relation to low expectations of motivation and engagement, and accompanying images of 'vulnerability', being 'at risk' and having 'complex needs' are also very influential.

Using insights from our case study of Entry to Employment programmes (e2e) for young people not in education, training or work, we highlight here some important recent shifts in depictions of the ways in which young people respond to life's problems and transitions. A key change from the late 1970s when mass youth unemployment first began, is that policy-makers and many education and welfare professionals now regard transitions as posing fundamental risks not just to social progression and employment but also to a sense of self and identity.[15] An ex-youth worker who trains personal advisers observes that policy-makers and many practitioners portray life experiences and events, such as being the child of single parents, permissiveness, poverty and exposure to some extremely risky situations, as if they are automatically a 'one-way ticket to a life of deprivation, ill-health and mental misery' (Turner 2007: 117).

Not only does this contrast with ideas in earlier eras that risk and even danger characterized many young people's rites of passage, sometimes positively, but it offers a small cautionary note to the idea that this fate is a typical outcome. This counter seems both hard and unrealistic in the face of the government's presentation of problems facing many families, children and young people. Numerous policy texts offer determinist ideas that children and young people inherit and then pass on attitudes and behaviours arising from deprivation, and contrast this bleak picture with optimistic possibilities of escape and transformation through education. In this scenario, educational achievement is indispensable to individuals' social and economic progress, and achievement is dependent on close forms of 'support'.[16]

These ideas have led to political investment in the transitions of children, young people and adults between education and welfare systems, and through all educational sectors.[17] Although the transition from school into training, work, education or unemployment has been a focus for political intervention since the late 1970s, school leavers with poor or no qualifications are seen now as profoundly and acutely 'at risk' and to have 'complex needs' that make them vulnerable to a host of risks including crime, drug abuse, marital problems, early pregnancy, unemployment and ill health.[18]

Policy-based images of what the Social Exclusion Unit called 'complex needs' are institutionalized in publicity to young people:

> Although e2e is not time-bound, it is based on the needs of each individual. You may need relatively short periods of time to prepare for entry to an Apprenticeship, employment, or further vocational learning opportunities. If you have *more complex personal and social needs you may require much longer periods before you are ready to enter and sustain suitable training and employment.*
>
> (website information, Oldminster College our emphasis)

The need for mentoring and personal assessment

e2e also epitomizes how these images have created closer forms of support and assessment. Assessment for young people leaving school or the care system deemed to be at particular risk of unemployment or other problems, and for those expelled from school, combines the welfare case management of social work, counselling and psychological assessments with the informal support and more recreational activities associated with youth work. These are based on high levels of emotional and psychological support, and detailed monitoring of their activities, formalized through the Connexions service, set up in 2001 to provide a youth support service combining vocational and training advice.

While mentoring is now commonly used in education, welfare services and workplaces around the world, young people seen as disaffected, alienated and difficult, and therefore 'unattractive' to other types of mentoring scheme often experience what Helen Colley calls 'engagement mentoring'.[19] This combines the searching out of individuals' interests and perception of needs with targets that seek to 're-engage' them with institutionalized norms, structures and pathways and to 'move [them]from a position of alienation and distance from social and economic reality, to a position of social integration and productive activity' (European Commission 1998, quoted by Colley 2003: 92). From this policy perspective, 'alienation', 'distance' and 'exclusion' are not material conditions, but, instead, psychological attributes and dispositions that require psychological or emotional intervention.[20]

For some young people, engagement mentoring runs alongside other approaches as part of a remit for advice and guidance services and programmes like e2e, continuing the Common Assessment Framework (CAF) introduced by legislation for *Every Child Matters* in 2003. The CAF typically requires practitioners to share information about children and young people and their families with other professionals and to target services and specific interventions at individuals identified as being at risk, including interventions such as cognitive behavioural therapy, motivational interviewing, brief solution-focused therapy and neuro-linguistic programming.

These interventions are meant to complement the main approach to fostering behavioural change for those outside the education and training system, namely the Assessment Planning Implementation and Review tool (APIR). In this process, young people and their advisers construct a personal version of a template that offers a graphical model in the form of a wheel with the client at the hub and each spoke representing a different feature of their life world such as friends, family, education and work. The adviser helps the young person sub-divide these sections further, through a series of concentric circles radiating out from the centre and encourages him or her to 'map' for themselves where they are positioned in the major aspects of their lives. A sequence of assessment, planning, implementation and review and aims to 'facilitate reflection' on where changes might be made and what 'resources' these changes might necessitate.[21]

Although not all young people in e2e or in vocational education have experienced these particular types of diagnostic and self-assessment, they are merely a more intensive version of approaches we see in the case studies of GCSE Business and Health and Social Care and e2e in Section Two.

In a more muted form, such approaches and their underlying images of young people are beginning to appear in the case study of BTEC National Diploma. In different ways, these courses all present attitudes, behaviours and dispositions, together with those of significant others, as 'resources' young people can draw on for help. They also institutionalize the idea that 'self-efficacy', motivation and engagement are resources that enable someone to identify other 'resources' and therefore integral to 'personal capital'. One effect is a shift from an acknowledgment that psychological and emotional attributes enhance opportunities in life and the labour market, to a growing acceptance that they are also 'skills' that require assessment.

Conclusion

Over 30 years, vocational craft subjects and general vocational courses based on strong forms of knowledge and skills needed for vocational or occupational roles, have been diluted in favour of a general 'education' of literacy, numeracy, personal and social skills, developed through topics with a vocational or occupational focus. Increasingly, vocational knowledge is little more than a vehicle for other 'skills'. Taken together, the trends summarized in this chapter have led to growing uncertainty about what forms of knowledge and skills young people need. This is reflected in our case studies and confirmed by a major review of the 14–19 phase, funded by the Nuffield Foundation.[22] As we show in some of our case studies in Section Two, this has produced extremely weak vocational subject cultures: while some are weaker than others, uncertainty about purpose and content of general vocational education, particularly in relation to academic general education and work-based qualifications, is now commonplace among teachers.

The effects on assessment and pedagogy of *A Basis for Choice* and Gilbert Jessup's book on outcome-based assessment have been inextricably linked. They offered particular images and related assumptions about what young people and adults characterized as 'non-traditional' learners would and should benefit from, the assessment and teaching methods that they would not or should not have to experience, and about what they are capable or incapable of achieving.

Associated value judgements about 'good' teaching and assessment are now commonplace and unchallenged. As we show in our case studies, the shift from didactic, whole-class teaching based on teachers' decisions about knowledge and content, towards small group and individual work, portfolio-based assessment and coursework projects based on outcome-based assessment specifications have changed the relationship between teachers and students, and their practices. A more open, criterion-based approach to formative and summative assessment has inserted other notions widely seen as progressive, such as the idea that students must have 'ownership of their learning' by understanding and using assessment criteria independently of teachers. This idea is now a standard feature of most if not all pedagogy in further and adult education.

As we show in our case studies, changing images of young people and adults as learners, with particular personal, social and educational 'needs' and 'barriers to learning' are also more prevalent. These images add the requirement for intensive one-to-one support to the drive towards transparent criteria. Yet, while images of vulnerability or of 'fragile learning identities', are undoubtedly powerful at the level of policy texts, our case studies show that their influence on expectations, beliefs and assessment practices is far from consistent between courses and contexts. This makes it important to evaluate why certain images take hold in some contexts and not others.

Finally, the constant policy development of the past 30 years is far from over. For example, the government department responsible for overseeing ALLN work, along with many of its myriad agencies, has been re-organized and re-branded three times since the launch of Skills for Life, and twice in the last 18 months. At the time of writing, the national literacy and numeracy strategy for schools has just been abandoned. By the time this book is published, a new government will have been in place for six months, attempting to service the largest debts of any British government in modern times. Educational activity that cannot unequivocally demonstrate its return on investment is highly unlikely to survive. It seems inevitable that the political and regulatory framework governing ALLN will change again, and yet the essential aims, purposes and features of their work are hardly different from what they were in the 1970s.

In different ways, this theme, of continuity of purpose contrasting with bewilderingly rapid changes in the policy and regulatory framework, has a powerful influence on all our case studies. The context summarized in this chapter also raises difficult questions about whether the forms of assessment and content experienced by students in vocational and adult education, and particularly in e2e programmes, are of real educational and social value as the recession deepens.

Notes

1. See James and Biesta (2007); Coffield et al. (2008); Avis (2009); Ecclestone (2002); Torrance et al. (2005).
2. However, see Ecclestone (2002); Torrance et al. (2005); Derrick et al. (2007); Hamilton (2009).

3. See for example Otter (1989); UDACE (1994); Jessup (1991).
4. For a detailed analysis of the rise and influence of the MSC, see Ainley and Corney (1990).
5. See Avis (2009); James and Biesta (2007); Ecclestone and Hayes (2008), for discussion of ABC, and Hyland (1994); Raggatt and Williams (1999); Ecclestone (2002) for discussion of the impact of assessment in NVQs and GNVQs.
6. See Hamilton and Hillier (2006).
7. For detailed discussion, see Hodgson and Spours (2008).
8. This section cannot do justice to the complex theoretical, political and technical debates about 'standards' of assessment in academic and vocational education but simply note at this point that such debates affect assessment systems in different ways. See Goldstein and Heath (2000) for detailed discussion, and Ecclestone (2002) for discussion of the political mess over standards in GNVQs between 1997 and 2001.
9. See FEU 1979; Avis (2009); James and Biesta (2007); Ecclestone and Hayes (2008).
10. We draw on earlier work that developed and applied this concept to further education, and explain it at length in the next chapter.
11. See Hyland (1994); Eruat (1994); Hodkinson and Issitt (1995).
12. See, for example, Otter (1989); UDACE (1994).
13. The NRDC has published research papers on all aspects of ALLN work, but has also aimed to make the results of its research available and as accessible as possible to practitioners, so as to have a positive impact on practice www.nrdc.org.uk.
14. See Field (2006).
15. See Ecclestone et al. (2010) for discussion.
16. See Williams (2009); Ecclestone et al. (2010).
17. See DfES (2003); Ecclestone et al. (2010) for discussion.
18. The Social Exclusion Unit, founded in 1997 produced a series of influential reports about the causes and effects of social deprivation and how government agencies should respond. For discussion of its claims and assumptions about young people, see Colley and Hodkinson (2001).
19. See Colley (2003) for detailed discussion.
20. See Williams (2009); Ecclestone et al. (2010); Ecclestone (2010).
21. Turner (2007).
22. See Hayward et al. (2005, 2009).
23. At the time of going to press (June 2010), the future of Diplomas is politically uncertain.

2   What formative assessment is, and what it is not

Introduction

Formative assessment or 'assessment for learning' is now widely and un-critically regarded throughout the British education system as integral to good teaching, student motivation and engagement and higher levels of achievement. For some supporters, good teaching cannot exist without good formative assessment. From its research-based inception as a key component of good teaching in the school sector, the well-known work of Paul Black and Dylan Wiliam, with colleagues from the Assessment Reform Group, is now seen universally as the basis for theoretical and practical work around formative assessment. It is one of the few academic ideas, supported by sound research evidence in the form of systematically worked-through theory and empirical data, to have had a major influence on policy and practice in the UK, and has been taken up by academics, teachers and policy-makers around the world.[1]

There has been widespread support for formative assessment, and large numbers of studies carried out in schools and higher education to support its development. Yet, many factors conspire against genuine understanding among various audiences trying to create effective assessment systems and militate against improving assessment practices. These include: rapid and repeated changes to policy and practice in curriculum and assessment systems in post-compulsory education since the late 1970s; lower levels of initial teacher education and continuing professional development than in the school sector; a heavily casualized teaching profession;[2] highly prescriptive, bureaucratic assessment systems; and funding tied to achievement, retention and participation rates. The introduction in 2009 of diplomas taught and assessed in partnerships between schools and colleges presents new challenges in assessment, not least because they are complicated and require teachers and assessors to combine different purposes and approaches.

Factors that hinder teachers from translating ideas from research and development into practice are exacerbated by the ways in which the ideas themselves have tended to become mantras, where apparently unproblematic definitions and activities assumed to be formative assessment conceal a great variety of underlying beliefs about purpose and outcome. This chapter aims to reiterate some key definitions and to distinguish between 'instrumental' and 'deep' purposes and outcomes for formative assessment. In the second section, we explore the crucial idea that formative assessment is not simply a set of methods or techniques but, instead, a way of organizing teaching and assessment activities around clear purposes and specific goals for learning. In the third section, we explore meanings of motivation and autonomy in order to counter somewhat simplistic uses of both notions that are widespread in policy, research and practice. Finally, we explore some typical problems of defining and interpreting what formative assessment is in practice.

1. Defining formative assessment

There is currently no watertight definition of formative assessment. It is often described as 'assessment *for* learning' as distinct from 'assessment *of* learning':

> Assessment for learning is any assessment for which the first priority in its design and practice is to serve the purpose of promoting students' learning. It thus differs from assessment designed primarily to serve the purposes of accountability, or of ranking, or of certifying competence. An assessment activity can help learning if it provides information to be used as feedback, by teachers, and by their students, in assessing themselves and each other, to modify the teaching and learning activities in which they are engaged. Such assessment becomes 'formative assessment' when the evidence is actually used to adapt the teaching work to meet learning needs.
>
> (Black et al. 2003: 9)

A widely quoted and influential idea about formative assessment comes from Roy Sadler who defines it as follows:

> In assessment for learning, the learner's task is to close the gap between the present state of understanding and the learning goal. Self-assessment is essential if the learner is to do this. The teacher's role is to communicate appropriate goals and promote self-assessment as pupils work towards the goals. Feedback in the classroom should operate from teacher to pupils and from pupils to teacher.
>
> (Sadler 1989: 119)

However, this should not imply a one-way route of feedback from teacher to student: feedback from a student about his or her own performance, or to other students about their performance (self- and peer assessment) are widely seen as integral to effective formative assessment. Some researchers observe that even when feedback from teachers is regular, detailed and helpful, students fail to improve: As Sadler argues:

> For students to be able to improve, they must develop the capacity to monitor the quality of their own work during actual production. This in turn requires that students possess an appreciation of what high quality work is, that they have the evaluative skill necessary for them to compare with some objectivity the quality of what they are producing in relation to the higher standard, and that they develop a store of tactics or moves which can be drawn on to modify their own work.
>
> (1989: 119)

Formative assessment embedded in pedagogy

For Black, all feedback is synonymous with formative assessment and feedback can take many forms. He argues that essential feedback comes from peer and self-assessment, in new approaches to discussion work and to teachers' written feedback, and in carefully constructed, open-ended classroom questioning.[3] An approach that embeds formative assessment in a holistic view of effective pedagogy comes from its depiction as 'encompassing all those activities undertaken by teachers and/or by their students which provide information to be used as feedback to modify the teaching and learning activities in which they are engaged'.[4]

Formative and diagnostic purposes and functions are therefore embedded in everyday teaching activities, such as questioning, oral feedback on answers and performance, and creating particular forms of dialogue between teachers and students and between students. Formative and diagnostic purposes are more obvious in explicit processes and techniques that might more easily be characterized as formative, such as tutorial reviews of progress, using records of achievement, or undertaking initial diagnostic tasks, and marking students' work.

Yet, characterizing methods in this way obscures the more subtle and sophisticated view that teachers need to think about such processes as part of a 'pedagogy of engagement', where they need to make students engage at a higher level cognitively than they either want to, or would choose to. This means capitalizing on what he calls 'moments of contingency', where learning might go one way or the other.[5] Rather than requiring a view of what is to be learned, or about what happens when learning takes place, this is, crucially, a *pedagogic* focus, a way of informing teaching decisions better and a way of finding new ways to break down complex learning activities into small steps (Black and Wiliam 1998).

From a pedagogic perspective, assessment activities cannot be understood as formative unless evidence from feedback is actually used to adapt teaching and learning activities, either there and then or in future planning (Box 2.1). This iteration between feedback, whether from students' written work or their answers to classroom or tutorial questions, can therefore be minute-to-minute as teachers and tutors think on their feet and respond to individuals or groups during classroom sessions or tutorials, or more considered as teachers plan new activities and lessons.

Box 2.1 Embedding formative assessment in pedagogy

Integral to this view is that teachers need to regard students' half-correct answers, their mistaken understandings or their wrong answers as essential to the sort of diagnosis that good teachers make to inform their responses and inputs, and to the feedback that teachers give them about those answers.

In our case study of AVCE Science, Derek Armstrong was a highly confident teacher, with a strong sense of expertise and great enthusiasm for his subject. He believed that teaching should enable students to construct their knowledge and understanding together and with him, to work actively to understand mistakes and misunderstandings, learn from them and then build new insights.

Far from the mantric use of ideas such as students 'taking responsibility for their own learning' routinely heard in vocational and adult education and evident in four of our six case studies (as well as in courses in our project that are not covered by this book), he encouraged students to 'be in charge of their own understanding', by which he meant that they needed to ask him or one of their classmates if they didn't understand anything. He stressed the advantages of getting students to come out to the front and explain things to their peers, observing that students who were very capable at maths could 'understand *why* they're doing it, rather than just doing it, and [were] able to explain that to others as well as – if not better than – I can, at times'. This built up the confidence of those doing the explaining, as well as providing a different explanation that often 'worked' for students when Derek's had not. Yet, he did not shy away from adding his own more expert view when this was needed.

In our ESOL case study, Ruth instinctively worked with an embedded idea of formative pedagogy:

We work within a structure which is driven by the scheme of work, you have to plan everything in advance and you have to save it to the shared drive.[6] I don't know how much people stick to them. But I like to go away at the end of a lesson and think 'OK, based on what happened in that lesson, what are we going to do next?', rather than just do the next thing on my scheme of work ... You can sometimes change a lesson completely because you realize for some reason what you have planned isn't going to work, or an idea comes up that you think is better. I call that 'seat-of-the-pants teaching', and often it goes really well.

(Ruth, ESOL teacher, Westhampton)

The 'spirit' and the 'letter' of formative assessment

The need to be clear about how formative assessment happens, and to be able to evaluate whether it is effective within specific subject domains and learning contexts are confirmed by research which shows that the same assessment activities or methods can lead to very different kinds of learning in different settings. In the Learning How to Learn Project in the Economic and Social Science Research Council's Teaching and Learning Research Programme (TLRP), Marshall and Drummond use the evocative terms 'spirit' and 'letter' of formative assessment or 'assessment for learning' (AfL) to capture how teachers practised it in the classroom:

The 'spirit' of AfL ... we have characterized as 'high organization based on ideas', where the underpinning principle is promoting pupil autonomy ... This contrasts with those lessons where only the procedures, or 'letter' of AfL seem in place. We use these headings – the 'spirit' and 'letter' – to describe the types of lessons we watched, because they have a colloquial resonance which captures the essence of the differences we observed. In common usage adhering to the spirit implies an underlying principle which does not allow a simple application of rigid technique. In contrast, sticking to the letter of a particular rule is likely to lose the underlying spirit it was intended to embody.

(Marshall and Drummond 2006: 137)

In this project, teachers working in the spirit of AfL encouraged students to become more independent, critical learners while those working in the letter of AfL adopted teacher-centred formative techniques in order to transmit knowledge and skills. However, as with all categories, these are not neatly separated from each other; teachers in this project often had a particular goal and focus of attention in mind, but shifted between these and others during a lesson (Marshall and Drummond 2006). As we show in our case studies, vocational and adult education teachers did the same.

We use the distinction of 'spirit' and 'letter' in our case studies because it illuminates the ways in which formative assessment might enable students to go beyond extrinsic success and instrumental processes that enable them to meet targets. Instead, the 'spirit' raises explicitly the goal of combining better performance with engagement and good learning habits in order to develop 'learning autonomy'. Differentiating between the spirit and the letter enables a contrast to be drawn in our case studies between techniques based on a transmission view of knowledge, usually the transmission of the concepts, knowledge and practical skills associated with clearly defined subject domains. The former usually means the transmission of externally prescribed specifications which encourages compliant, narrow responses, and techniques that aim explicitly to transform understanding, engagement and attitudes towards learning a subject.

2. Principles, purposes and activities

Purposes

Given that ideas about formative assessment are now widespread, it might seem strange to discuss purposes and to differentiate formative from summative and diagnostic assessment. Yet, as we show in the case studies in Section Two, the broader political and social factors discussed in Chapter 1 and the features of many 'learning cultures' of vocational education and ALLN discussed in the next chapter, mean that we cannot assume agreement, let alone proper understanding, on what formative assessment is or what it's for.

In a strictly technical sense, formative assessment can be summarized as being used for the following purposes:

- to diagnose starting points/current levels of strength and weakness in relation to learning outcomes and/or the final demands of a particular programme or qualification;
- to review progress in relation to strengths and weaknesses;
- to set targets and goals for future learning and achievement;
- to guide and advise learners about ways forward, gaps, strengths and weaknesses.

Summative assessment is used for the following purposes:

- to confirm and record achievement and competence for an external audience;
- to provide a basis for accountability and quality assurance for external audiences.

It is possible for teachers to use the outcomes of summative assessment for advice and feedback for future performance. Ideally, the insights gained from formative assessment are private between the teacher and student: they are not designed for other audiences. However, many institutions and providers of programmes require teachers to communicate the outcomes of formative assessment to parents, inspectors and others, thereby confusing both the purposes and activities of formative and summative assessment.

Formative assessment involves *diagnosis* at different points:

- at the beginning of a programme, in initial guidance or formal 'diagnostic assessments;
- during lessons and sessions, through dialogue and question and answer;
- during tutorials and reviews;
- when reading and marking assignments;
- during group work, through listening to students talk to each other;
- from specific 'diagnostic' activities: tests, quizzes, 'fear in a hat'.

Albeit rather 'medical' in its associations, the idea of 'diagnosis' is an integral part of formative assessment. It can reveal strengths and weaknesses, gaps in understanding and barriers to learning. Teachers have to decide how much to record as outcomes of a diagnosis but the crucial factor is that diagnosis should provide information to enable teachers to adjust teaching and learning inputs, for whole groups or for individuals.

Principles

The Assessment Reform Group (2002) promotes ten key principles of formative assessment. Assessment for learning should:

1. be part of effective planning for teaching and learning so that learners and teachers should obtain and use information about progress towards learning goals; planning should include processes for feedback and engaging learners.

2. focus on how students learn; learners should become as aware of the 'how' of their learning as they are of the 'what'.
3. be recognized as central to classroom practice, including demonstration, observation, feedback and questioning for diagnosis, reflection and dialogue.
4. be regarded as a key professional skill for teachers, requiring proper training and support in the diverse activities and processes that comprise assessment for learning.
5. should take account of the importance of learner motivation by emphasizing progress and achievement rather than failure and by protecting learners' autonomy, offering some choice and feedback and the chance for self-direction.
6. promote commitment to learning goals and a shared understanding of the criteria by which they are being assessed, by enabling learners to have some part in deciding goals and identifying criteria for assessing progress.
7. enable learners to receive constructive feedback about how to improve, through information and guidance, constructive feedback on weaknesses and opportunities to practise improvements.
8. develop learners' capacity for self-assessment so that they become reflective and self-managing.
9. recognize the full range of achievement of all learners.
10. promote fundamental care principles.

Formative activities

Data and insights for formative purposes can come from a range of activities that teachers and students might normally associate with 'teaching' such as classroom questioning and feedback, group work and peer assessment on a piece of previously assessed work, from summative assessment outcomes and from draft or interim assessments. It is therefore the purpose of the assessment that makes it formative, not the method, timing or activity: a timed examination can be used solely for formative purposes, for example. Data and insights for formative purposes can come from:

- initial guidance interview;
- initial diagnostic assessment (tests, assignments, etc.);
- questions asked individually or in class to diagnose understanding and to build understanding with students;
- written feedback and advice that focuses on the task and not the grade, feelings or ego of the student;
- oral feedback to answers to questions asked of students or to questions that students ask;

- drafting assignments or a performance for feedback from teachers, self or peers;
- using exemplars of good and poor quality work to assess the quality of one's and others' work in relation to the assessment criteria;
- tutorials or reviews – group and individual, peer or teacher-led;
- questions at the end of sessions to find out what was easy or difficult, what students think they still need to learn.

Some activities, like questioning and giving feedback are commonly associated with good teaching but having a formative purpose in mind can enhance the quality of questions and class feedback. Questioning and feedback are therefore crucial to good formative assessment but also one of the more complex areas of teachers' practices to change.

Such activities can be very formal or be quite informal or unobtrusive. Yet, as our case studies show, even these potentially useful techniques can obscure the purpose of learning, become tedious and ritualistic, give students an unrealistic view of what 'learning' really is, or be little more than attempts to make the summative assessments less onerous. More controversially, we show in some of our case studies that they can give students too much of a say about activities and content they might not be qualified to evaluate!

Divergent and convergent assessment

Two useful related concepts are those of 'divergent' and 'convergent' formative assessment, developed through in-depth observation of primary school teachers by Harry Torrance and John Pryor (1998). They draw an important distinction between formative assessment practices based on behaviourist theories of learning, which break down cognitive and practical learning into a hierarchy of tasks and competences, and socio-constructivist ideas about learning that focus on processes, interactions, collaborative activities and the specific types of communication, dialogue and questioning that lead to learning.

The former is prevalent in the standardized assessment tests of the National Curriculum in schools while a much more utilitarian version of it is prevalent in the outcome- and competence-based assessment systems of vocational education and many work-based training qualifications. The latter remains a theory, albeit becoming more coherent, at the level of academic research that aims to reconcile psychological ideas of cognitive development with the social practices and interactions that develop learning.[7]

In Table 2.1, Torrance and Pryor identify ideal types of each approach from their observation of teachers in primary schools.

Table 2.1 Convergent and divergent assessment

Convergent assessment	Divergent assessment
Assessment which aims to discover *whether* the learner knows, understands or can do a predetermined thing. This is characterized by:	Assessment which aims to discover *what* the learner knows, understands or can do. This is characterized by:
Practical implications (a) precise planning and an intention to stick to it	*Practical implications* (a) flexible planning or complex planning which incorporates alternatives
(b) tick lists and can-do statements	(b) open forms of recording (narrative, quotations, etc.)
(c) an analysis of the interaction of the learner and the curriculum from the point of view of the curriculum	(c) an analysis of the interaction of the learner and the curriculum from the point of view of both the learner and the curriculum
(d) closed or pseudo-open questioning and tasks	(d) open questioning and tasks
(e) a focus on contrasting errors with correct responses	(e) a focus on miscues – aspects of learners' work which yield insights into their current understanding – and on prompting metacognition
(f) judgmental or quantitative evaluation	(f) descriptive rather than purely judgmental evaluation
(g) involvement of the pupil as a recipient of assessments	(g) involvement of the pupil as initiator of assessments as well as recipient
Theoretical implications (h) a behaviourist view of learning	*Theoretical implications* (h) a constructivist view of learning
(j) an intention to teach or assess the next predetermined thing in a linear progression	(j) an intention to teach in the zone of proximal development
(k) a view of assessment as accomplished by the teacher	(k) a view of assessment as accomplished jointly by the teacher and the pupil
This view of assessment might be seen less as a formative assessment, than as repeated summative assessment or continuous assessment.	This view of assessment could be said to attend more closely to contemporary theories of learning and accept the complexity of formative assessment.

Source: Torrance and Pryor (1998: 115).

3. Meanings of motivation and autonomy

A typology of motivation

In the light of the ubiquitous use of terms like 'learning', 'motivating', 'engagement' and 'independent learning', discussed in Chapter 1, and confusion and misunderstandings about formative assessment, a more nuanced understanding of the forms of motivation and autonomy that assessment promotes is crucial for better meanings of 'learning'.

In order to go beyond an old and somewhat unrealistic dichotomy between 'intrinsic' and 'extrinsic' motivation, German researchers have undertaken longitudinal studies of the ways in which students combine strategic approaches to learning based on external motivation, with self-determination and personal agency. This work uses well-known psychological constructs of motivation, such as students' and teachers' attribution of achievement to effort, luck, ability, the difficulty of a particular task or to other external factors, and the extent to which students have a sense of agency or locus of control.

The resulting typology offers a systematically ordered spectrum of constructs that illuminates individual behaviours and activities in different contexts while recognizing that motivation is affected strongly by social factors in a learning group, and by family, peers and work colleagues. The typology proved useful and illuminating in a study of vocational education students' experiences of, and responses to, assessment.[8] We have also used it to analyse data from our case studies in this book. Descriptions and definitions here draw on Prenzel's original categories and insights gained from these two studies.

Amotivation

Amotivated learners lack any direction for motivation, and are, variously, indifferent or apathetic. Sometimes this state is an almost permanent response to formal education or assessment and therefore hard to shift, or it appears at points during a course. There is a sense that amotivated learners are drifting or hanging on until something better appears. However, it is important to recognize the obvious point, that for all of us at different times, our deepest, most intrinsic motivation can revert to states where we are barely motivated or not motivated at all! In this context, surviving the pressure of targets or trying to achieve something difficult requires the reward or punishment of external motivation.

External motivation

Learning takes place largely in association with reinforcement, reward, or to avoid threat or punishment, including: short-term targets, prescriptive outcomes and criteria, frequent feedback (this might be about the task, the person's ego or feelings or the overall goal) and reviews of progress, deadlines, sanctions and grades. In post-compulsory education, external motivation sometimes takes the form of financial incentives (payment to attend classes or rewards for getting a particular grade) or sanctions (money deducted for non-attendance on courses).

External motives are sometimes essential at the beginning of a course, or at low points during it. They are not, therefore, negative and can be used strategically as a springboard for other forms of motivation or to get people through difficult times in their learning. Yet, if left unchecked, external motives can dominate learning all the way through a course and lead to instrumental compliance rather than deep engagement.

Introjected/internalized motivation

'Introjected' is a therapeutic term where someone has internalized an external supportive structure and can articulate it as her or his own: in a qualification, this might comprise the vocabulary and procedures of criteria, targets and overall assessment requirements. Good specifications of grade criteria and learning outcomes and having processes or tasks broken into small steps enable learners to use the official specifications independently of teachers. Nevertheless, although introjected motivation enables students to articulate the official requirements and criteria almost by rote, it is not self-determined.

For learners disaffected by assessment in the past, introjected motivation is powerful and, initially, empowering. However, like external motivation, it can become a straitjacket by restricting learners and teachers to an emphasis upon the formal requirements, especially in contexts where contact time and resources are limited.

Identified motivation

Learning occurs when students accept content or activities that may hold no incentive in terms of processes or content (they might even see them as a burden) but which are necessary for attaining a pre-defined goal such as a qualification and short-term targets. It links closely to introjected motivation, and goals that students identify with can be course-related, personal and social (or all three) as a means to a desirable end.

Intrinsic motivation

Learners perceive any incentives as intrinsic to the content or processes of a formal learning or assessment activity, such as enjoyment of learning something for its own sake, helping someone else towards mastery or being committed to others outside or inside the learning group. It is often more prevalent among learners than teachers might assume and takes idiosyncratic, deeply personal and sometimes fleeting forms. Intrinsic motivation is context-specific: someone can therefore show high levels of intrinsic motivation in one task or context and not in another. Learning is highly self-determined and independent of external contingencies.

Interested motivation

Interested motivation is characterized by learners recognizing the intrinsic value of particular activities and goals and then assigning their own subjective criteria for what makes something important: these include introjected and identified motives. Like intrinsic motivation, it relies on students assigning deeply personal meanings of relevance to content, activities and contexts. It is accompanied by feelings of curiosity and perhaps risk or challenge, and encouraged by a sense of flow, connection or continuity between different elements of a task or situation.

High levels of self-determination, a positive identity or 'sense of self' and the ability to attribute achievement to factors within one's own control are integrated in a self-image associated with being a successful learner. Interested motivation relates closely to Maslow's well-known notion of 'self-actualization', where identity, learning activities, feelings of social and civic responsibility and personal development are fused together. It is therefore often correlated with good peer and social dynamics in a learning group.

Interested motivation characterized ideas about learning and personal identity among some young people in Ball et al.'s (2000) study of transitions into post-compulsory education, training or work. The processes and experiences of 'becoming somebody' and of having an 'imagined future' were not only rooted strongly in formal education but also in their sense of having positive opportunities in the local labour market and in their social lives. Formal education therefore played an important and positive, although not dominant part, in their evolving personal identity (Ball et al., 2000).

Fluctuating motivation

Despite the descriptive and analytical appeal of these types, it is, of course, crucial to bear in mind that they are not stable or neatly separated categories. Nor can motivation be isolated from structural factors such as class, gender and race, opportunities for work and education and students' and teachers' perceptions of these factors. In formal education, students might combine aspects of more than one type, they might change from day to day, they might show 'interested' motivation strongly in one context (such as a hobby) but not at all in the activities required of them at school, college or university.

The factors that make someone an interested or barely motivated learner are therefore idiosyncratic, very personal and changeable. It is stating the obvious to observe that the most motivated, enthusiastic young person can show high levels of interested motivation in year one of a two-year vocational course but be barely hanging on through external and introjected motivation by the end of year two, simply because they are tired with a course and want to move on. Some need the incentives of external rewards and sanctions and to be able to internalize the official demands and support structures as a springboard to develop deeper forms of motivation.[9]

Nevertheless, these caveats do not detract from a strong empirical connection shown in Prenzel's studies as well as in our project between intrinsic and interested motivation based on high levels of self-determination and positive evidence of the conditions listed below and, conversely, amotivation or external motivation and poor evidence of these conditions:

- support for students' autonomy, such as choices for self-determined discovery, planning and acting;
- support for competence, through, for example, effective feedback about knowledge and skills in particular tasks and how to improve them;
- social relations such as cooperative working, a relaxed and friendly working atmosphere;
- relevance of content including applicability of contents, proximity to reality, connections to other subjects (here it is important to note that 'relevance' is not limited to personal relevance or application to everyday life);
- quality of teaching and assessment situated in authentic, meaningful problem contexts, adapted to students' starting points;
- teachers' interest and expression of commitment to students.

A typology of autonomy

Assessment systems in vocational, adult and work-based education have made autonomy an explicit goal.[10] In a context where teachers and designers of qualifications present independent learning or autonomy as a holy grail, being clear about what it really is becomes essential.

Yet, autonomy is an even more slippery concept than motivation. An earlier study of formative assessment in vocational education combined Prenzel's typology of motivation with a typology of autonomy that offers three categories: *procedural* or *technical autonomy* in the form of command of technical processes, the official requirements and a body of subject-related language; *personal autonomy* where students become more self-directing, based on insights into their strengths and weaknesses and their choices for action in a particular field; *critical autonomy* where learners can relate ideas in a subject context to evaluations of, and changes to their practice as part of a broader, socio-political awareness.[11] Critical autonomy, where students engage analytically with concepts, practices and debates in a subject links closely with a definition of 'learning autonomy' as the transformation of cognitive skills and insights into the concepts and practices of a subject discipline so that students can genuinely think for themselves.[12]

Although critical autonomy and intrinsic and interested motivation might be educational ideals, the chance to have some control over a procedure or activity, such as action planning, working alone without a teacher or negotiating ways of working is crucial for some, if not all, students. In situations where courses have uncertain progression to work or higher education, and attract students with poor experiences of education, young people and adults value opportunities to work alone, without a teacher, to create and review action plans and to master the use of assessment checklists and criteria. It is possible to argue that external and introjected motivation, technical or procedural autonomy can be springboards for deeper forms of motivation and autonomy.

At a theoretical level, motivation and autonomy are inextricably linked and they can be related to practices that, as we argued in the first section of this chapter, promote either the spirit or letter of formative assessment. For example, feedback, classroom questioning, reviews of progress and setting targets that transmit pre-defined criteria and procedures, with poorly motivated students, are likely to encourage external, introjected and identified motivation and procedural autonomy. In contrast, the spirit of formative assessment aims to transform knowledge and understanding, based on critical autonomy and intrinsic and interested motivation, through feedback, questioning and diagnostic activities and 'critical conversations' about a topic between teachers and students, and between students.

Yet it is important to reiterate that external motivation, technical autonomy and instrumental engagement might be essential in the early stages of a course or at various points throughout it. If the overall purpose is deep engagement and transformation of understanding, instrumentalism is not problematic. It becomes problematic when this purpose is absent.

The typology, potentially, offers a more nuanced basis to explore motivation and autonomy in a particular assessment context, and to show the ways in which assessment practices can reinforce, deliberately or unwittingly, particular forms of both. Like many typologies, its implications for changing practice and conditions in order to encourage deeper forms of motivation and autonomy are less clear since formative assessment activities are only one factor in shaping a learning culture. Nevertheless, better understanding of motivation and autonomy is an important step in doing this. We return to examples of motivation and autonomy in the case studies and to their implications in the final chapter of the book.

4. Problems in practice

Mechanistic interpretations

Formative assessment sounds straightforward at the level of definition! Many policy-based texts, and, indeed, lists like those we have used in the first section of this chapter, present formative assessment as unambiguous and unproblematic. Although some of the more subtle and complex interpretations of formative assessment discussed in this chapter are well understood and widely used by researchers and many teacher educators and staff developers, they are not widespread among teachers in post-compulsory education. Nor, as we discuss further in Section Three of this book, are they widely known in teacher education for vocational and ALLN teachers.

There is, for example, widespread misunderstanding among practitioners and institution managers in post-compulsory education that some activities are 'formative' and others 'summative'. There is also a tendency to see formative assessment as teacher-led techniques for feedback, diagnosis and review where, despite an accompanying rhetoric of 'engaging students with learning', the techniques and associated formal paperwork are often solely to 'track' students towards their summative targets. Formative assessment is also widely seen as synonymous with continuous or modular assessment where summative tasks are broken up into interim ones.

Yet, countering these mechanistic ideas with a more holistic depiction of formative assessment as integral to pedagogy highlights difficulties in helping teachers change their practice. Not least, the dominance of summative targets leads them to associate activities such as classroom questioning, oral and written feedback, self- and peer assessment on practice examination questions with 'teaching' rather than with diagnosis of misunderstandings and half-understandings, useful and meaningful feedback and for informing teaching activities.

Further confusion arises because activities that are ostensibly the same can be based on *transmission* of the teacher's expertise, knowledge and advice and the prescriptions of those designing the assessment specifications. Alternatively, formative assessment can be based on *transaction* between teachers and students about processes, the content of an activity or task or about its goals. More rarely, if our case studies are typical, formative assessment might aim to *transform* students' and teachers' understanding of concepts and processes associated with learning a subject offers a higher degree of challenge. It is therefore important to pay attention to the language that teachers, qualification designers and students use, as well as to their practices.

Different educational goals

An overlooked problem in all the advice typically given to teachers, is that emphasis on techniques, purpose and principles does not illuminate the underlying focus and educational goal.[13] Our case studies show how teachers' goals for using formative assessment reflect, usually implicitly, a meaning of learning which is being communicated to students. Apparent agreement about meanings and principles, translated into activities that are ostensibly the same in different contexts, can conceal very different learning goals and beliefs about students' dispositions and abilities. The case studies also show that teachers in different subject teams, or sometimes in the same team, might all aim to improve assessment practices such as classroom questioning, but have very different goals, and therefore produce very different effects.

The lack of a subject

Mechanistic interpretation of techniques is not the only difficulty. One of the biggest differences between policy and practical interpretations of it in post-compulsory education and those initiated by the Assessment Reform Group in schools, is that the former have been driven largely by broader goals of motivation, inclusion and participation rather than progression in students' cognitive understanding within a clear subject domain.

The goal of cognitive progression within subjects such as English, Mathematics, Geography, or Science in the research-based developments summarized in the widely read 'Inside the Black Box' series, is a key feature of formative assessment for school teachers.[14] Questioning, written feedback on written work and on classroom answers, self- and peer assessment, are all supposed to enable teachers to diagnose misunderstandings and misconceptions about subject concepts, tasks and content. Injunctions to focus on task not a student's ego or affective state, to explore assessment criteria so that students understand different examples of good, mediocre and poor quality and to encourage students to indicate difficulties are all, in theory, based on assumptions that enhancing subject understanding is the main goal.

Yet, as our research confirms in following chapters, the goal of cognitive progression cannot be assumed in vocational education and parts of ALLN. Indeed, numerous factors conspire against it as an educational goal. In a context where the content of vocational education has been widened over 30 years to encompass a growing range of personal dispositions, social, life and work 'skills' as well as some knowledge about different jobs and occupational areas, techniques that look like formative assessment might have a range of purposes. These include:

- finding out students' affective responses to process, teaching style and format;
- encouraging an instrumental commitment to maximizing grade achievement;
- using the close setting of targets about behaviour to discipline young people in basic habits of attendance, time management and social skills as part of an induction into further education;
- using praise to bolster egos and identities seen to be fragile, and to minimize criticism;
- using dialogue, feedback and review as a means of engagement and inclusion rather than progression in a subject or skill;
- using detailed feedback on suggested improvements to coach students into filling the gaps between performance and the prescriptive assessment specifications.

As we show in our case studies, all of these techniques and their underlying purpose are evident in varying degrees, in vocational education course and ALLN programmes. One of the most common confusions is between students' self-assessment of 'learning' and their evaluation of the content, method and effect on their motivation of teaching. But, as we also show, the purposes in the list here are also widespread and they move formative assessment further away from the ideas about the need for teachers to better understand and plan for cognitive progression, that were the impetus for research interest and subsequent developments.

Conclusion

It is possible to agree on broad distinctions between formative and summative assessment, and to identify some of the key processes and activities that comprise formative assessment. Nevertheless, activities that appear to be formative in purpose, can be instrumental and ritualistic, or genuinely able to engage students in learning a subject, whether practical or academic, or both.

Formative assessment is part of learning and not the simple monitoring and tracking of progress toward summative goals. It should enable students to improve their skills, knowledge and understanding and to compare their current performance with their past performance (ipsative assessment, or self-referenced assessment). Adapting teaching and learning activities might be teacher-initiated or student-led: a student might decide for him or herself how to proceed and what activities she or he should undertake.

Formative assessment is therefore much more than a series of teacher-led techniques for feedback, diagnosis and review, continuous assessment that merely breaks up summative tasks into interim ones or detailed advice about how to 'plug gaps' between current performance and the demands of the summative crtiera. Rather it requires the involvement and engagement of students with these processes, and the adaptation of teaching activities that avoid a mechanistic series of steps towards the superficial attainment of objectives. This requires formative assessment to have the following characteristics:

- Its outcomes should enable teachers to make instructional decisions and enable students to set goals, evaluate their performance and change their approaches to learning.
- Activities with formative purposes should involve students actively in their learning and in trying to improve it: formative assessment is not therefore didactic and does not mean the teacher does all the work.
- Activities and processes should engage students actively in becoming motivated and independent in achieving the purposes of formative assessment.

Research studies provide useful theories and concepts that can help researchers and practitioners interpret more precisely and realistically the purposes and effects of everyday practice. Yet, despite the appeal of ideas in this chapter, they are notoriously difficult to translate into everyday practice. Earlier studies with school teachers show that such ideas have to be interpreted within specific subject domains and teachers have to work over a period of time, with experts, to identify in some detail how to change patterns of questioning, feedback and dialogue in the classroom in relation to the cognitive demands of their subject.[15]

Until teachers and other interested parties observe how techniques and activities in one context can have very different purposes and effects to the same ones in other contexts, it is difficult to clarify what is, and is not, formative. In our view, this is essential for clarifying the underlying educational goals of these practices. Yet, there are tendencies towards ritualistic adoption of an apparently unproblematic 'good idea' and the corresponding ubiquitous use of bland rhetoric about formative assessment, and associated ideas about 'ownership of learning', 'engagement' and 'independent learning'. This means that misunderstanding of what formative assessment is and is not is one reason why instrumentalism is becoming endemic in vocational education and ALLN. Yet, as our case studies show, instrumentalism is also inextricably linked to the tendency to overlook subject content and an endemic use of bland rhetoric about learning.

Notes

1. The Assessment Reform Group involved leading British academics in the field of assessment between 1989 and 2010. It produced numerous, highly influential reports and other publications that advocate a focus on formative assessment or 'assessment for learning' as a key factor in improving the quality of teaching and assessment (see www.arg.org.uk).
2. Approximately 50 per cent of FE college staff are on casual, part-time or temporary contracts; in ALLN, the figure varies greatly between providers but can be as high as 90 per cent.
3. See Black (2007); Black and Wiliam (2009).
4. Black and Wiliam (1998: 7).
5. In our case study of ESOL classes at Westhampton College in Chapter 9, Ruth, one of the teachers participating in the project, calls this 'going with the teachable moment'.
6. See note 4 on p. 34.
7. See, for example, James (2005) and discussion in Chapter 1, of this book.
8. Prenzel et al. (2001), applied to a study of Advanced level vocational education in Ecclestone (2002).
9. See Ecclestone (2002).
10. See Jessup (1991); Otter (1989); McNair (1995).
11. See Ecclestone (2002).
12. See Black et al. (2003).
13. See, for example, Hargreaves (2005); Stobart (2008).
14. A series of highly popular pamphlets for teachers, published by NFER, explore formative assessment inside the 'black box' of numerous subjects: Geography, Science, English, Maths and others. See www.nfer-nelson.co.uk.
15. See Black et al. (2003); Marshall and Drummond (2006); James et al. (2007).

3 Learning and assessment cultures in lifelong learning

Introduction

No evaluation of assessment and teaching activities can overlook the powerful influence of contextual factors on practice and on its underlying beliefs and values about what counts as 'good' practice and 'worthwhile' educational purposes. Yet, while it is commonplace to offer an account of 'context', researchers and practitioners vary greatly in what they consider to be salient factors within particular settings. In addition, as the case studies in Section Two show, there are profound differences between vocational education courses and those in ALLN. There are also some worrying tendencies towards homogenization across these two once very different areas of educational provision. Not least, as we argued in the introduction to this book, it has become less common, even non-existent, to discuss fundamental educational purposes and subject content that implicitly and explicitly lie behind practice.

As our summary of developments in assessment policy suggests in the first chapter, policy has had profound effects on teachers' formative and summative practices in ALLN and vocational education classes. Some effects arise directly from specific policy decisions, such as the introduction in ALLN of mandatory standardized national tests for literacy and numeracy learners at certain levels of study, or the decision that ESOL learners should take the same test as native speaker literacy learners. Some policy decisions affect teaching contexts indirectly. In ALLN, for example, an overall reduction in the national funding tariff led colleges or local authorities to reduce class hours from three hours per week over 36 weeks per year to two hours per week over 30 weeks, or to merge two classes into one. In vocational education, changes to funding have led to the reduction of class contact and the removal of general education options that are not formally assessed.

Policy over time, in both vocational education and ALLN, has led towards greater political regulation and control of the forms of teaching, assessment and content seen to be 'legitimate'. Policy also produces unintended effects. For example, increasing emphasis in funding and performance measurement on summative achievement has led to widespread teaching or coaching to the test, producing a curriculum that is much narrower than originally intended.

Research can enhance understanding of the nuances of policy and practice and can evaluate the subtle ways in which they affect attitudes and outcomes of pedagogy and assessment. There is, for example, a growing body of high quality work on policy and practice as they affect further education colleges. This shows that the historical evolution of FE and current policy combines with students' and teachers' attitudes, dispositions to learning and their previous experiences to shape teaching and assessment practices in subtle and sometimes contradictory ways.[1] There is also a body of in-depth analysis and evaluation of the ways in which assessment systems exert a powerful influence on teaching practices in post-compulsory education and on views about good practice. These are reinforced through inspection criteria, regulation by awarding bodies and other managerial pressures.[2] In adult literacy, language and numeracy, research has focused on the impact of Skills for Life programmes on the ethos, practices and outcomes of adult basic education, with similar themes to those of the literature on further education, of the impact of managerialism, target-setting and changes to funding regimes.[3]

The research referred to in this chapter is confirmed by findings from our project developed in the case studies in Section Two. It shows that it is both possible and necessary to identify the general factors that create a further education or adult education 'ethos', a vocational education ethos, an adult literacy and numeracy one, an English for Speakers of Other Languages ethos, and so on. This ethos combines with other factors to produce what some researchers have analysed as 'learning cultures'. In this chapter, we summarize the main features of a 'learning culture', highlighting especially influential factors such as the 'learning and assessment careers of students'. This is a precursor to analysis in our case studies of teachers' assessment practices, the underlying values and expectations of students and teachers, and their effects on the purposes and outcomes of those practices.

1. A socio-cultural understanding of teaching, learning and assessment

Using the concept of the 'learning culture'

It is common to define 'pedagogy' as the theory and practice of teaching, thereby enabling researchers and teachers to focus on techniques and strategies within specific domains of knowledge. Yet, as Hall et al. point out:

> Understood from a socio-cultural perspective, pedagogy is also and crucially concerned with what is salient to people as they engage in activity and develop competence in the practice in question. It takes account of two phenomena and their dynamic relationship: a) the social order as reflected in, for example, policy and its associated cultural beliefs and assumptions and b) the experienced world, as reflected in both the enactment and the experience of the policy, including the beliefs underlying the approaches used in its enactment and the beliefs mediating how it is experienced.
>
> (2008: viv)

The relationship between historical and political contexts and participants' identities, dispositions and activities in a particular context is as much part of pedagogy as specific techniques and strategies. This relationship cannot be isolated from judgements about the effects of those techniques and strategies. In a large-scale study of pedagogy in different countries, Robin Alexander argues that teachers' theories, ideas and value judgements about their role in curriculum development, the design of pedagogy and assessment, cannot be divorced from broader considerations. These include questions about central government control over curriculum content, educational purposes, teaching and assessment methods, the quality of teacher education and social judgements about the purpose and content of education and about what is regarded as personally and socially useful knowledge (Alexander 2001).

Of course, it is easy to reach agreement at a general level about the importance or obviousness of these influences, or to assert impatiently that these are merely 'common sense'! Yet, it is not until we examine how broader factors interact with local ones in specific sites or contexts that researchers can really understand, and help teachers understand, the impact of different strategies and techniques. More importantly, analysing this interaction and its effects can encourage people to question fundamental questions of educational value and purpose that lie behind any practice.

From a socio-cultural perspective, students do not merely learn (or not learn) knowledge, skills and practices. Related questions are what they learn through the assessment practices they experience, how they shape and influence those practices, and what they and other participants in a context consider to be important processes and outcomes.

In order to address these questions in a range of very different contexts, we draw on the concept of 'learning culture' developed in the

Transforming Learning Cultures in Further Education (TLC) project through the well-known work of Bourdieu and defined as:

> a particular way to understand a learning site[4] as a practice consti-tuted by the actions, dispositions and interpretations of the par-ticipants. This is not a one way process. Cultures are (re)produced by individuals, just as much as individuals are (re)produced by cul-tures, though individuals are differently positioned with regard to shaping and changing a culture – in other words, differences in power are always at issue too. Cultures, then, are both structured and structuring, and individuals' actions are neither totally deter-mined by the confines of a learning culture, nor are they totally free.
>
> (James and Biesta 2007: 18)

'Learning culture' 'aims to understand how people learn through their par-ticipation in learning cultures, [and] we see learning cultures themselves as the practices through which people learn' (James and Biesta 2007: 26).

A learning culture is not the same as the features of a course or pro-gramme, or a learning 'site'. Instead, it is a particular way of understanding any course/programme by emphasizing how the interactions and prac-tices that take place within and through it are part of a dynamic, iterative process in which participants (and environments) shape cultures at the same time as cultures shape the values, beliefs and actions of participants. Learning cultures are relational and their participants include parents, college managers at various levels, policy-makers and national awarding bodies, as well as teachers and students. 'Learning culture' is not therefore synonymous with 'learning environment' since the environment is only part of the learning culture:

> a learning culture should not be understood as the context or environment within which learning takes place. Rather, 'learning culture' stands for *the social practices through which people learn*. A cultural understanding of learning implies, in other words, that learning is not simply occurring *in* a cultural context, but is itself to be understood *as* a cultural practice.
>
> (James and Biesta 2007: 18, original emphasis)

It is important to identify how certain practices within a learning culture implicitly or explicitly reveal the values of the broader culture at different points in history. In that sense, the policy reforms of teaching and assess-ment that people experience are never neutral, and nor are judgements about 'good' and 'bad' practice. It is, therefore, not enough to 'deconstruct' or analyse practice, or to relate this analysis to broader factors, because this does not necessarily reveal values about educational purposes or pose alternatives. As we argued in the Introduction to this book, we aim to go beyond detailed analysis to evaluate educational purposes and outcomes, and to make value judgements about them.

Key dimensions of a learning culture

Influential dimensions of a learning culture include:

- the social positions of class, race and gender, age and the dispositions and actions of the students and tutors;
- the location and resources of the learning site which are not neutral, but enable some approaches and attitudes, and constrain or prevent others;
- the time tutors and students spend together, their interrelationships, and the range of other learning sites students are engaged with;
- the effects of college management procedures, together with funding and inspection body procedures and regulations, and government policy;
- wider vocational and academic cultures, of which any learning site is part;
- wider social and cultural values and practices, for example, around questions of social class, gender and ethnicity, the nature of employment opportunities, social and family life, and the perceived status of further and adult education as parts of the wider education system.

These dimensions interact with the 'reified' elements of a learning culture, such as official texts, syllabuses, learning materials, assessment specifications from awarding bodies, the physical environment and its resources and organizational structures. In vocational education, 'reified elements' are especially detailed and prescriptive, enforced through strong systems for awarding bodies that regulate teachers' assessment judgements, and by inspectors. They impose constraints and procedures and mean that participation in implementing or complying with them is not merely a metaphor for student and teacher activity: participation also reproduces and enacts particular social and power relations (James and Biesta 2007).

A cultural understanding of learning illuminates the extent to which students and teachers act upon the learning and assessment opportunities they encounter and upon the assessment systems they participate in. The ways in which they do this, and what they choose to highlight, ignore or pay lip service to, are influenced by implicit and explicit values and beliefs about the purposes of a course or qualification, together with certain expectations of students' abilities and motivation and associated expectations about what students will and will not put up with.

Of course, while teachers and students are the key actors or participants in a particular situation, operating within implicit and overt systems of expectations, they are far from alone! Inspectors, awarding and funding body officials, college managers, parents, colleagues, are also powerful participants with influential expectations about purposes and practices. And, as we see in some of the case studies in Section Three of this book, so too are mentors and other learning support staff.

So, although teachers engage with their tasks on the basis of ideas about what it means to be a teacher, and students embark on courses with ideas about 'appropriate' behaviour, these ideas are likely to change as the course progresses, both for individuals and the whole group. They are also influenced by expectations about appropriate teacher and student behaviour from other participants in the learning culture. Other influential factors are the nature of relationships with other students and teachers, students' lives outside college and the resources available to them during the course, such as class contact time, staff and student ratios and the availability of support staff for individual students.

These factors make students and teachers active agents in shaping expectations and practices around the formal demands of a qualification, and these expectations influence and constrain what is possible for those working inside the system. Yet, because many expectations exist at the level of dispositions, they manifest themselves as cultural ways of doing and being that are considered to be 'normal' and therefore unproblematic. In turn, this means that learning cultures are governed by values and ideals, by normative expectations about what comprises 'good' learning, teaching and management (see Box 3.1). Many of these values and expectations are not only implicit but may also be contradictory, realistic or inaccurate. In addition, they vary across and between learning cultures ostensibly with the same purposes and practices.

Box 3.1   Contextual factors in a learning culture

Four brief examples here illuminate some of the features of learning cultures explored in the case studies.

1.   In Mid-Counties college, managers had put staff in a health and social care department into 'special measures' following an internal

> inspection. The fear of teachers in our project from BTEC Public Services and BTEC Health and Social Care that 'poor' rates of achievement among their students would invoke sanctions threatened by college managers if they did not raise them, dominated every aspect of the changes they made to their formative assessment.
>
> 2. In the AVCE Science course in a highly successful and well-regarded community school, our focal teacher's powerfully held beliefs about the purposes of education and therefore about his role meant he refused to 'coach to the criteria', whatever pressures on achievement the school placed on its staff. Yet, as we show later, his beliefs combined with his effective formative assessment to produce very high rates of achievement in the school.
>
> 3. In one e2e course, the charisma and exhaustive levels of personal and emotional commitment from the programme leader, together with strong images that all e2e participants are 'vulnerable' and need a highly supportive, individualized environment, were central to the students' motivation, and to the subtle combination of emotional support and discipline in e2e formative assessment practices.
>
> 4. In all the ALLN classes in our project, a strong public service ethos from the years before forms of strong accountability and regulation were introduced vied with pressures to push students through the Skills for Life tests and tutors' and students' expectations of close, highly supportive and not too-challenging, individual attention.

2. Students' learning and assessment 'careers'

Dispositions to learning

Earlier studies of primary school children's and 16–19-year-olds' experience of and reactions to schooling show the powerful socializing influences of teaching and especially of assessment, both formative and summative.[5] Our case studies of 14–16-year-olds doing an Applied GCSE in Business and a group following a school/college link course for GCSE Health and Social Care, and another study of 17-year-olds in the second year of a BTEC National Diploma in Public Services show that by the time they get to Level 3 study, young people have strong expectations about assessment, support, feedback and 'acceptable' teaching methods. These expectations, in turn, are powerful shapers of their teachers' ideas about students' expectations, behaviours, abilities and dispositions.

Dispositions to learning are shaped both in the past and present and are both stable and open to change. They include expectations, values and beliefs about education, learning and assessment practices, and actions. As a large-scale study of teaching, learning and assessment in further education shows, participants can influence the nature of the field and the learning culture through striving to change and/or preserve certain characteristics or practices.[6] In one course, a distance learning for basic IT skills site had to cater for very diverse students with a desire to learn at home without face-to-face contact, where the way in which they and the tutors interacted through telephone and emails were integral to a distinctive set of practices that made up the learning culture. However, as James and Biesta (2007) argue, much of the impact made by individuals in a learning culture is the result of their presence and actions within it, whether they intend to influence it or not. Teachers and students can play more or less influential roles in a particular learning culture.

For the tutors in our study, deliberate changes to assessment practice were a more focused example of the sort of interventions they designed as an everyday part of their job. Yet, as previous studies show and ours confirms, students sometimes also work on the culture intentionally and can influence it in powerful ways.

Earlier work cited here drew extensively on the ideas of Pierre Bourdieu and argued that 'habitus' is integral to teachers' and students' roles and dispositions.[7] Although Bourdieu focused on social class, as a battery of often subconscious 'durable, transposable' dispositions to all aspects of life, habitus applies equally to factors of gender and ethnicity, nationality or local community. Dispositions develop from social structures operating within and through individuals, rather than something outside of us. Just as mind and body are not separate, neither are the individual and social structures.

Another way of understanding the significance of habitus for practices and what individuals learn, or do not learn, is that students have a significant existence prior to entering the site and prior to becoming part of the research. It is through prior experiences that the dispositions that make up the habitus were developed. These largely tacit dispositions orientate people in relation to anything they do in life, including learning. According to James and Biesta, we should understand these dispositions as a product of accumulated lived experience, at home, school and work, in leisure and in local communities. Dispositions are developed further through particular teaching and assessment experiences, but also through other parts of a student's life that run in parallel with, and sometimes overlap, activities in college. Sometimes existing dispositions are reinforced, modified or changed or new dispositions can be formed. From this perspective, one way of understanding learning is as a process through which a person's dispositions are confirmed, developed, challenged or changed (James and Biesta 2007) (see Box 3.2).

Box 3.2 Dispositions as the focus of 'learning'?

Most of the teachers in our case studies regarded dispositions towards learning, and towards the self as a learner as the most important goal and outcome of 'learning'. Yet the idea that dispositional change or development should be the focus of learning is not value-free. Some brief examples here are developed in the case studies in Section Two of this book.

1. The focus in e2e learning sites was to cajole and motivate young people into creating a positive disposition towards themselves in monitoring, improving and assessing personal discipline, behaviours and attitudes. In this sense, the self and its attitudes, attributes and behaviours form the 'subject content' around which formative assessment is organized.
2. The focus of learning in AVCE Science was on positive dispositions and cognitive ability in acquiring a body of knowledge and skills associated with science.
3. In some of the ALLN classes, teachers' concern was with positive dispositions and attitudes towards coming back into an educational context. In others, teachers had to develop positive attitudes towards literacy and numeracy as a springboard to learning specific concepts and skills.
4. In both e2e and ALNN, teachers had to work out the effects of individuals' dispositions on these goals, while in AVCE Science, although teachers knew their students well, there was much less of a personalized expectation that they would work with them as individuals.

Choice and progression

A significant factor affecting students' and teachers' attitudes to assessment is the nature of 'choice' for a particular track. In vocational education, whether at age 14 or 16, students tend to choose progression routes that both reflect and reinforce an image of themselves as a 'type' of learner suited to particular 'types' of assessment. In further education (FE) colleges, large numbers of vocational teachers teach in the tracks that they themselves have experienced as students, thereby reinforcing stereotypes and perceptions about vocational students. For example, a growing number have done vocational A-levels or their predecessor GNVQ, or a BTEC National Diploma, sometimes followed by a vocational degree, and have internalized many of the assumptions about effective assessment summarized above.

In many general vocational education courses, colleges offer a secure, tightly-knit group within which some students can overcome feelings of failure from school and create a new sense of themselves as a successful learner. Growing numbers of students want to continue a familiar set of teaching and assessment activities from their previous vocational qualification at school. Numerous studies show that their choices are made in a socio-economic context of poor job opportunities and correspondingly uncertain ideas about further or higher education. It is therefore far from evident that students have chosen a track to meet vocational aspirations: instead, they frequently have uncertain, erratic goals and little insight about how their vocational qualification would help them 'progress' to the next stage.[8]

Other studies confirm that choices to study post-school qualifications are strongly differentiated. Dispositions and attitudes, and the often-stereotyped expectations they both produce and emerge from, create particular ideas about suitable opportunities and institutions. These cannot be isolated from employment prospects, the effects of educational differentiation in a local area, students' social class, gender and cultural background and their image of institutions and courses as appropriate for 'people like them'. As Ball et al. (2000) demonstrate, student decision-making and institutional marketing are both predicated on images of what counts as an appropriate learning identity and culture (see also Ball et al. 2005).

Personal development for 'second chance' learners

Earlier studies of assessment systems in further education show that teachers' and students' motivation are influenced very strongly by official targets to raise attainment of grades and to improve retention on courses and progression to formal education at the next level.[9] In many courses, 'learning' and 'achievement' are synonymous, where assessment 'delivers' achievement, mirroring the language of inspection reports and policy texts. Vocational tutors reconcile official targets for delivery with educational goals and concerns about students' prospects, and regard achievement as largely about growing confidence and ability to overcome previous fears and failures. For many vocational education teachers, personal development is often therefore more important than the acquisition of skills or subject knowledge.

Some, but not all, students on vocational courses have a strong sense of identity, even a disposition, as 'second chance' learners and many tutors empathize with this from their own educational experience. This leads to particular ideas about what students like and want, what 'good' assessment is, and what teaching methods and style are 'appropriate' (see Note 9).

Comfort zones

One effect of prioritizing personal development and of particular expectations about what students like and want from 'learning', is a tendency to create 'comfort zones' and to 'protect' students. Earlier studies highlight the extent to which teachers aim to minimize assessment stress or pressure.[10] In keeping with beliefs about 'progressive' or 'student-centred' pedagogy, teachers and students like working in a lively, relaxed atmosphere that combines group work, teacher input, time to work on assignments individually or in small friendship-based groups and feedback to the whole group about completed assignments. In her study of Level 1 vocational students, Liz Atkins found that tutors embellish their ideas about effective teaching with strong images of 'vulnerable', 'at risk' students who do not need or want too much pressure. In parallel, although these students believed they worked hard, high levels of collaborative, relaxed work interspersed with socializing led to very little serious work.[11]

In these earlier studies, the majority of students in vocational courses worked strategically in a comfort zone, adopting a different grade identity from the high achievers. Most did not aim for Distinctions (or A-grades), but for Passes (E-grade) and then perhaps a Merit (C-grade). They were unconcerned about failure, since, as teachers and students knew, not submitting work was the only reason for failure. A minority were high achievers, gaining peer status from consistently good work, conscientious studying and high grades. In Ecclestone's (2004) and Torrance et al.'s (2005) studies, they referred to themselves in the same language as teachers, as 'strong A-grade students', approaching all their assignments with confidence and certainty and unable to imagine getting low grades. Crucial to their positive identity as a successful student was that less confident or lower achieving students saw them as a source of help and expertise. In some courses, successful students drew consciously upon this contrast to create a new, successful learning identity.[12]

Motivation and autonomy

The rhetoric of motivation, engagement, independent learning and student autonomy is integral to ideas about progressive and student-centred learning and assessment. In vocational courses studied in earlier research, goals for retention and achievement, together with teachers' goals for personal development and students' desire to work in a conducive atmosphere without too much pressure, encourage external, introjected and identified motivation and much-valued procedural autonomy. Students used the assessment specifications to aim for acceptable levels of achievement, with freedom for what Inge Bates describes as 'hunting and gathering' information to meet the criteria, to escape from 'boring' classrooms and to work without supervision in friendship groups.[13]

For many students, introjected and identified motivation and procedural autonomy were crucial to confidence and to an emerging identity as a successful student. Familiarity with the assessment requirements and a comfort zone of achievable grades meant that some students could move to the next level of study, and aim for deeper autonomy. Procedural autonomy also enabled students to develop the confidence to ask questions of teachers, initially about official requirements and then about broader aspects of learning.

These findings raise important questions that we pursue in the case studies below, about the relationship between what teachers in these earlier studies, and even more extensively in our research project, referred to as 'independent learning' or 'taking ownership of their own learning', and an instrumental approach to formative assessment based on coaching and feedback. Earlier studies showed that for less confident students, command of the minutiae of the assessment requirements could lead to more subtle insights rooted in a struggle to understand the subject rather than just its procedures or requirements.[14]

For a minority of students, procedural autonomy and an initially instrumental approach enabled them to flourish and then to go on to develop deep forms of motivation and fleeting signs of critical autonomy. In all the studies of assessment cited in this chapter, a minority transformed prescriptive procedures to develop educationally worthwhile outcomes. Yet, this was a very small minority: the majority of their peers aimed for comfortable, safe goals below their potential capacity, based on high levels of instrumental compliance and coaching by tutors to 'fill the gaps' in the criteria. There were also strong indications that the official specifications enabled students to put pressure on teachers to 'cover' only relevant knowledge to pass the assignment, or to pressurize teachers in difficult subjects to 'make it easy'.

Box 3.3   A 'public service ethos' in the learning culture of 'Larkshire' adult education centre

We discuss the impact of Larkshire's learning culture on assessment in literacy and numeracy programmes in Chapter 5. Here we draw out some key elements.

The learning culture that the centre, teachers and students participate in creating, while at the same time being shaped by, is an integral part of a wider and very long-established local authority public service ethos. This is reproduced and reinforced on a day-to-day basis primarily through the social interactions in the centre.

Larkshire is a small community-based AE centre in a country town about 15 miles away in opposite directions from two very large cities, owned by the County Council as one site in the largest local education authority adult education services in the country, covering a mainly rural area. The main building is the size of a large family house of two storeys, which originally was perhaps a local police station. It has offices, a small café area and about six teaching rooms, none of them large enough for classes of more than about 10–12 students. There is a prefab outbuilding, which has two much larger classrooms, and where a crèche is provided. The buildings are surrounded by about an acre of open space, much of which is used for car parking, but also has flowerbeds, a grassed area with benches, and one or two trees. There is a bus stop immediately outside the centre, served by regular buses between the two cities. The centre offers many courses including arts and crafts, independent living, and introductory courses to professional training programmes such as 'Crime and Society', as well as adult literacy and numeracy. Some weeks it is open on Saturdays for weekend and one-off educational events. The building has been modernized internally, and is a very clean and bright environment.

There is a palpable ethos of friendliness and support. The centre is served particularly well by administrative and premises management staff, who are almost always the first point of contact with students. Bureaucracy is kept to a minimum and seems not to be high profile, though standards are officially high: the county service received excellent inspection grades in both 2003 and 2007.

This is typical of 'traditional' adult education settings, where the importance of formal achievement is enriched by a concern for access to learning on any terms, and the quality of the experience, based on an awareness of the marginal position of education in many students' busy lives and the difficulties they often experience in enrolling and attending regularly. In adult basic education, a public sector ethos also includes commitment to the idea of all students' potential to learn successfully, an awareness of the high probability of low confidence levels among many students, and a consequent emphasis on establishing an atmosphere of trust and co-operation between all the participants.

Conclusion

Researchers, staff developers, teachers, managers, policy-makers and inspectors who hope to 'improve' practice have to understand what forms and ways of learning are made possible within a particular learning culture and what forms of learning are made difficult or sometimes impossible. According to James and Biesta (2007: 83), the concept of 'learning culture' helps us to understand practice and its effects on learning outcomes because:

- It shows how complex interrelationships influence learning.
- It shows that both external and internal factors influence learning in any site.
- It enables a clearer identification of any barriers to effective learning, as well as synergies that promote it.
- It shows more clearly what can be achieved to preserve and enhance effective learning and what might action those changes.
- It makes clear the extent to which learning effectiveness lies within or beyond the scope of a particular tutor or teaching team.
- It raises awareness of possibly undesirable learning, and facilitates considered judgements about the value of learning, as well as its effectiveness.

It is clear from discussion so far that the concept of learning cultures has to account for the subtle, local and often idiosyncratic features of practice, expectations and outcomes of very different courses and classes, as well as courses and classes that might, on the surface, appear to be very similar. However, our research showed that there are also general characteristics of what might be called a 'further education' learning culture, an 'academic' or 'vocational' learning culture and an 'adult literacy and numeracy' culture. These general features interact with local expectations, practices and outcomes, and, in turn, these local features interact with the general ones.

There are therefore common features of vocational education and adult basic skills learning cultures, but also powerful differences between different types of programme and institutional setting within a highly diverse, segregated and differentiated lifelong learning sector, or system. Our case studies illustrate this interplay and its effects. For example, the two Applied GCSE courses, in completely different institutional settings, show a remarkably homogeneous set of characteristics in terms of expectations and practices, as do the three e2e learning cultures. In ALLN, our case study of ESOL classes at Westhampton shows that there is a distinct 'ESOL' learning culture, even though it occupies the same qualification and funding regime and is taught in the same types of settings as literacy and numeracy programmes. A comparison between the BTEC National Diploma in Public Services in two FE colleges shows strong common features in the two learning cultures, but also important differences. Further comparison between the GCSE learning cultures and the BTEC courses to which some of their students are likely to progress, shows the powerful socializing influence of the assessment regimes. Finally, the learning culture of AVCE Science and the learning cultures of two ESOL classes show how teachers can resist the instrumentalism that we see as highly problematic in the others.

The concept of learning culture also exposes how mantras about 'good' assessment and teaching practice reflect particular official constructions, reinforced in the 'reified elements' of a learning culture, such as inspection reports, teacher training and professional development materials, and assessment specifications and materials produced by awarding bodies. There are other normative constructions. As our first chapter argued, repeated injunctions to change pedagogy in further and adult education over the past 30 years or so have responded at different times to different concerns about the state of the employment market and people's readiness for it, problems with social cohesion, youth motivation and engagement. Changing assessment practice has been integral to these injunctions, reflecting the British government's tendency to use summative assessment systems to engineer changes in teaching and curriculum content throughout compulsory schooling, further and adult education.[15]

Finally, research on the learning cultures of further education, cited in this chapter, shows that some kinds of learning are made possible as a result of the configuration of a particular learning culture, while others become difficult or even impossible. This raises the question of what influence teachers can have on the characteristics of the learning cultures they work in and help to shape. In a context where the much promoted idea that formative assessment raises achievement and improves motivation and autonomy cannot be taken at face value, our case studies illuminate why certain assessment activities have different effects in different learning cultures, and what factors lie inside and outside teachers' control.

Crucially, our findings also show the need to explore essential educational questions of what sort of person a learning and assessment culture is, or should be, creating, and the forms of knowledge, skills and dispositions that assessment and teaching practices foster, overlook or discourage.

Notes

1. See James and Biesta (2007); *Journal of Vocational Education and Training* (2004); Coffield et al. (2008); Ivanic et al. (2009).
2. See Ecclestone (2002); Torrance et al. (2005).

3. See Brookes et al. (2004); Derrick et al. (2007).
4. In the TLC project, the term 'learning site' was used, rather than 'course', to denote more than classroom learning.
5. See, for example, Reay and Wiliam (1999); Filer (2000); Pollard and Filer (1999); Torrance and Pryor (1998); Ecclestone and Pryor (2003); Ecclestone (2007).
6. For an in-depth analysis of Bourdieu's key concepts that make up a cultural theory of learning, see James and Biesta (2007: 19–21); also *Journal of Vocational Education and Training* (2004); Colley (2006).
7. We do not develop Bourdieu's ideas in our own project but, instead, use it more loosely via the work cited here.
8. See Ecclestone (2002); Davies and Biesta (2006); Davies (2007); Bathmaker (2002); Atkins (2009).
9. See Ecclestone (2002); Torrance et al. (2005); Ecclestone (2007).
10. Ecclestone (2002, 2007); Torrance et al. (2005); Bathmaker (2002); Atkins (2009).
11. Atkins (2009); see also Bathmaker (2002).
12. Ecclestone (2004).
13. Bates (1998a, 1998b).
14. Ecclestone (2002, 2007); Torrance et al. (2005).
15. See, for example, Hargreaves (1989); Ecclestone and Daugherty (2005).

Section 2

Formative assessment in practice

4 Questioning and feedback embedded in teaching:

Resisting instrumentalism in AVCE Science

Introduction

Our case studies of AVCE Science at Moorview Community College and the ESOL classes at Westhampton stand out as only two examples of formative assessment that were truly in the spirit of deep engagement with subject content and process, based on clear ideas about autonomy and motivation, and embedded in everyday classroom pedagogy. Crucially too, these two cases studies are the only ones where the teachers actively resisted a prevailing culture of instrumentalism. It therefore illuminates those factors in a learning culture that encourage constructive rather than disempowered resistance.

In AVCE Science, discussed here, the strategy introduced by Derek Armstrong, our focal teacher, was almost identical to strategies adopted in other case studies. Yet it had very different purposes and outcomes. This confirms that a technical focus on specific methods or approaches is only a tiny part of encouraging formative assessment as part of teaching that is educationally worthwhile. The case of AVCE Science shows a need to develop the subject expertise, confidence and enthusiasm of teachers as a crucial factor in resisting instrumentalism.

Our research focused on the second-year Level 3 AVCE Science course[1] (Advanced Vocational Certificate of Education, more commonly known as a 'Vocational A-level'). The group comprised sixteen Year 13 students aged 17/18, with roughly equal numbers of boys and girls, taught by three teachers involved in our project: Derek Armstrong (Physics), Emma Scott (Chemistry) and Jane Wilkins (Biology). We explore formative assessment through the strategy introduced in our project by Derek. Moorview Community College has a corporate, successful, energetic ethos with high expectations, expressed in the laminated notice displayed in every classroom: 'Opportunity, Achievement, Endeavour, Excellence'. Although this ethos led to a pervasive focus on targets and exam grades, the school also emphasized, and was strongly committed to, wider educational achievements, for example, in sport and the arts.

Derek's approach to formative assessment highlights what we consider to be excellent formative assessment practice for reasons that we explore in this chapter. First, although 'vocational' courses at the school were typical in being generally accepted by students, their parents and certain teachers as being of 'lower' status than the academic single subject courses at GCSE or A-level at Moorview, once on the course, the issue of status became irrelevant to the three teachers and their students, who all praised the AVCE in contrast to single-subject science A-levels. Second, there was a much stronger sense of what 'vocational' meant than in other vocational courses discussed in this book, rooted in a coherent subject curriculum. The AVCE Science students had learnt science from Year 7, and built up a conceptual framework over time and, although their course was termed 'vocational', it was rooted in accepted academic disciplines. In strong contrast to the case study of another Level 3 course, BTEC National Public Services in this book, neither students nor teachers equated 'vocational' with 'practical' activities as opposed to didactic teaching or written work although there were laboratory experiments elements in the three science subjects of AVCE. Instead, the meaning these students attributed to 'vocational' stemmed strongly from the way teachers linked scientific knowledge to real-life situations and to careers. The title 'vocational' here also encompassed the fact that the course included a greater ratio of coursework to exams than the single-subject A-levels.

The nature of teaching and assessment on this vocational course, and the beliefs about learning that informed it, illuminate particular factors that affect the quality of formative assessment in all learning cultures to a greater or lesser extent. In the first section, we show how these teachers and students were not circumscribed by prescription nor by particular expectations of 'types' of students, as can so often happen with vocationally labelled courses. The second section explores the various factors shaping the learning culture of AVCE Science, and the relationship with both formative and summative assessment activities. In the third section, we evaluate the aims and effects of the strategy Derek adopted for the project. In the fourth section, we explore how this learning culture enabled formative assessment to be more of a springboard for deeper forms of learning than seemed to be the case in other learning cultures. The chapter concludes by exploring the implications of the case study for improving practice and for wider questions about what comprises an educationally worthwhile vocational qualification.

1. Clear aspirations for vocational education

Converging goals

At the start of the course, the expectations and aspirations of the teachers differed from those of many of their students. All three teachers were academically well-qualified, with a good degree in their subject and a PGCE, and also professionally experienced: Derek had taught for eight years at Moorview, Emma for seven, and Jane for two (with two previous years teaching at an inner-city comprehensive). The teachers were confident and enthusiastic about their subject areas, teaching subjects that were part of the accepted academic canon translated into a vocational syllabus. In this respect, AVCE Science was different from other general vocational courses, in that its vocationalism was derived from the content and concepts of academic subjects which were then applied to everyday life. This took account of students' interest in scientifically-related jobs and topics rather than being derived from the activities of an occupational area or as a simple, more appealing alternative to the 'onerous' writing and reading young people associate with academic subjects. We return to the broader implications of what many interested parties regard as the 'special case' of Science in the final section of the book.

Leaving aside for the moment the stronger subject roots of vocational Science compared to other courses, a crucial characteristic of this learning culture, and very notable in contrast to others in this book, was the complete absence of 'diminished' images of a 'type' of student who will or will not put up with particular activities or content, or who are perhaps seen as 'vulnerable' or 'at risk', or merely 'disaffected' or 'disengaged'. The AVCE teachers expected their students to achieve, and encouraged high career aspirations while also accepting that students did not usually arrive on the course with such high GCSE grades as those taking separate A-level science subjects, and that significant numbers were disappointed not to be doing 'straight' A-levels. Positive images of students' potential were linked inextricably to teachers' subject enthusiasm and expertise.

Initially at least, there were more varied expectations and aspirations among the students. For certain students, AVCE Science had been a second choice when they failed to achieve high enough grades to take a single-subject science A-level while others saw the course as a positive choice. However, once on the course, students soon developed a high level of enthusiasm and commitment and a desire to study science *per se*, rather than solely for 'vocational relevance'. The aspirations of many students changed during the course. Most did not initially aim for higher education but soon became motivated to apply to study in a vocational branch of science (such as forensic science), or a different field (such as architectural technology) where the vocational A-level grades would help them achieve the necessary points score.

Strong ideas about education

The teachers all had strong theories of learning, and Derek's in particular appeared to be especially influential in shaping both students' expectations of different subjects and their future aspirations. Rooted in his confident sense of expertise and great enthusiasm for his subject, he believed that teaching should enable students to construct their knowledge and understanding with each other and with him, to work actively to understand mistakes and misunderstandings, to learn from them and then build new insights. Classroom observations and student interviews revealed that this espoused theory was also his theory-in-use.

This theory and its enactment had a number of positive features. He routinely asked students to explain a point to the rest of the group, rather than always doing this himself; he refused to spoon-feed the students; they tackled problem-solving together. In contrast to the somewhat mantric use of ideas such as students 'taking responsibility for their own learning', seen in other case studies in this book, he encouraged students to 'be in charge of their own understanding', by which he meant that they needed to ask him or one of their classmates if they didn't understand anything. He stressed the advantages of getting students to come out to the front and explain things to their peers. He observed that students who were very capable at maths could 'understand *why* they're doing it, rather than just doing it, and [were] able to explain that to others as well as – if not better than – I can, at times'. This built up the confidence of those doing the explaining, as well as providing a different explanation that often 'worked' for students when Derek's had not. Yet, he did not shy away from adding his own more expert view when this was needed.[2]

Although, unsurprisingly, students did not conceptualize their learning in exactly the same way as their teacher, and placed a higher premium on their grades, there was a discernible interest in the subject, together with appreciation of the way their understanding and appreciation of science was developing:

> Some of the teachers teach you the subject and some of the teachers just help you learn it. Mr Armstrong will help you learn it and understand it.
>
> (Nick, AVCE student, Moorview)

A crucial feature of Derek's theory and practice of questioning and feedback was his insistence that he would not simply 'teach to the test':

instead, he emphasized constantly the importance of developing students' understanding of the value of scientific knowledge, and ability to become more independent learners, as an essential preparation for university. He believed strongly that an advantage of the vocational over the academic A-level was that it taught students to be 'in charge of their own learning'. This involved his belief that students should acquire self-knowledge in order to be able to learn effectively, in particular knowing when to ask for help: 'I think students must know how good they are, and know what their limitations are.' His teaching and assessment practice encouraged dispositions that could lead to deeper learning, rather than simply success in meeting targets:

> I'm a lot more comfortable with saying, 'You're actually getting a grade that is much more appropriate to what you've done, rather than one which we could have forced you to get, by making you do exactly what we know needs to be done', which obviously we know happens more and more in education because it's all results driven.
>
> (Derek, AVCE teacher, Moorview)

Indeed, he was one of only six in our project sample of 49 teachers not being prepared to compromise to meet a target-driven educational culture and the only one to express it with great passion and confidence:

> There's no point in jumping through hoops for the sake of jumping through hoops and there's no point in getting grades for the sake of getting grades. I know that's not the answer, because the answer is – no, we should be getting them to get grades. But that's never as I've seen it and it never will be.

He was also unique in being unashamed of his confidence, expertise and authority and in seeing it as central to students' achievement. While his theory of teaching and assessment might seem to be typical of student-centred approaches seen in our other case studies, where much activity referred to as 'learning' was collaborative and minimally dependent on teacher input, there was an overt mutual acceptance of the importance of the teacher as leader: 'I believe they all know they can't do it without me.' When asked what motivated his students on the AVCE, Derek's answer was unequivocal: 'I'm going to say it – me, me, me, me.'[3]

His aims were not to simply get students through the course. Ultimately, he wanted them to enjoy science and see its relevance in their lives and the world outside, and be capable of independent study if/when they moved on to university. He wanted to encourage a deeper level of understanding, not simply the 'facts', and acknowledged the advantages of the AVCE in its current resourcing of three teachers, group size of only 16 and a reasonably generous time allocation.

Instrumentalism, enjoyment and 'becoming somebody'

An ethos of teaching and learning interacted with, and was also shaped by, expectations of motivation: the links between student motivation and the various dimensions of a learning culture are therefore symbiotic and iterative. Drawing on Prenzel's typology of motivation, our study showed that expectations of positive achievement for all students interacted with, and were also shaped by, expectations of students' motivation. Teachers showed high levels of *intrinsic* motivation, where engagement with topics and ideas was rooted in their intrinsic value rather than for *external* reward (such as grades), and also *interested* motivation, where a sense of personal and learning identity is bound up with the subject, its activities and possibilities. They expected students to develop intrinsic and interested motivation too.

Students wanted a qualification in order to achieve their individual goals, and the goals stemmed from interest in the course/science. They also showed strong intrinsic interest in specific topics:

> The qualification is the over-riding factor, but they continue to look at Applied Science courses at degree level, which tends to suggest the subject itself is motivating.
>
> (Derek, AVCE teacher, Moorview)

As with the vast majority of school teachers, the language of ability was evident in the AVCE teachers' accounts of practice, but belief in students' ability to learn and achieve was more prominent than the more fixed beliefs found in the typically strong stereotypes of vocational students seen in other studies discussed in Section One and also evident in our other case studies. Derek focused on the positive rather than the negative; indeed, his reference to 'the two weakest students' was to praise their considerable effort which was leading to the achievement of high grades. He combined realism with high expectations for his students:

> We have very well-motivated, interested kids, who like *all* kids doing this type of course, which is an A-level course for students who aren't really designed for A-level, find it hard going and there are dips and troughs.

Images of the students among all three teachers were largely positive. Students were described as: 'lovely', 'great to teach', 'lively' and 'motivated', and they liked engaging with topics and issues in the subject. There was no talk of, 'fragile' learning identities or low self-esteem, 'typical' vocational students 'preferences' for certain types of learning and therefore, no expectation that students would or could not cope with the written demands of the course.

Students wanted a qualification in order to achieve their individual goals (*external* motivation), especially at the start of the course, but the goals stemmed from interest in the course/science and their sense of 'becoming somebody' in a subject with progression and future possibilities (*intrinsic* and *interested* motivation). Motivation appeared to stem from a symbiotic relationship between teachers' expertise and enthusiasm, the supportive group dynamics, the focus on collaborative learning, and students' own vocational goals. However, deep levels of motivation, even among the most enthusiastic students in any course, are rarely constant, and our interviews showed that motivation fluctuated with individuals and over time.

Derek's pedagogy was rooted in a belief in students' potential for becoming deeply interested in his subject, and a refusal to make physics predominantly task-focused:

> I allow one motivation, that's interested[4] motivation . . . I strongly believe that the only way to have motivated students is to have an interest and if I'm not going to have interested and motivated students, then there is *no* real point in them doing the course.

There was therefore a general consensus between teachers and students that science was intrinsically interesting as well as practically relevant. Derek's teaching focused on topics, which led, in turn, to assignments or exam practice, rather than being primarily assessment-based.

2. Assessment for learning the subject of science

Resisting a simplistic view of 'assessment for learning'

Like all vocational courses, assessment in AVCE Science was partly through assignments, partly through exams. Yet, in complete contrast to the total fusion of teaching, formative and summative assessment seen in other general vocational courses, the prime focus of AVCE teachers was not on the assessment, whether formative or summative. Instead, assessment stemmed from teaching subject content with attention to how students might best learn it, rather than being about generic dispositions and attitudes to learning, as it was for teachers in our other case studies. For Derek, formative assessment was about how students learned Science.

Formative assessment was therefore integral to Derek's teaching, although he did not explain it in these terms. Indeed, he was dismissive of what he termed 'jargon' (for him this included the terms 'formative assessment' and 'assessment for learning'), perhaps to a large extent because teachers at Moorview had been subjected to a battery of in-service training events on 'assessment for learning'. He and the other two AVCE Science teachers had not found this helpful but, instead, patronising and simplistic.

Despite his antipathy to jargon, it was clear from his practice, however, that a sophisticated approach to, and understanding of, formative assessment were deeply embedded within it; there was constant reciprocal feedback between him and his students, and he amended his teaching in response to that feedback. He showed subtle but sophisticated skills in particular aspects of formative assessment such as classroom questioning that enabled students to admit mistakes or uncertain insights so that he could build on these collaboratively, and he used peer and self-assessment judiciously. Again, in contrast to the coaching to the minutiae of each criterion seen in other vocational courses, he integrated critical and positive feedback with teaching:

> I don't think there is any point in scribbling on a piece of paper, 'This isn't done right. This is how it should be done.' I think you've actually got to go through and do it *with* them. They've got to know where the issues and the problems are for themselves.

A further practice was individual tutorial time with students on their coursework assignments. As we show below, Derek's decision to change his approach to coursework was another stark difference from how tutorials were used in our other case studies.

'Interested motivation'

Instrumentalism, compliance, external motivation and deeper ideas about learning and education seemed to co-exist comfortably and symbiotically in AVCE Science. Derek recognized the value of external motivation stemming from aiming for particular grades in coursework, and from having the goal of a university place. He explained that, concerning coursework, if students could say '"We just want to sort this and get such and such a grade", you know that's going to work'. Yet, crucially, he also refused to play the 'grades only game', as already illustrated. Derek made no secret of the fact that he did not want 16 identical pieces of work, not just because it would be 'very dull to mark', but largely because that would not reveal fully what each student had understood. He refused to simply dictate to students what was needed because that would encourage the kinds of assignment clones[5] that he was vehemently against ('I *hate* that so *much*', his emphasis). He had turned firmly away from falling into that 'trap', asserting 'I'm not going to allow myself to do so.' He was scathing about the way many institutions now taught solely to the task, the extent of which he had realized through his recent work as an awarding body moderator. Instead, he preferred to encourage students' independence as learners but again in contrast to how 'independent learning' was used in our other case studies, he meant something quite different from merely working without him, or being able to move without help through the technical demands of the assessment criteria.

Indeed, his students appeared to enjoy challenges in learning, were not risk-averse, and did not assume that their teachers would 'get them the grade'. Learning and assessment were understood to be a partnership by the students as much as by the teachers. Within this aspiration, motivation had a sense of Prenzel's category of 'interested', where students were gaining a sense of subject-based identity, with related attitudes and subject knowledge that was more than the general maturation and transition to adulthood valued by students and teachers in the BTEC National Diploma in Public Services, discussed in Chapter 7.

In theory, there was potential for negative tension in formative assessment activities between Moorview's target-driven, achievement-orientated ethos and the AVCE Science teachers' commitment to their subjects, but in practice this did not materialize. Instead, as described, these teachers saw formative assessment as being about how students learned and as part of a continuum of teaching and assessment techniques deeply embedded in their day-to-day practice. Derek used formative assessment to help students construct their knowledge, rather than solely to achieve targets. As he put it, 'I can teach them to enjoy the science – but I wouldn't call that formative assessment.' Yet, as we have already stressed, in a highly instrumental culture it is important to reiterate here that his declaration, 'My primary concern has never been their final grade', was not a sign of a cavalier attitude: all his students achieved high enough grades to gain their choice of university place.

3. Improving grades and subject knowledge

Using the grade criteria with students

All three teachers in the AVCE Science team for our project chose their formative assessment strategies in order to improve summative assessment: in this respect, the initial imperative was instrumental. Because Derek's exam marks were always higher than his coursework marks, and it was the opposite for his colleagues Emma and Jane, he adopted a new assessment strategy that was different from theirs. Emma and Jane chose to approach exam revision in a more focused and structured way, in particular with the way they approached and used practice exam questions. Derek considered that his use of individual tutorials for all coursework was an inefficient use of time, encouraging over-dependence on himself as the provider of answers.

He therefore decided to take a different approach to coursework. This involved making detailed use of an explanatory grid for the assignment criteria, in order to engage students with what the criteria really meant in terms of quality, alongside helping students become more independent in assessing their own work. In contrast to the teaching seen in other case studies, Derek assessed students' understanding of the E, C and A grade criteria through constant question/answer, peer discussion, making judicious use of the smartboard, and getting students to check the criteria against what they had written on their handouts concerning their own assignments. An earlier stage in the strategy was getting students to rewrite the grade criteria in their own words, to make it clearer what they had to accomplish.

Derek's and his students' expectations for this strategy were ostensibly similar, namely that this new way of focusing on the coursework criteria would improve understanding of what was required for the assignment. The students, however, interpreted 'understanding' in a different way from their teacher. Both teacher and students were concerned that students should improve their coursework marks, Derek specifically aiming for them reaching the C or A grade criteria, but for students Vanessa and Nick this was the only goal, i.e. this strategy was in the 'letter' of formative assessment for the students. In other learning cultures, as case studies of NPDS and GCSE Business and Health and Social Care show, these expectations exerted a strong influence on teachers' assessment strategies. The way Derek conceptualized his strategy was much more than this.

Resisting instrumentalism

Derek also aimed to increase students' depth of understanding of the topic under discussion (energy resources and the environment) and to encourage independent working. He wanted students to develop the skills of critical self-assessment, rather than over-reliance on himself as the teacher. Derek spoke about making the coursework criteria more 'meaningful' to students, about the importance of helping them to work 'more independently' and that alongside encouraging students to aim high, the point of his strategy was to encourage them, for them to realize, 'Well, it's not actually as difficult as you think it is.' He refused to give students a 'check list', 'because that's *not* preparing, that's *not* what the course is about and *they* should be working more independently. So in doing what I did today, it wasn't a list' (his emphasis). His aims were both long- and short-term:

> They are getting close to being students that will cope reasonably well at university... and I think that's a lot of what this sort of work's about.

Derek considered his strategy had been partially successful. He thought that students still returned too readily for individual explanations of coursework criteria even after the class where they had rewritten the criteria in their own words, so in future he would devote more time to this work earlier in the year. Nevertheless, he hoped students would take away lessons from it that would be useful for their university studies the following year. Although Vanessa and Nick did not talk about such long-term benefits, they both sounded more confident about what they could now do with their coursework, now they had 'more direction'. Optimistically, their more restricted view would serve as a springboard for deeper learning once at university.[6] Pessimistically, if this experience is not capitalized on, instrumental expectations are very likely to remain.

4. Resisting the pressures of instrumentalism

The spirit of subject content

By comparing our case study of AVCE Science with similar courses in other research projects, it appears that very few learning cultures indeed encourage deep approaches in formative assessment that focus on a subject.[7] It seemed that the high level of synergy and the expansive nature of the learning culture of AVCE Science both encouraged and encompassed practices in the 'spirit' of formative assessment, and hence as a springboard for this type of learning. The strategies used in our project were no different in this respect from the ongoing formative assessment practices already embedded in the teaching on the course.

In other learning cultures, Derek's strategy might have been used purely as an instrumental exercise, in the 'letter of formative assessment', but here it was very much in the 'spirit of formative assessment', encouraging habits of learning alongside intrinsic interest in science rather than extrinsic success in meeting targets. Derek believed that if he adopted a more didactic approach, some students might gain higher coursework grades, although his course always more than met his school's targets. Such a view, however, presents a potential ethical dilemma: should teachers' priority be to help their students to gain the highest possible grades when doing so might be detrimental to developing students' deeper understanding, or should such deeper understanding come first? As explained earlier in this chapter, Derek was highly critical of the current educational ethos and remained more comfortable with the philosophy of encouraging student independence in learning, even if that meant that not all students gained the highest grades that might be possible.

There was a high degree of convergence between teacher and student expectations. Teachers expected students to achieve, and students developed enthusiasm to do so. The system of 6th-form selection had guaranteed a certain level of achievement and motivation and, by this second year of the course (Year 13 students), the few students who had decided that AVCE Science was not for them had left after their AS year. This helped in making the group very cohesive, while of course consisting of individuals with varying predispositions and dispositions (for example, Nick's love of rugby was greater than his interest in science – 'rugby's my life'); in these ways there was divergence as well as convergence.

Highly significant in producing cohesion were the ways in which teachers' and students' ideas about learning converged over time. Students had generally begun the course expecting the work to be reasonably easy and thus restrictive and 'safe', rather than challenging. In fact, through the teachers' pedagogy, they had come to accept challenge and risk, not in *what* they were learning, but in *how* they were learning. Instead of experiencing predominantly the straightforward 'transmission' kind of learning they had initially expected, they found themselves explaining work to their fellow students, joining in Derek's explanations, and losing any initial inhibitions about asking questions of Derek and of one another. Problems were not seen as indicators of their lack of ability.

Understandably, grades were important to both students and teachers, but Derek's refusal to compromise over the value of wider scientific knowledge and his insistence that he would not 'teach to the test' also influenced how students felt about their learning. Derek's beliefs and commitments were very powerful factors in this learning culture. Hence, alongside its collaborative nature, it was rooted in a strong belief on both sides that the teacher was the most crucial factor in learning.

Strong vocationalism

We noted in earlier in this chapter how the confidence of teachers in a subject that is rooted in an academic canon was translated productively into a robust meaning of 'vocational' science. This arose partly from the syllabus specifications (especially some of the more overtly vocationally focused units like Pathology) and the balance between coursework and examinations. There was no sense that students could not 'cope' with exams. Nevertheless, the status of the course at Moorview was lower than that of single-subject A-levels because of its 'vocational' label and the wider-ranging GCSE backgrounds of its students. Despite this, by the final year of the course, the majority of the students were aiming at HE, largely to study subjects with a scientific vocational focus, such as forensic science.

A strong meaning of 'vocational' was central to the learning culture, enhanced by teachers being able to teach throughout the college and therefore getting to know many of their students well during their school careers. These contextual aspects were highly influential in producing a collaborative learning culture in which both vocational and academic aspects co-existed comfortably.

Resource and structural dimensions were also crucial, including a high teacher/student ratio, small group size and fairly generous teaching time allocation, as were the students' dispositions to learning. Aged 17/18, students became more focused on vocational goals in their last year at school. For some, 'horizons for action' had broadened during Year 13 through their relationship with the course, and they were now aiming for university, which had not been a consideration when they started the course in Year 12.[8] Moreover, while some students were choosing to study at their local university, as is often the case with Level 3 vocational students, others planned to study further afield. There was, therefore, a strong ethos among students and teachers of progression in a clear route to something desirable and interesting. This reinforced the strong subject culture of Science, applied approvingly by teachers and students to real vocational and life contexts.

High expectations

The understanding, interaction and collaboration which characterized the AVCE Science course meant that students developed and maintained positive dispositions to learning as the course progressed, although not all to the same extent or level.[9] Although overall dispositions to learning became more positive, there was always individual variation. Teachers and students considered effort to be as important as 'ability' in students' achievements, alongside their own teaching skills. As Derek said,

> I believe they all know they can't do it without me [and] they all know that the more effort they put in, the better grade they will get, and that is clearly exemplified by some of the academically weaker members of the group who are *very* contented with the course.

Yet it is important not to overplay positive aspects of motivation and dispositions to learning. Despite some evidence of *intrinsic* and *interested* motivation, students did not maintain stable levels of these. Towards the end of Year 2, even the most enthusiastic students were 'getting through' with the future external reward of finishing the course and getting to the next stage. This confirms that 'types' of motivation are not stable or individual 'traits' but fluctuate and vary over time and in different contexts.

Expectations and a strong sense of 'vocational' meant that the learning culture of AVCE Science was characterized by a high level of synergy while also being reasonably 'expansive' on an 'expansive/restrictive' continuum. In other words, the teachers, even within the restrictions of the syllabus, took opportunities to promote an interest in scientific problems, questions and topics which was reflected in the interest and motivation of the group as a whole. In other vocational courses explored in this book, teachers' and students' purposes were very varied, and where vocational knowledge and purposes were weaker and less coherent, in AVCE Science, these features were narrow and more focused.

Moreover, the vocational relevance of the AVCE contributed towards the expansive nature of the learning culture. The course was not vocational in the sense of providing work placements (although it did include relevant trips and experimental laboratory work), and much of it demanded 'academic' skills (such as logical thinking, structuring a report and so on). However, both Nick and Vanessa praised the course for the way it related constantly to 'life'. Vanessa mentioned the links with nutrition and pollution, while Nick referred to how his learning had enabled him to understand his uncle's heart bypass operation and how the anaesthetic worked when he needed stitches after a rugby match. For certain students, like Vanessa, there was also a more direct link between the course and her vocational goal of a degree in forensic science – the unit on pathology. The course indeed appeared to be 'vocational' above all in the way the teachers related the knowledge they taught to real-life experience. As Derek summed up:

> I think the real life concepts that we try and pull out in everything works very well. I think we're *incredibly* fortunate to have time to teach *learning*, as opposed to time to teach *content*.
>
> (original emphases)

Conclusion

While it is common for teachers to say, often simplistically, that formative assessment is 'just part of what we do' or that 'learning is co-constructed with students', Derek's approach helped students gain realistic grades and developed their enthusiasm for, and knowledge of, scientific principles and topics alongside the skills of self-assessment. The AVCE Science learning culture illuminates well the factors that enable formative assessment to be embedded in subject-based pedagogy in educationally powerful ways.

Students' willingness to admit to misunderstandings or half-understandings, and teachers' use of these as the core of effective formative assessment were significant. The AVCE learning culture encouraged students to view a problem as an interesting question to be explored collectively, with Derek firmly in charge, rather than seeing it as an indicator of lack of ability.

Significantly, formative assessment was far from being predominantly grade-focused, despite the strong institutional ethos. Integral to this, was the total absence of the bland and ubiquitous rhetoric of 'learning' that is now invoked routinely in many parts of the education system. Instead, the spirit of formative assessment was very evident in AVCE Science, rooted in strong values and beliefs about the need for confident teaching and coherent subject content as the basis for skilled classroom pedagogy.

The case study also confirms that the frequently heard claims to be 'student-centred', 'independent learners' or developing 'learning to learn' skills have to be underpinned by strong subject expertise and confidence if they are not to become vacuous ends in themselves. Integral to this was that, despite the lower status of vocational courses at Moorview, AVCE Science teachers and students appeared to cast off such lower status very rapidly. Enthusiasm for a strong meaning of 'vocational' education meant that linking scientific knowledge to 'relevant' topics and to students' careers also broadened their horizons and was not in conflict with academic content, higher-level analytical skills and the encouragement to study further.

In contrasting Derek's method with other case studies that also encouraged students to engage proactively with grade criteria, we argue that broader professional values and expertise were able to co-exist with a highly prescriptive assessment system because they enabled instrumentalism to be a genuine springboard to deeper learning and motivation.

Nevertheless, challenging the idea that instrumentalism is either inevitable or realistic is far from easy. We observed above that our presentation of the AVCE Science case study at conferences, seminars and professional development courses invokes the response that Derek is 'old-fashioned' and 'too didactic'. Others have commented, including representatives from awarding bodies, that (1) science is 'different' from other vocational subjects in its strong content base and (2) many teachers are neither as expert or as confident as Derek and so we should not present the teacher as central to any learning culture.

This raises a salient question: if teachers and their expertise are not central to a learning culture, how can they question and enhance their own professional values and subject expertise in a climate that encourages instrumentalism or accepts it as 'inevitable' or 'realistic'? What conditions have to prevail for them to do this, and which ones can they realistically influence in the majority of vocational education courses?

Notes

1. AVCEs replaced General National Vocational Qualifications in 2000, enabling them to be presented as 'Vocational A-levels'. See Chapter 1 for fuller discussion of changes and developments in the vocational curriculum.
2. Analysis of effective questioning and feedback shows that these features are quite rare and yet essential for the classroom culture created by teachers, and together with overt attention to developing students' skills in dialogue, using a richer vocabulary than normal through focused discussion, are crucial to formative assessment embedded in teaching.
3. It is interesting yet salutary to note that when we have presented findings about Derek and his approach, values and beliefs at staff development and research conferences, audiences of teachers, awarding body officials, and staff development managers initially respond that he is 'didactic' and 'teacher centred', 'arrogant' and 'uncaring' for not wanting to get his students the best grades possible, and therefore a 'poor' teacher. Yet, his grades were among the best in the school and his students were highly motivated for the subject as well as grade achievement.
4. Unsurprisingly, Derek's use of 'interested' motivation is not the same as the one we have adopted from Prenzel's typology, discussed in Chapter 2 of this book; here he means 'intrinsic' motivation.
5. 'Assignment clones' refer to the practice that has emerged since the days of GNVQ of creating assignment briefs that enable students to work closely to tasks tailor-made to enable them to address each grade-related criterion in the specifications, and, in turn, enable awarding body moderators to judge that teachers' grading decisions are 'standardized'. One effect is to produce highly formulaic and homogeneous work from students that teachers find boring to mark but easy to show awarding body officials at standardizing meetings that they have 'moderatable evidence' (see Ecclestone (2002); Torrance et al. (2005); and the BTEC NPDS case study in this book).

6. In an earlier study of formative assessment in Advanced GNVQ, the predecessor to AVCE, Philip, a high achieving Business student who progressed to a Business degree in a local university, worked out for himself how to move from what had been a very instrumental approach to a deeper one in the less prescriptive, more holistic approaches he encountered there (see Ecclestone 2002).
7. See studies cited in Section One of this book: Ecclestone (2002); Torrance et al. (2005); James and Biesta (2007).
8. We discussed the notion of 'horizons for action' in Chapter 3: see also Hodkinson et al. (1996).
9. See Chapter 3 for discussion of 'dispositions'.

5 Coaching to the grade in 14–19 vocational education[1]

Introduction

Our case studies of GCSE Applied Business at Moorview Community College, and GCSE Health and Social Care as part of a 'link' course between a local school and Oldminster College, are stark examples of formative assessment that teachers regarded and practised unproblematically as 'coaching to the criteria'. Nevertheless, it is also evident, and as our other case studies also show, that individual teachers' values, beliefs, motivation and expertise remain crucial shapers of the two learning cultures discussed here. They also show how close forms of coaching for grade achievement are embellished by individual mentoring. These are powerful socializing influences on students' 'learning and assessment careers', with implications for the expectations they are likely to have if they progress to similar courses at a higher level, either at school or college.[2]

The other crucial feature of both the Applied GCSE learning cultures discussed here was highly uncertain meanings of 'vocational.' As we showed in Section One of this book and in our case study of BTEC National Diploma in this section, meanings of 'vocational' at both Level 3 and Level 2 have become hazy, diffused and over-loaded. Intertwined with this problem are powerful stereotypes of a 'type' of student suitable for vocational courses in which ability, personal and educational attitudes and their preference are more influential than vocational aspirations.

Our two learning sites were very different. Applied Business took place in Moorview Community College which, as we showed in Chapter 4 on AVCE Science, was an institution with high expectations of achievement combined with a strong community and general education ethos. Our research with the GCSE Applied Business course followed three 'mixed-ability' groups of roughly equal numbers of boys and girls in the second year of their course (Year 11): Groups 1 and 2 (with 23 and 21 students respectively) were taught by Laura Newton, our focal teacher, and Group 3 (with 20 students) by William Marwood, Head of Department. The students were all aged 15–16. In GCSE Health and Social Care, our research followed four students attending Oldminster College for a day a week as part of a school/college link course and the focal teacher of a team of three, Mary Radnor. We focus here on the tutor Mary, and Hannah, one of the students.

This chapter illuminates the key factors shaping a 'coaching to the criteria' learning culture, drawing out similarities and differences between the two courses. The first section explores how students and teachers regarded the purposes of vocational GCSE courses, the types of students and their motivation. The second section examines the various factors shaping each learning culture, and their relationship with both formative and summative assessment activities. The third section describes the strategies adopted by the teachers involved in the project, their rationale and the hoped-for effects. The fourth section evaluates the ways in which the learning cultures affected the outcomes and effects of the strategies. Finally, the chapter raises implications for pedagogy and assessment, teacher professional development and wider educational questions. In particular, insights from the case study support some key findings from the recent extensive Nuffield Review of 14–19 Education, and a challenge to the almost total absence of political and professional debate about the purposes and content of 'vocational' education.

1. Expanding the purposes of vocational education?

Diverse aspirations

In both courses, teachers' and students' initial expectations of the course were quite different. In GCSE Business, one of the two teachers in our project had wider, more idealistic views of the course as providing students with a broad picture of the world of business and its relevance to everyday life. A different overall aim prevailed at Oldminster College where there seemed to be stronger expectations among staff and students in GCSE HSC that, if students were successful, the course would lead directly to a Level 3 course at college in a related subject, such as a BTEC National Diploma in Health and Social Care or Public Services. Not least, this was because both tutors were experienced in vocational courses in a further education context rather than a school one.

A crucial motivator for students was that vocational GCSEs enabled them to receive two GCSEs at the end of two years. As with the AVCE Science course, there was an implicit acceptance by teachers, parents and most students that vocational courses were of lower status than single-subject courses. However, in contrast to AVCE Science where the issue of status diminished rapidly after the start of the course, it remained a significant factor in GCSE Applied Business. And, while a distinct understanding of 'vocational' emerged on AVCE Science, albeit far removed from the general understanding of practical, 'hands-on' learning, there was much less clarity as to what 'vocational' meant in Applied GCSEs.

Although it had potentially strong life and work applications, both courses had a somewhat nebulous subject base that were not well recognized outside subject specialists. Unlike their other GCSE subjects, 'vocational subjects' were new to 14-year-olds; they had no previous conceptual framework to build on. It was, moreover, a new 'vocational' subject, the meaning and status of which carried mixed messages and interpretations about, for example, 'practical' activities as opposed to didactic teaching or written work, and the application of topics to work or life-related contexts.

There was a tacit acceptance by teachers and students that such courses were easier and therefore suitable for 'non-academic' young people. This was largely because of the kinds of written tasks involved and the greater ratio of coursework to examination (two-thirds coursework, one-third examination) than because they were more practically orientated. Certainly GCSE Applied Business was not vocational in the sense of being practical or 'hands-on'. It could be described as officially but not practically vocational: that is, it involved writing about vocational topics rather than undertaking vocational tasks, it did not include any work experience, and there were very few visits to companies.

In contrast, although the interviewed students expected the course to be 'useful' in a non-specific way, they had largely chosen it because they wanted to avoid assessment through written examinations. Some had no better alternative; it was merely an option to fill a timetable. In GCSE Business, only a few students had chosen the course because they thought they might like a business career and even here, like many vocational students, they had only a very hazy idea of what this would involve. Some had also chosen it because it was a double award. The age (15/16) and level of maturity of these students were, of course, significant factors in their aims and aspirations for the future. Some were eager to progress to the next stage of their education; others were less keen. Even among the more enthusiastic, there was also some wariness about leaving behind the more familiar aspects of their education.

Two contrasting factors affected expectations on both sides in GCSE HSC. One was that the school could off-load those young people it deemed to be disaffected, difficult or disengaged onto a course run by the college, and could insist that students remained enrolled at college rather than taking them back into school or finding alternative courses. The other was that 'care' was familiar to the entirely female group where students did have vocational aspirations: some wanted to be primary teachers, others to work in the care system because, according to their college tutor, Mary, 'they probably don't know anything else. They're used to babysitting, they're used to their own brothers and sisters and things like that' and this was confirmed by student data. Another strong expectation was Mary's view that 'people who come into care . . . actually need it more themselves. I've *always* said that, so that is never going to change' (original emphasis). As her colleague Deborah also observed: 'Of course they come to health and social care thinking they're going to look after babies, but they're not, they can't.' Students often chose HSC for practical, hands-on vocational experience and were very disappointed at the amount of written work expected of them.

The two teachers for GCSE Applied Business, Laura and William, were both experienced and well-qualified teachers. However, despite their best intentions of conveying the importance and excitement of the world of business, their teaching was largely concerned with meeting targets. Their theory of learning was primarily of learning as the transmission of knowledge and objectives from teacher to student, at least for students at this stage (Level 2) and age.

In GCSE HSC at Oldminster, Mary Radnor had a special needs background and had also been a local authority health officer. She thought that, through a combination of subject coaching at the college and participating in our project, she was moving away from a more general approach of support and 'nurturing' to encouraging more independence:

> I'm not supposed to tell them what to do, and that's difficult for me, because the bit of special needs I've had to shed in this job is telling people what I think is a good plan of action. And I'm quite glad to get rid of that, actually, because over the years . . . special needs grinds you down, because people always look to you for an answer . . . I'm . . . getting to the point where I'm getting closer to retirement and as I wind down, I . . . don't want to be answerable to other people's questions, and this technique [your project] has brought in and what I've learned from subject coaching is turning the tables of responsibility back on to the person who is needy and saying 'Well, how can I help you help yourself?'

Despite their reservations about which students schools were sending to college, both teachers were highly committed to teaching a younger cohort.[3]

Modular 'learning'

Applied Business students saw knowledge as largely separate 'chunks' being 'delivered to' them, implying a corresponding 'modularization of learning'. Indeed, while praising the pace of the course, Sarah's (Group 3) language bore this out: 'You can take more time to, like, let it set in, before you have to move on to the next unit and get some more chucked in' (Sarah, GCSE Business student, Group 3, Moorview).

However, while teachers in both courses were critical of the current 'spoon-feeding' culture of secondary education, they felt trapped within it. It seemed particularly difficult for them to resist this 'spoon-feeding' route with a combination of younger students, a vaguely defined subject base, and the low status of vocational GCSEs. They saw the prevailing educational culture as one where students expected teachers to 'get them through' the course; learning was seen less as a partnership where student effort was crucial, more as almost entirely the teacher's responsibility.

In GCSE Business, students regretted that there was little collaborative or interactive learning during this second year of the course. The Moorview message was that collaboration was not part of GCSE learning and, in order to discourage plagiarism from the internet, students were subject to stern warnings about work being 'their own'. This resulted in students spending much time working individually at computers, with little peer learning and virtually no didactic teaching. Coursework requirements, in the students' eyes, did not necessarily equate to learning. As one of the students explained:

> I did find it more interesting when we were learning as a class ... I just felt like I was learning more then instead of sort of teaching myself as we were going along.
> (James, Group 3 GCSE Business student, Moorview)

Enjoyable learning was also linked to the teacher's willingness to help by, making learning 'easier', as Jim's enthusiasm showed:

> I love Miss Newton. She's a brilliant teacher, excellent. It's very easy – she's made layouts so we have to find whatever we need to do in the book and type it on the computer and it just makes ... learning a lot easier and also if you do something wrong, she doesn't snap at you. She won't shout at you ... She just *looks* at you and you know from that just to be quiet. It's a nice way of learning.
> (Jim, Group 2, GCSE Business student, Moorview)

This 'type of student'

There were largely weak expectations of achievement and engagement between the two teachers, and between the teachers and their students. This was evident in many frequent references to students' 'ability'. At Moorview, both Laura and William referred to 'able' and 'weak' students, but while Laura also used the terminology of achievement ('lower' and 'higher' achievers), William's language revealed more fixed views of abilities and the ways students learned, referring, for example, to some as 'your spoon-feed people', and to the simplest version of the criteria as 'an "idiot sheet"...where...the lower ability students can just meet the basic standards'. Nevertheless, he was also open to evidence of potential, as when he entered three Year 10 students for Applied Business AS-level alongside their GCSE. These students had responded well to working on their own, and had unwittingly been following this higher level course on the computer. In the AS, taken a year earlier than would have been usual, they were also progressing successfully.

The majority of students regarded effort as being as important as ability, if not more so. Although one student had labelled himself as non-academic, he linked such a disposition to learning with lack of motivation and concentration rather than directly with ability. He rationalized the reason why he was not achieving as well as had been predicted:

> I'm not really an academic child [because] I seem to like drift off...I define an academic child as someone who can easily work and who is somebody that can – how can you put it? – keep...motivated I'd say, just constantly keep motivated on the job that's in hand.
>
> (Jim, Group 2, GCSE Business student, Moorview)

Crucially here, his image of vocational is equated with demotivation and an ability to stay 'engaged'. This is similar to an image among many vocational teachers, where some, particularly those in FE Colleges, identify strongly with their students' attitudes, preference and difficulties.[4] Mary's own learning experience influenced strongly how she applied ideas about teaching and learning to her students:

> Well, I'm a practical learner. I also have low-level dyslexia, and so does my son, and I've spent *years* adopting personal strategies for the things I need to learn, with as little writing as possible...I'm a kinaesthetic learner and I'm a kinaesthetic teacher ...Learning through doing things – absolutely...not sitting in a classroom, endlessly, endlessly, endlessly tied to a classroom.
>
> (Mary, HSC teacher, Oldminster)

Individualized working

Approaches to teaching and learning did not lead to cohesive groups in either GCSE Business or HSC. In the former, Groups 1 and 2 were more cohesive than Group 3; lack of cohesion seemed to stem from the presence of distinct sub-groups within each class. Each of the three Applied Business groups contained some students who were clearly *amotivated* (namely, they had no motivation at all, not even through external sanctions or rewards). The presence of amotivated and/or disruptive students was most obvious in Group 3, together with the higher achieving sub-group. The physical layout of the teaching rooms contributed towards lack of cohesion, especially William's room which was partially divided into computer booths, into which the less committed students retreated. This removed them physically, socially and cognitively from the main interaction between teacher and students.

In both GCSE courses, higher achieving students disliked having to be in a class with those who were unmotivated, comparing Applied Business unfavourably with the 'tiered' groups of their other GCSE subjects. As James said, 'I would have preferred it if I had been with ... people that had chosen it because they wanted to, not because it was what they fell back on' (James, Group 3, GCSE Business student, Moorview). However, the more motivated students sat apart from their unmotivated colleagues and their own motivation did not appear to have been affected by them. They were fatalistic about their amotivated peers, believing such students could not be motivated by anything at Moorview (neither by teachers, nor courses, nor the rest of the group). The teachers considered that the motivation of this sub-group could be increased, but only by external factors beyond teachers' control, like a more supportive home background, or a more practically orientated vocational course that included relevant work experience.

According to students, one reason for improved motivation in Year 2 of GCSE Health and Social Care was that less committed students left after the first year. In contrast to emphasis on individual work within groups at Moorview, tutors at Oldminster channelled motivation to get good grades into intensive one-to-one tutoring. Mary considered that peer pressure was a powerful factor that affected motivation and achievement adversely, so an advantage of an individual tutorial system was that it could improve motivation, in 'the privacy of a one-to-one situation away from the group where they can see what the tutor thinks will be good for them to do'. The combination of lower-achieving students where, according to Mary, 'the guys that *we* get are not the stars. The stars are kept back by the school' and she believed that the prevailing culture that 'it's not cool to be clever' made it difficult for many students to remain motivated.

2. Feedback for grade achievement

Boundaries and constraints

One strong interpretation of our GCSE data is that the dependency of students on detailed feedback that is so evident in our case study of the

National Diploma in Public Services (NDPS) begins at 14. Yet, unlike some teachers on the BTEC course at Oldminster, tension between broader ideas about learning and subject content, and the demands of official systems, was almost non-existent in both courses here. Teachers and students considered formative assessment solely as the direct route to, and motivator for, summative assessment. Laura and William equated it predominantly with oral and written feedback to help students improve their coursework marks through redrafting. The visible form was the 'cover sheets' that provided an individual progress record for each coursework unit and an accompanying language of 'targets', 'meeting criteria', 'evidence' and 'levels', the same language that teachers used to describe learning.

Both teachers at Oldminster focused on grade achievement. Deborah, the course leader, thought that students did not realize how demanding this was:

> I'm coming from a place of 'This is what you need to know, this is how we're going to do it, this *is* how we're going to get you through. Jump, jump, jump, jump' and I don't think they like that.

Mary saw formative assessment as partly synonymous with paperwork records, a grid to keep track of marks and targets 'as a result of *needing* to keep feeding them the grades and to keep track of the fact that they may be underachieving' (Mary, HSC teacher, Oldminster, original emphasis). She disliked writing comments on work, preferring instead to provide lists on a separate piece of paper: 'They go away with . . . things that might be missing and then they cross them off and chuck them away.'

Deborah described her way of working as 'supporting learning', with 'learning' synonymous with formative feedback that was '*very, very* prescriptive about *what* exactly they need to do to improve their grade' (Deborah, course leader, HSC, Oldminster, original emphasis).

For the students too, formative assessment, feedback and learning all merged into one entity. The kinds of comments that students made about feedback (i.e. helping them with their coursework) were very similar to those they made about teaching/learning, in particular about what made a good teacher and how their teacher helped them. For example, the readiness of the teacher to help was a vital aspect of good feedback: 'All you basically have to do is stick your hand up. She'll come running if you want her' (Jim, Group 2, GCSE Business Moorview. Almost identically to their older peers in our case study of BTEC National Diploma, GCSE students thought feedback was indispensable:

> Feedback is the main thing . . . I don't feel as if I'm learning anything unless I'm having feedback, being given feedback. It doesn't

matter whether it's positive or negative, but at least you can sort
of steer yourself in the right direction.

(James, Group 3, Business, Moorview)

They appreciated both written and oral feedback and most found knowing
interim marks motivating.

The high-achieving institutional ethos of both our sites was a strong
contextual feature of the GCSE learning culture. An uneasy contrast between this ethos and the nebulous vocational nature of the course found
a resonance in instrumental grade-driven pedagogy. At Moorview, the
mixed ability, rather than settled groups, and tight adherence to the
boundaries of the syllabus, also contributed towards a learning culture
that was both instrumental and restrictive.

Yet, in light of the age and maturity of students, and with an applied
course heavily dependent on precise official criteria, this was perhaps both
unsurprising and appropriate. A fairly fixed approach could lead to students feeling confident with this 'new' subject and achieving well in the
coursework units because they were clear about what they had to do.
In this context, instrumentalism could, potentially, be a springboard for
deeper learning, once a safe base had been established.

A narrow curriculum

Predictably perhaps, and despite the positive view that students had of
their teachers' formative feedback, the downside of such restrictiveness
was that students showed little appreciation of the wider issues relating
to the worlds of business or health and social care. In these learning cultures, the dynamic interaction of teachers' and students' dispositions to
learning, the specification of the syllabus and the strong emphasis on
raising grades, the make-up of the groups, the physical properties of the
classrooms, and heavily individualized approaches all reduced possible
expansiveness.

In GCSE Business, there seemed to be learning opportunities that were
not taken up. For example, students spoke thoughtfully about what they
had gained from their work experience in various organizations, and what
they were learning from their part-time jobs, but this was not brought into
the course in any way. Indeed, any expansiveness seemed to arise outside
the parameters of the course itself. For example, Laura had encouraged her
students to enter a regional business enterprise competition for schools,
where they set up their own companies, and Jim (Group 2) spoke enthusiastically about his company which was the Moorview winner chosen to
compete in the final. This was the only time when there was evidence of

intrinsic motivation for business studies, apparently encouraged by the teacher's enthusiasm rather than by the course itself.

The Business students did not talk about the 'relevance' of their course, except in a general way ('It'll be useful if I decide to go into business'). Despite constraints, teachers gave small examples of where they had been able to make the course more expansive at times for individual students by relating it directly to their lives. For example, Laura had encouraged a demotivated student who worked as a chicken farmer to relate his occupation to assignments and, according to her, he produced 'brilliant' work. Similarly, William had done the same with a student who worked on a fishing trawler. Notwithstanding this professed commitment, both teachers considered it unrealistic to think of doing this for everyone in their groups, because of time constraints.

Grade dependency

With learning firmly equated with grade achievement, it is unsurprising that (discounting the amotivated students) motivation was seen as *external* (driven by points and grades) and possibly also *introjected* (where students were motivated by their ability to internalize and use an external support structure such as the detail of the assessment specifications and criteria or a system for coaching to the criteria, either by teachers or, as in the case of Health and Social Care, by teachers and mentors, working one-to-one), rather than by *intrinsic* or *interested* motivation. Laura used target grades to motivate, and always related her feedback to a grade result:

> If they didn't know what mark the work they had done was worth, then it wouldn't be as motivational ... They're only interested in what they can do to improve once they know the grade isn't as good as they would want it to be, or they only need a few marks to get into the next grade boundary.

This instrumental approach was not completely negative. Laura cited examples of a positive effect on their peers when students increased their grades as the course progressed. Melanie's comment was typical of the higher achieving students: 'I've pushed myself more because I've been achieving good grades' (Melanie, Group 2, GCSE Business student, Moorview). The grade was the means to a vocational end for some students, but more often in the sense of a step towards A-levels and possibly HE rather than towards a specifically business-orientated career. It was part of doing well at school, in order to increase life chances on leaving school: in this sense, students seemed to have internalized the dominant policy discourse.

However, this was not the case for the lower achieving students, where the grade-dependent culture seemed to be having a negative impact. An inability to achieve good grades appeared to be contributing towards these students' disruptive behaviour in class and lack of willingness to engage with the tasks set.

At Moorview, William mentioned the importance of 'equipping students for life' and 'understanding how the world works', of students' learning being about more than achieving the grade. Yet both his students' views and other statements he made indicated that this was not his 'theory-in-use'. Indeed, there was considerable discrepancy between this more holistic view of learning and the spin-off from William's emphasis on the importance of coursework:

> Fairly soon – they get wise ... 'cos I keep telling them the important thing is getting this coursework right – [and] you can't get them to do anything in the classroom, unless they can see the actual benefit.
>
> (William, Business teacher, Moorview)

In effect, therefore, his espoused theory of learning and theory-in-use[5] for GCSE Applied Business students was functional. Any hint of a desire to broaden students' knowledge outside the course criteria was kept firmly in its place:

> Certainly with the Applied ... , you know, we teach straight to the scheme, so it is nice every now and again, if something's in the news we can extend it a little bit, ... but at the same time, *always* emphasize, you know, "It's nice to know this, but you're not actually going to be tested on it" ... So we try and tailor *everything* to them completing the coursework because, basically, I don't want to waste their time.
>
> (William, Business teacher, Moorview, his emphases)

3. Intensifying support for better grades

Student markers in GCSE business

At Moorview, both teachers wanted to make grade achievement both more effective and motivating, and chose the same new formative assessment strategy for the project though they approached it in slightly different ways. The task consisted of reading sample pieces of course work and, through paired discussion, awarding them marks according to the criteria. Laura's groups were given two pieces, a 7/10 and a 10/10 piece, the latter included to show that such a piece did not mean total perfection, which

Laura hoped would be motivating for some students. William, in contrast, thought the 10/10 piece would be demotivating for most of his group, and so used only the 7/10 example. The strategy was introduced to the students as a way of developing their ability to be self-critical of their work, through improving their knowledge of the coursework criteria. With all groups there was initial criticism of the task from some students, but the interviewed students' understanding of their teachers' aims were largely in line with Laura's and William's intentions.

In all groups (although most obviously in Group 3), the strategy rapidly evolved into an instrumental marking exercise, where the marking was seen as an end in itself without exploration of *why* students had decided on a particular mark. To their teachers' surprise, students' mark allocation was highly accurate. However, the students equated higher marks largely with quantity so that improving coursework remained a question of 'adding in more', rather than realizing what kind of 'more' was needed. In practice, the strategy had come to focus on the instrumental aspect of allocating marks for both teachers and students. With Laura's less disruptive groups, the strategy had more potential for deeper learning, through her specific questions to the group in the second half of the lesson, intended to lead to more independent self-assessment of the coursework currently being completed.

The strategy offered an opportunity for self- and peer assessment, rather than heavy reliance on the teacher, but this opportunity was not taken up in any meaningful way at the time. While Laura hoped that the new strategy would serve as a springboard for deeper learning, the students' priority at this stage was to complete their coursework rather than develop their ability to be self-critical. Although there was potential for certain practices to become springboards in Applied Business, it would not be easy within the current learning culture.

Certain students saw this potential for themselves. Sarah, one of William's 'higher ability' students, pointed out how the strategy could have been used to develop a deeper response:

> I would go round to – like, go to everybody individually and just say, "What would you give it and *why*?" So you actually get some response.
>
> (Sarah, Group 3, GCSE Business, Moorview)

This matched Laura's own view as to how she could develop the strategy to become a springboard in the future; she would aim to rely more on student rather than teacher feedback:

> [I would] ask the student what *they* think of the piece of work and
> you know, if they would . . . make improvements, what *they* would
> suggest, and *then* give the teacher feedback.
>
> (Laura, Business teacher, Moorview, original emphasis)

Both Laura and William planned to use the strategy with their next co-
horts, but would introduce it earlier in the course so that students had
time to develop a more self-critical approach.

Despite good intentions, teachers' labels of students' ability coloured
their expectations of how students coped with the introduced strategy
and what they would gain:

> I think the lower ability ones . . . just felt that it wasn't really their
> job to mark work and I don't think they quite, at first, understood
> the relevance of doing it, and I think they would still now find
> it difficult to try [to apply] what they learned today to their own
> work, whereas the higher ability ones could see that.
>
> (Laura, Business teacher, Moorview)

In fact, the higher ability interviewed students were already working much
more independently than their classmates. James, for example, appeared
to have developed his own kind of self-criticism, and his approach to
coursework was not entirely mark-determined:

> Because I'd rather just get on with what *I* think is improving it
> than looking . . . at the mark that I've been given . . . I just want to
> improve it to *my* standards before I look at the mark and see what
> I've got.
>
> (James, Group 3, GCSE Business, Moorview)

Most students in each group, though, continued to ask their teachers for
advice individually as to how to improve their coursework marks, rather
than working out their own improvements.

Introducing individual tutorials in health and social care

In the same vein as GCSE Business teachers, and addressing the aim of
more effective grade achievement, Mary and Deborah chose to introduce
individual tutorials in order to provide more oral feedback on students'
written work and to ensure that written feedback was understood and
could be acted upon. Their aims were affected by resource constraints:
the provision of another member of staff had already been agreed for
HSC which meant the new tutorials would be feasible. When the third
teacher in their team had been appointed, they had planned that in every
session, one member of staff would teach each group, while the third

would take students out of both groups for these tutorials. In practice, this proved impossible to implement on a regular basis due to one of the team's unexpected and prolonged sick leave, and HSC, once again, had only two instead of three teachers.

However, one school invited Mary to come in on seven consecutive Mondays to help eight HSC students individually (in 15-minute individual tutorials either weekly or fortnightly), with the stated aim of raising their grades.

Mary's tutorial continued her well-established approach to feedback and target setting and contrasted her tutorial with more open-ended approaches:

> It was a deliberately structured tutorial with an aim that they would go home with some homework, whereas most tutorials are, 'Where are we up to now? What targets shall we achieve?' I actually got them to do things and have things *done* by the next time they come back. So I would look [i.e. in future] at the tutorials as trying to find out what the barriers are that are stopping you in class, and just offering an alternative route to achievement, because no matter what those tutorials are, the schools still want results.
>
> (Mary, HSC teacher, Oldminster, original emphasis)

She encouraged them to think about 'what they needed to do, what they'd got missing and what else they had to add'. She also started to get students to complete a sheet 'to show what they'd done in the lesson and what still needed to be done between now and the next session'.

Mary continued to criticize students being 'spoon-fed' at school and contrasted such spoon-feeding with how students learnt at college: 'Here I have got *them* to create their own targets.' Despite her assertion that she did not like being achievement-led, she now felt that, because HSC students were 'not *mature* enough to work outside the box', her practices had to be achievement-led. As she explained,

> So, in order that *they* achieved, we did what was necessary for achievement . . . Time has put that constraint on. We started saying, 'Do this, do this, do this, do this, do this.' They loved it and in one week we turned it around.
>
> (Mary, HSC teacher, Oldminster, original emphasis)

Although Mary blamed the schools for creating a grade-led culture, it seemed that the college also promoted this approach by regarding students as 'customers'.

Mary's language at times appeared to conflate broader questions about learning with gaining maximum points. She described the handouts that she had used in her assessed observation as focusing on 'self-motivated targets', which she amplified as students asking themselves 'What have I done today?' Her hope was that their reply would be:

> Getting the points. The school target for me is that I get as *many* points for their GCSEs as they can. They [i.e. students] then look at exemplification of what it is, the criteria...that they need to produce, and then they work out what they're going to do and how they're going to do it. That's what I put in place.
>
> (original emphasis)

Hannah also thought that individual tutorials, along with completing work in lesson-time, would have helped such students to enjoy the course and consequently become more motivated:

> A lot of people obviously like one-on-one help, and I think that the people that haven't done it, that aren't enjoying the course, do need a bit of help to just want to do it...Plus most people don't do it at home, so if they get it done in the lesson, then it's done then, and they don't take it home because they probably won't do it...So, you know...really I think that everybody should have the tutorials.
>
> (Hannah, GCSE HSC student, Oldminster)

Hannah described the tutorials:

> Well, Jane takes the class and then Mary will just call in a person at a time, and then when you go in there, she goes through the bits and pieces that you've done, and then she tells you how you can improve it and tells what grade you've got for it so far and if you want to improve it, how to.

She was grateful for individual help in college but most praise was reserved for the individual tutorials with Mary at their school, which were highly appreciated by all students who experienced them. This caused resentment, however, because this special treatment was not equally available to all: 'Sometimes it's just unfair because we don't get that; if everyone had, like, a chance, then we'd probably, like, know where we all are' (Sharon, GCSE student).

It seemed, however, that individual tutorials were not enough. The same school also had a mentoring scheme for certain students. Of the four students we interviewed for the project, three attended this school with the individual sessions that students referred to as the 'Mary tutorials': Alison, Hannah, and Wendy. Alison and Hannah both also had mentors in school. This was the only school offering a mentoring system for GCSE students and the individual 'Mary tutorials' for HSC.

Hannah felt that working with her mentor had helped her to learn more effectively by being more focused; the mentor had helped her

> to not distract others and just to listen and try and concentrate on the teacher speaking and things, and to not try and get distracted by others, so ... [That] hasn't been too hard actually. It's just not listening to them, isn't it? It's just like focusing yourself on the teacher, on what the teacher's saying.
>
> (Hannah, GCSE HSC student)

She explained this 'really good help' more specifically:

> I mean, it's just how to get ready for your exams and helping you start making revision cards. They're just really helping you try and get that grade that you need, so ... They do *push* you a bit, but at the end of the day they're just trying to do what they think's best for you, so. But I do find it helpful.

Conclusion

The 'new' formative assessment strategies that teachers introduced for our project fitted the ethos and practices already established in Applied GCSE learning cultures and the implicit or overt forms of motivation they already encouraged and reinforced. The strategy did not seek to transform motivation, but to work with it.

In all three groups of GCSE Business and the school-college link group for Health and Social Care, the learning cultures were overwhelmingly instrumental, where students rapidly learned to 'play the game'. The only high level of synergy within both learning cultures was a grade-dominated one, which seemed attributable to two main factors: a weak vocational subject, leading to less potential for an enthusiastic subject focus from the teacher, and teachers', together with assumptions that students' motivation was externally driven and an associated view among teachers that they could do very little or nothing to influence this. On both courses, an institutional ethos of achievement combined with other significant factors to lead teachers and students to agree on grade achievement as the sole acceptable goal. Instrumentalism was therefore already an entirely rational, pragmatic response.

Powerful perceptions and expectations of what counted as 'vocational' and the kind of status attached to it were a key factor in shaping the learning cultures of the two Applied GCSEs. 'Vocational' courses were generally accepted by students, their parents and certain teachers as 'lower' in status than the academic single subject courses at GCSE or A-level. As Laura explained, when talking about her students' planned progression routes and their choice of the 'academic' A-level Business Studies over the AVCE route:

> All the students that are coming back are quite able and I think that they see the Applied A-level [i.e. AVCE] as not so good...I think that it is sold at school as a lower qualification. There's... three tiers of entry. There's the BTEC, the Applied and the straight.
>
> (Laura, third interview)

On the surface, vocational seemed, simply, to be synonymous with the greater ratio of coursework to exams and one effect was that opportunities to relate the course to students' lives were not taken up to any great extent. 'Vocational' also meant, in these two courses at least, being coached to the grade criteria to a quite extreme extent in the case of the Health and Social Care students, and a little less so in Business.

The dominance of highly instrumental goals for achievement in both learning cultures illuminates the ways in which certain expectations of a 'type' of young person who will choose (or, as is increasingly likely, be selected by the school to do a vocational GCSE instead of general GCSEs) combine with resource and organizational constraints and unclear, diverse purposes for 'vocational' learning at this level. In these conditions, expectations become fixed stereotypes that are reinforced by the socializing process of being coached to achieve; students take this socializing process and the stereotypes it creates and arises from, to the courses they progress to. The case study of BTEC National Diploma shows the effects of these expectations and stereotypes.

It is hardly surprising that teachers struggled to maintain broader values about the purposes of education and the specific meanings of vocational education within the restrictive learning cultures discussed here. Although time spent through our project to consider the impact of a highly instrumental learning culture on reducing educational aspirations to grade achievement was seen by teachers as positive, the fact that their strategy worked dominated. At Moorview, most students gained an A–C grade: 20 of 23 in Group A, and 20 of 21 in Group B.[6] In both courses, teachers regretted the effects on broader purposes but only Laura seemed to want to challenge the prevailing culture.

Nevertheless, as in other learning cultures discussed in this book, there were glimpses of deeper possibilities: again like those other examples, these were tiny and fleeting. For example, GCSE Business student Jim was motivated to look at teachers' comments before his mark, to see if he could improve his work to his standards, in a more holistic way. Of course, it is always easy to dismiss these glimpses as 'typical of high ability students' but we argue that all the fleeting examples of something deeper are worth trying to capitalize on!

Finally, though, our interpretations of data discussed here lead back to a concern that, however strong the pressures to make assessment in GCSE Business and Health and Social Care highly instrumental, they reflect and reinforce acceptance on all sides of a paucity of students' aspirations. Of course we recognize that some of the students were challenging, demotivated and unwilling to take part in teaching and assessment activities without intensive support. In addition, staff changes on the Health and Social Care course led to real difficulties in getting students through their targets.

Notwithstanding these caveats, the powerful language of motivation, 'typical' students, ability and preferences shaped the learning culture. This created a view on both sides that students simply cannot and will not get through without coaching, and, as we saw in the case of some of the school students, mentoring too. In this context, 'autonomy' is reduced to students 'owning' and being motivated by spoon-feeding.

Notes

1. Applied GCSEs and Advanced Vocational Certificates of Education as 'vocational' alternatives to general academic subjects are now subsumed into the Diplomas, introduced at both levels in 2009. However, at the time of going to press (June 2010), the political future of Diplomas is uncertain.
2. The concept of 'learning and assessment careers' among primary school children and young people on vocational courses is explored at length in Ecclestone and Pryor (2003).
3. Although numbers of 14–19-year-olds are increasing in FE colleges, many lecturers do not believe this is a good thing.
4. In earlier studies, this was an important feature of vocational education courses, see, for example, Ecclestone (2002); Torrance et al. (2005).
5. We discuss the useful concepts of 'espoused theory' and 'theory-in-use' in Chapter 7.
6. It is important to note, however, that Group 3 did not improve their grades; 6 of 20 gained A–C. For these students, emphasis on grade achievement was demotivating.

6 Discipline and support for 'vulnerable' learners in e2e programmes

Introduction

Assessment practices in programmes like e2e emerge from a long tradition of 'alternative' approaches to pedagogy and assessment for young people deemed to be disaffected and alienated from formal education. In some respects, e2e continues the counselling-based, individualized self-assessment that began in careers education and unemployment schemes in the late 1970s and continued through the 1980s. These were widely seen at the time as progressive alternatives to traditional assessment, and they fused assessment and pedagogy in new ways. In such programmes, analysing yourself in terms of useful and less positive character traits, and thinking about how others regard you, were key features of pedagogy and outcome-based assessment methods. These were rooted in areas such as Rogerian counselling and transactional analysis, leading to an influx of a new type of teacher trained in counselling and youth work rather than traditional teaching.

Entry to Employment (e2e) schemes are the latest in series of initiatives over the past 30 years to provide an alternative for young people who do not want, or are not able to follow, mainstream qualifications. Approaches to teaching and assessment in e2e have their roots in programmes introduced in the 1970s and 1980s to respond to rising youth unemployment, such as the Youth Opportunities Programme (YOP) (1979), the Certificate of Pre-Vocational Education (CPVE) (1985), and the Education and Technical Vocational Education Initiative (1988). They are also influenced by practices from discrete programmes for those with special needs and learning disabilities, and from careers education and guidance. e2e is targeted at young people Not in Employment Education or Training (NEETs) or young people with Behavioural Emotional and Social Difficulties (BESDs). These labels encompass a very diverse range of individual and social problems including: exclusion from school, poor achievement levels, mental health problems, homelessness, substance misuse, physical abuse, and learning and physical disabilities.

The following upbeat description of what students can expect from e2e is an extract from a college website in one of the colleges in our project:

On e2e you can:

- *Improve your skills and learn about teamwork*
- *Get advice on work and training*
- *Get help with your CV and how to succeed in a job interview*
- *Build your confidence and motivation – we have fun as well as work hard!*
- *Try out different work situations and prepare for employment.*

Your programme will be designed just for you. You'll be expected to attend between 16 and 30 hours per week, including work experience. At the end of the programme you could go onto an Apprenticeship or go onto a full-time course. It's up to you ... You will be expected to undertake learning in three interdependent core areas: basic and key skills, vocational development, and personal and social development.

Young people are selected by the personal guidance and advice service to attend, with a penalty of losing welfare benefits if they do not, for a period of up to 22 weeks. For some, attendance is a condition of living independently, returning to families or living with carers. Young people are offered financial bonuses for joining, completing a formal induction programme with a compulsory Individual Activity Plan, achieving particular goals and staying the whole course.

The programme is in two stages. A diagnostic stage of 4–6 weeks includes an activity day each week, with trips and other recreational activities that both ease young people into the course and provide tutors with opportunities for diagnostic assessment of behaviour, social skills, dispositions and attitudes. Stage Two lasts for about four months and young people attend the centre for $2^1/_2$ days a week, following an individually planned programme that might include basic skills (using the 'Skills for Life' national tests), preparation for employment, and the ASDAN[1] Further Education Award programme. The latter incorporates a number of 'challenges', namely tasks/activities within a wide-ranging choice of 12 modules (e.g. Rights and Responsibilities, Independent Living, Jobsearch, International Relations), with key skills.

An important contrast to earlier programmes in which e2e is rooted is the prevalence of images of young people 'at risk' in the transition from school to employment or further education that permeate contemporary policy texts. A particularly influential example is the Social Exclusion Unit's 1999 report *Bridging the Gap*, with its images of the damage done by cycles of social, economic and psychological deprivation, where further education is crucial for enabling particular young people to 'turn their lives around'. As we show in this chapter, such images are powerful in tutors' ideas about the participants they deal with, even if they have not read the report themselves. A further difference from earlier programmes is that many, although not all, e2e participants have already experienced intensive assessment and support.[2]

In this chapter, we show how ideas about alternative assessment that began in the 1970s, discussed in the first section of this book, have become strong forms of personalized target-setting rooted in images of 'vulnerable' and 'at risk' young people. In e2e, this has created a highly disciplinary yet emotionally supportive assessment regime. The three case studies of different e2e learning sites in our project illuminate common features in a discernible 'e2e' learning culture that create this regime, and which affect tutors' reasons for choosing particular strategies for formative assessment. We show how the policy context and the expectations of tutors and young people combined to produce very similar practice and outcomes across all three sites. We focus here on six interviewees: George and Craig (Southern Counties), Tyler, Charles and Louise (Oldminster College) and Zara (Mid-Counties), and four tutors: Marianne (Oldminster College), Rob and Ann (Southern Counties) and Mary (Mid-Counties).

Separation is a key feature of e2e learning culture; on the one hand, it allows a sense that the provision is special and personalized, on the other, it leads to intense pressure on tutors and a sense of isolation. The physical environments of our three sites varied in shabbiness and degree of separation. In Southern Counties, e2e occupied a new, well-resourced and comfortable building, while at Oldminster College, it was hidden away in a dingy building in a city shopping centre, and had a friendly but shabby, run-down feel to it. In Mid-Counties, e2e was located in a suite of rooms within a college department and young people had more of a sense that they were part of a wider student body. All settings conveyed similar messages of informal, individualized, supportive programmes designed mainly around one-to-one interactions and small group work, with computers and small private areas for counselling and reviews of progress, access to a kitchen area, and discrete accommodation not used by other college students.

Our analysis begins by exploring the roles, motivations and expectations of tutors and young people on e2e. In the second section, we outline changes to self-assessment and target setting made by the project tutors, focusing on Oldminster College, and evaluate their outcomes and effects. In the third section, we highlight how the e2e learning culture turns the self and its attitudes, dispositions and behaviours into the subject and outcomes of 'learning'. Finally, we suggest small ways that formative assessment in e2e might be improved or extended, and raise broader questions about how to make e2e educationally worthwhile.

1. Personalized support and assessment

Welfare workers or lifecoaches?

e2e blurs the lines between social work, youth work, counselling and teaching. As the programme leader in Southern Counties pointed out, college managers regard staff working on e2e as 'support workers' since they do not teach a curriculum subject. In addition, e2e is funded as a work-based learning programme rather than general FE and so staff do not share the same term closures as the rest of the college, nor the same conditions of service. However, by the end of our project, one college, Southern Counties, was considering changing different conditions of service, in recognition of the 'real teaching nature' of e2e tutors' various activities.

Tutors recognized their complex, highly demanding roles and some talked about the profound tension between their values and beliefs and the time-constrained, target-driven programme they had to get e2e participants through. Marianne's professional biography was rooted in helping disadvantaged participants, starting with setting up a project at Oldminster College for excluded Year 11 participants. Her life and her responses to it influenced her values and attitudes to education very strongly. As a single mother with two small children, she took a Return to Learn course and became a learning support assistant, which led to A-levels, a degree, a further education teaching qualification, and a career in youth work. She had always worked while studying and, at the time of our project, was studying for her PGCE alongside her full-time post. Her espoused and practised theory of learning was marked by compassion for young people and a strong belief in the power of education to change lives – as it had for her. She used the vocabulary of 'self-esteem' and 'confidence' more than 'learning' when talking about her e2e participants:

> I still have the same compassion and empathy for . . . the learners, because I know what's happened and maybe the damage that's been done and the way they feel and . . . [the importance of] building up their confidence and their self-esteem . . . and getting them to enjoy learning again, and re-engaging. That hasn't changed at all. But the focus for me is, you know, 'I've got to get you . . . from A to B to C.' I'm under pressure more . . . [because] we're target- and funding-led.

For her, young people's needs were to gain confidence and self-esteem, to develop employability skills like punctuality. She emphasized the individual nature of the learning so that she and her colleagues could encourage individuals to take 'small steps', resulting in achievements which 'make them feel so much better'. 'Progression' targets were, simultaneously, to meet the formal targets of moving to employment, training or further education, and idiosyncratic and personal.

At Mid-Counties, Mary had previously been an A-level lecturer at the college. She regarded her role as completely different from lecturing, 'more of a guide or coach really'. Her philosophy of learning focused on 'individual development in a holistic sense' and about the need for 'soft skills of confidence, self-esteem and social awareness' to come first, before educational goals and objectives, where learning in a more educational sense would follow. Her view of soft outcomes also encompassed very basic social training:

> The soft outcomes...so one learner might be having good eye contact, that might be something we see as an achievement from one day to another, so the quiet things that we discuss in terms of how we...connect with young people. And this assessment...is from one human being to another and how this human being interacts in work and the course and we can normally gauge their confidence quite well in terms of body language and those little questions that are being asked of us, like 'What time do I have to be back here'? If someone asked and turns up – even that's an achievement.

'Vulnerable' young people with 'complex needs'

The language of 'nurturing', 'engaging', 'supporting', 'creating safe spaces' was central to all four tutors' accounts of their goals and activities to achieve them:

> It's important to develop a safe environment...we have a lot of young people who have been bullied in the past either at school or home...from a [safe environment] we can build up a relationship...provide breakfast for them and that is both to give them a good start...but it's also part of the nurturing.
>
> (Rob, tutor, Southern Counties)

This language and its underlying images of young people were integral to e2e learning cultures in our three sites and, as we showed in Section One, such images are embedded in policy texts. Tutors saw young people on e2e as 'vulnerable', 'fragile' and 'at risk', recognizing that 'vulnerability' and being 'at risk' are both technical terms from social work, mainly for young people from the care system. The formal assessment of 'vulnerable' and 'at risk' comes from social work and is supposed to encompass conditions such as homelessness, drug abuse or living in violent homes. Yet, 'vulnerability' has become a generic term. As Marianne and Mary both pointed out, a host of other difficulties such as being bullied, lack of confidence and social skills, also make young people 'vulnerable' and so, as Marianne observed, 'they're all vulnerable'.

At Southern Counties, Ann described e2e participants as 'scared of learning', so that mere completion of activities and, crucially, success in them, were central to 'engagement'. For Marianne, inclusion and self-esteem were a crucial springboard from which many other things might follow:

> We see them desperate to be included and want to be accepted... it's very individual you know. The idea is that they start to work independently and to believe in themselves.

For e2e tutors, social and personal skills, including confidence and experiencing success were foundations for other goals.

At Oldminster, neither Louise nor Charles had any formal educational qualifications and neither had attended secondary school regularly. Louise lived with her mother and step-father and had a sister and step-brothers who joined them on a regular basis. She had enjoyed primary school, but her attendance at secondary school had declined rapidly from Year 9:

> I used to mitch sort of in Year 9, then I was doing it all the time in Year 10 and I used to never go in Year 11 ... I was excluded in Year 8, Year 9, Year 10 twice and Year 11. I got kicked out at the end of Year 11.
>
> (Louise, e2e participant, Oldminster)

Charles had a history of broken family relationships, drug-taking and truanting and had been diagnosed as dyspraxic at the age of 9. He was now in care. He had truanted seriously from the age of about 14, and spent some time in a pupil referral unit before coming to e2e. The e2e learning site represented a significant return to the formal education system for both young people.

Both Louise and Charles said they came to e2e because they 'liked coming here' even though, as for them and other young people we interviewed in e2e, getting out of bed in the morning was frequently a problem. Their motivation appeared to be external, with Louise's linked loosely to a desire to achieve in a way she had not done at school – 'That's why I wanted to come e2e to get my grades up[3].... you look back at it and you think, "What have I done?"' (Louise, Oldminster). Attending e2e was a condition of Charles being able to live with his carers; he had initially been unwilling to undertake the programme, but he had changed:

> Well, I came here, like, with the intention not to do it, 'cos, like, they just put me on there 'cos I had to do something to live where I am now. But now I'm, like, I'd rather stay here, 'cos it's, like, quite fun during the day.

Young people were highly self-aware of their various 'issues', a word used often by both participants and teachers, presenting themselves in similar terms to those used by tutors, sometimes accounting for their situation with emotional or psychological assessments. Despite initial unwillingness to attend, Charles's motivation changed and although he was not sure why, he thought 'just probably I've sorted my head out and I've got that self-esteem'. 'Self-esteem' was also used by George at Southern Counties while Chris, also at Southern Counties, was adept at using the official language of his reviews and target setting:

> My communication skills with people in authority have progressed and my relationships with most participants have improved ... I can go out and meet people, and I worry less.[4]

Another crucial feature of the learning culture was its difference from school, both for its personal, individual focus and being with people 'like me':

> I thought it would be different from school ... I find it much easer ... because most of the people here are in my position [whereas] in my English class there would be loads of them there that are quite clever and they can sit and listen for a long time and then there's me and a couple of others that can't do that ... but here we're all the same.
>
> (Zara, e2e participant, Mid-Counties)

The holy grail of personalized motivation

Although the subtleties of each person's educational motivation are lost in the mist of time, a powerful image among tutors and young people alike is that they 'all' have a history of *amotivation* and it is a hard task to turn this around or to uncover indications of possible positive motivation from those experiences. According to Marianne, 'They're never well motivated.'

Of course, poor motivation is a reality and it would be wrong for us to present it as insignificant or as anything other than a serious challenge for tutors. Yet, it is also institutionalized in e2e from the outset. Unlike other courses, and leaving aside the absence of alternatives to college for many young people, they do not 'choose' e2e but are selected to attend. A prime motivator is financial reward in the form of an educational maintenance allowance (EMA) and over which tutors have some control as a 'bargaining tool', alongside other incentives:

> [T]hey will get a £25.00 start-up bonus but... after the 4 weeks I will give them feedback on how they've done. If they've been late and they haven't attended or whatever... I'll say, 'I'm not paying your bonus until [you've achieved]... I'm going to set you a target for 2 weeks... to attend every day, be punctual and then I'm going to release that £20.' So there's lots of incentives... we negotiate with them on what we think is a suitable target... to get that money.
>   So... there're three £25.00 bonuses and one £50.00 bonus at the end.
>
> (Marianne, e2e programme leader, Oldminster)

Encouraging *external*, *introjected* and *identified* motivation underpinned tutors' strategies in a constant interplay between monitoring, finding tiny targets that might trigger a change in attitude or behaviour, disciplining, building confidence and cajoling.

A particular challenge was that motivation to encourage positive aspirations for work or further education occupied a profoundly difficult place between realism and fantasy. Louise expressed an aspiration to become a hairdresser, but was hazy about exactly what qualifications she needed. She had previously had a part-time job in a budget clothes shop and was currently applying to work in the clothes section of a large branch of Tesco's. She was particularly keen to earn her own money as she was enjoying learning to drive and wanted her own car. Her progress was set back by her rapid boredom with hairdressing and then shoplifting from a placement at Tesco's, followed by becoming pregnant.

Perhaps because employment aspirations were vague, they played a very minor part in the predominantly external motivation that kept Louise and Charles on e2e, for Louise, fuelled by an expressed desire not to do anything 'boring' and her defiant resistance to anything difficult:

> I can write all right, it's just that when it comes to big words in reading, I won't do it and I won't even try either... if I can't do something, I won't bother and won't even try and do it.
>
> (Louise, e2e participant, Oldminster)

In reality, sustaining external and identified motivation relied heavily on participants' emotional identification with tutors: this was particularly evident at Oldminster where Marianne herself, and her relationship with them were the core of their motivation:

> She's just really nice. Like, if I've got problems and that and I talk to her, she's always, like, helping me out and that ... And she makes me feel better ... 'cos she's always, like, saying, 'Oh, you're really good at this and you're good at that', which makes me feel better about myself.
>
> (Louise)

Yet while essential for many young people on e2e, as it was for Louise, this positive relationship with Marianne was not a new or unique motivator in Louise's system of close support. Instead, it was an additional strand to close support already provided by her mother. Who also set targets, imposed sanctions, and helped Louise find information for e2e work, as she had done throughout her school career.

Tutors searched constantly for motivational triggers or for diagnoses of the much-cited 'barriers to learning' that might motivate participants; this was often highly pressurized:

> I feel ... I'm letting them down because I'm not finding the right way to teach them and what is engaging them, but I've been with them six or seven months and I've tried loads of different strategies, so how long and how far can I go with them? ... I'm really dedicated to them and it's been turbulent for me.
> (Marianne, e2e programme leader, Oldminster)

Tutors used tiny steps in progress as a motivator, making young people aware of these through personal reviews and group sessions, constantly comparing their social/academic learning with that of previous weeks or months:

> I'm getting them to recognise, 'I haven't just been sitting there doing nothing. I *have* actually been doing something.' So it's all the little tiny things that help motivation – 'Oh, you look nice today. Look at your hair,' you know. We're really keen to big them up and promote them ... as much as we can.
> (Marianne, e2e programme leader, Oldminster)

This struggle was intensified by not being able to use peer dynamics as support or role models. Not only does a roll-on, roll-off programme make establishing a 'group' more difficult but many young people were unwilling to work with peers or to even be around them too often:

I'm just beginning to get used to crowds. I don't like a load of people.

> (Chris, e2e participant, Southern Counties)

I hated school, there is a lot less people and a lot easier here.

> (George, e2e participant, Southern Counties)

This antipathy, together with positive one-to-one relationships with tutors, was crucial to e2e's learning culture:

Most of them [school teachers] have got a frown on their face or start setting detentions – we get. . . . leeway here as well. If you get quite naughty, a bit cheeky, we don't get told off. We just get sat down in a room and basically discuss what's happening, but you need a one-to-one, not sit down and write from a book.

> (Chris, e2e participant, Southern Counties)

For most of the young people we interviewed, intense personal support paid off. Charles had started e2e knowing what he *didn't* want to be: 'I'd rather not just, like, be a bum, really. I don't want to end up on the streets and that.' Towards the end of his programme, he had begun to consider a job as a dog-handler (he was very keen on dogs and parrots; his mother had four dogs and two parrots) or else he thought he would like to be a pilot (he liked heights). He seemed to have no awareness of the discrepancy between the levels of these occupations; his aspirations were linked solely to what he liked. Nevertheless, although as we noted above, he put better motivation down to 'sorting his head out' and 'getting that self-esteem', a real spur came when he found how much he loved his dog-handling work placement, a motivation that led to him learning Latin terms and wanting knowledge about animals and how to look after them.

2. Continuous self-assessment

'Ownership' of target-setting

In e2e, 'continuous' assessment reaches new heights through a pedagogy based on constant, detailed tutor and self-assessment of dispositions, attitudes and behaviours. Informal and formal assessments underpinned tutors' search for ways in which to respond positively to each person's school, family and work experience, and to work out how this might have affected motivation, personal development and attitudes to learning. Diagnostic assessments, carried out by tutors and young people themselves, encompassed everything from the breakfast club to recreational or leisure trips, as well as formal sessions and reviews of progress. Assessment and feedback encompassed the minutiae of behaviour, both social and personal, and psychological traits like confidence and self-esteem. These are embedded into the course from day one. As Marianne explained:

> The minute they walk in, the minute the task is set in induction, I'm assessing them, their personal and social behaviour because, you know, that tells me a hell of a lot about them.

In introducing a bowling trip, she explained:

> I said to them, 'Why do you think we're going bowling?' And they said, 'It's not just a bit of fun, is it, Marianne?' And I said, 'No, it is fun, but what do you think it's going to show me . . . about you?' And they said, 'Oh, what we're like when we go out.' I said 'Exactly, and how you behave around people, and how you work in a group, how you mix in a group.' So that's one form of assessment that I do, and I'll just take them for coffee afterwards and sit and chat with them and see, you know, how they interact with each other.
>
> (Marianne, e2e programme leader, Oldminster)

Some young people enjoyed self-assessment. In Southern Counties, occasional group work identified and confirmed individuals' targets before each went off to work on his or her plans for the day. In one activity, they had to draw a detailed, creative map of their lives and hoped-for future, to help them to identify where they 'need to go' and 'how they will get there'.[5] George found this both motivating and absorbing, and while he was given encouragement by the tutor, the map was clearly his own and he was very proud of it:

> We've been making roundabouts with roads coming off it, what we want to do in our lives, what we've got planned ahead of us for our future, what's important to us . . . It's nice to sort of look at yourself in a different way and see what you actually do like and sort of think about it. Just, I don't know, sort of think about your future a lot more, just sort of get a lot more out of yourself in that situation.
>
> (George, e2e participant, Southern Counties)

Sometimes the status of a diagnosis was unclear. For example, some young people came with a formal statement about a condition such as ADHD or dyslexia, while at other times, participants informed tutors of a condition or problem and tutors were not always sure if this was authentic or not.

Notwithstanding these difficulties, Marianne wanted to improve self-assessment:

> I'd like them to be more involved in their self-assessment, in a group, in class, to be confident enough to do that. To look at 'what I'm good at, what I'm not good at, what I need to improve'... because they're setting themselves the targets for their own improvement, or getting a job.

Reviews to make young people identify targets and plan their next steps focused heavily on proving where they had 'engaged' or 'shown a positive attitude': such behaviours were a formal auditing requirement from the Learning and Skills Council. Yet young people either, as Marianne observed ruefully, 'refuse to do it or they write the wrong thing'.

At Oldminster, Marianne and her colleague Adrian designed a Progress and Learning Sheet to help young people identify weekly targets, assess progress on each and assess their feelings and reactions to various activities. Tutors in Mid-Counties chose an identical strategy, deciding to streamline official requirements and to motivate young people through a different approach to self-assessment.

All the e2e tutors in our project couched goals for their new strategy as enabling young people to be more 'aware of their own learning', to help them 'take ownership of their own learning' and make it easier to diagnose what might motivate individuals and then design appropriate activities. Mary saw individual plans as central to personal and social development:

> Learners gain more responsibility over following and setting their own targets and leading their own individual learning plan, rather than being led by it.
>
> (Mary, tutor, Mid-Counties)

In explaining her new form to the young people at Oldminster, Marianne said:

> This is for you to recognize where you might need some help, or what you've done really well, what you've not done, what you might want to improve and maybe add – we've thrown in a few little things about how the course might be improved as well.

At Oldminster, young people had to assess:

- What have you done this week?
- What do you want to do?
- What new things have you learned this week – and that could be about yourself!
- What have you enjoyed, hated or found boring?

- What did you learn in this lesson about the topic?
- What did you like?
- What did you find difficult?
- What did you find boring?
- What did you learn about yourself?
- What did you learn about your learning?[6]

As Marianne explained:

> When they have the review once a month ... there's a section we encourage them to fill in, good, bad, and good again – we try to end on a positive – but something they like about the programme, something they don't like, something they would like to change, or something they have learned about themselves.
> (Marianne, e2e programme leader, Oldminster)

The targets that arose from these self-assessments encompassed attributes, attitudes and behaviours, elided into what tutors called 'personal skills' which included everything from arriving on time, maintaining eye contact, having a positive attitude to oneself, self-esteem, or not reacting negatively if 'someone talks on placement in a way they're not used to' (Mary, tutor, Mid-Counties).

Although young people interviewed cited the same sorts of achievements as signs they were 'learning', they found filling in weekly self-assessment sheets, either as the main focus of a lesson or as part of a review, neither engaging or interesting. At Oldminster, both Charles and Louise said 'we just tick anything' while others wrote 'don't know', 'nothing', 'can't remember'. They saw the purpose as 'so they can see how we're getting on, what we feel about what they're like ... the work they're giving us and that' (Charles). In the face of resistance after one month of the new strategy, tutors changed to fortnightly use.

In part, problems arose because accounting for behaviour and attitude with the same set of questions becomes dull for most people! Questions also mixed self-assessment with evaluation of how the course might be improved so that, even within the goal of monitoring and accounting for behaviour, young people could displace problems they might be having onto 'boring teaching' or 'too much teaching'. In a context of heartfelt concern about young people's vulnerability, this reinforced teachers' guilt at not finding the 'right' motivational strategy for each young person. It also diverted attention from the limited subject content on offer, emphasising instead motivation, behaviour, dispositions and attitude.

Despite antipathy, the simple act of completing feedback sheets and related self-assessment activities was an achievement in itself and, in Tyler's case, a review of his sheet was a springboard for identifying changes in behaviour, confidence and attitude after an army taster programme and this motivated him to get involved in setting new, intrinsically motivating targets.

3. The self as the 'curriculum', process and outcome of learning

Empty meanings of 'learning'

At the end of our project, Marianne saw formative assessment in a much broader sense than she had at the start, in contrast to Mary, who confirmed her initial view that formative assessment was self-assessment and tutors' feedback to young people and, in turn, the 'feedback' tutors got from 'the learners' from their activity plans.

Apart from the case study of AVCE Science, our other examples in this book show (and other studies cited in Section One confirm) that e2e is typical in lacking a coherent theory of pedagogy. One obvious reason is that tutors have to respond to a huge range of needs and difficulties in an emotionally demanding, target-driven programme. Lack of theory about pedagogy is exacerbated in e2e by its almost total absence of a 'curriculum' or even coherent subjects. Although participants do some literacy and numeracy with the ASDAN certificate and other small certificated 'bits' of learning, these are little more than a vehicle for motivation: there is little intrinsic value or purpose in their own right. Instead, they are instruments to diagnose psychological or behavioural barriers to a work ethic or to being motivated to 'engage' in learning, and the motivation to be included.

The most significant difference between e2e and other programmes is that the disciplined, engaged, motivated self is the 'curriculum' subject, process and outcome of learning and assessment, and any subject-related certificates are solely an instrument for engagement. Yet, our study of vocational GCSEs in Chapter 2, shows similar tendencies to some of those we saw in e2e.

The intensely personalized nature of tutoring and assessment meant that tutors struggled to find a coherent idea or approach to pedagogy. Marianne talked at different times about 'motivational self-talk', 'learning styles' or 'thinking skills' and once Charles found a subject that truly engaged him, she wanted him to think about 'learning to learn'. Mary sometimes used the language of neuro-linguistic programming.

Although the term 'learning' has become simultaneously more vacuous and ubiquitous throughout further education, policy terms such as 'learning to learn', 'meeting individual needs', 'learning journey' and 'distance travelled', 'engagement', 'barriers to learning', 'taking ownership of learning' dominated e2e tutors' depictions of learning far more strongly than they did in the other sites encompassed by our study. This led tutors to observe that young people are 'learning all the time' and that 'everything is learning', so that 'taking ownership' meant taking responsibility for 'monitoring your own targets', 'being able to identify what you have done this week', or 'deciding what you want to do'.

In turn, autonomy or what tutors called 'independent learning' was little more than being able to manoeuvre within very tightly drawn targets, and working individually with a lot of one-to-one review, counselling and support. Autonomy was also characterized by informal and friendly relationships between tutors and participants; e2e participants saw it as significantly different from school and therefore accepted the discipline, monitoring and accountability in return for good relationships and high levels of compassionate support. A crucial feature of the motivational aspect of 'independence' was freedom from any formal input.

'Therapeutic' and disciplinary assessment

The antipathy of e2e participants towards testing and exams, something they shared with almost all young people in our project, was a strong influence in the learning culture. The policy context, with its attendant language and images of 'vulnerable' NEETs, is a powerful shaper of this regime, permeating tutors' and young people's accounts of their problems, needs, motivations, likes and dislikes. All three e2e sites addressed the central goal of preparing young people for work and further education by focusing on the re-shaping of individual emotional and psychological traits and behaviours, defined as 'needs' and, in turn, recasting 'meeting needs' as 'learning'.

Participants' expectations from previous experiences of formal assessments, perhaps through social work, engagement mentoring or personal advice, were shaped in e2e through funding targets based on accountability for individual student outcomes.[7] Although targets competed with tutors' humanitarian and liberal humanist beliefs and practices, causing great frustration, tutors could reconcile these differences. Intertwining discourses of 'complex needs', 'vulnerability' 'risk' and 'personalization' created a therapeutic and disciplinary assessment regime that focused upon where the self and its attitudes, dispositions and emotional responses.

It might seem that the intensely instrumental learning culture led the assessment strategy implemented by our e2e tutors to be in the letter rather than the spirit of formative assessment. Yet, when each young person's behaviour, attitudes and dispositions are the purpose, process and outcome of learning, attempts to improve responses and attitudes made tutors' new approach entirely in the spirit of the subject. In contrast to our other case studies, they implemented and evaluated their new feedback sheets as much more than a simple route to better grades, without deep engagement with subject content or learning process. Instead, it was a conscientious, integrated approach to their everyday work with young people on e2e and an attempt to get young people to engage with the subject, namely themselves! Whether or not it was educationally worthwhile, or effective, is something we return to in our conclusion.

Compassion and emotional labour

We showed in Section One of this book that FE teachers' roles now require much more 'emotional labour' and increasingly have a more emotional focus. e2e epitomizes that change and the demands it places on tutors, and we noted at the beginning of this chapter that recognition by managers at Southern Counties of what the e2e programme leader described as the 'true teaching' nature of their roles has led to a college-wide review of what 'teaching' comprises.

Our project showed that e2e tutors had to use very high levels of emotional labour. Psychological insights and compassion are other outcomes of the tradition of alternative curricula and assessment initiatives from which e2e derives. Yet, arguably, their work is much more intense and pressurized than in those earlier programmes. Each one had to strive constantly for idiosyncratic ways to cajole, persuade and bribe each young person to engage with self-assessment. This was time-consuming, *ad hoc* and frustrating, handicapped by tutors' lack of specialist knowledge and easily derailed by resistance. Understanding the complexities of each young person's emotional and psychological make-up, their dispositions to learning, why they found literacy difficult, whether they really did have ADHD or dyslexia as a formally diagnosed condition, as well as responding to daily setbacks or crises, were emotionally draining. Yet, while tutors were highly compassionate and supportive, sometimes at a cost to their own health, the very diverse needs and problems they had to deal with might also have reduced their ability to offer proper therapeutic or psychological interventions to those who really needed it.

Despite pressures, tutors found it extremely rewarding when participants made small or large steps in progress. The case studies showed fleeting glimpses of experiences that motivated participants to learn for its own sake; Charles loved dog-handling and suddenly found a motivation to learn even Latin terms and to study the subject in-depth. It is perhaps in these occasional successes in a specific topic that formative assessment might best be focused to maximize motivation and learning real knowledge and skills as a springboard to other things. For Tyler, the turning point in his motivation came when the initial tedium of filling out the sheets suddenly changed because Marianne was able to point out in his weekly review with her how much he had enjoyed an army taster course.

Conclusion

The logic of e2e's subject matter, the constraining and highly prescriptive auditing requirements of the funding body, and the disparate, often very profound needs of e2e participants, limit possibilities for radical change in e2e's learning culture. Nevertheless, our project showed *ad hoc* examples of young people becoming motivated by subject content or new practical experiences, rather than by studying and assessing themselves. These were tiny and fleeting signs, just as they were in other case studies.

While not wishing to overlook how fleeting these signs were, this does perhaps suggest small ways in which e2e tutors might shift the emphasis from the self and its attitudes, and from things that were or were not motivating about the teaching or the programme, towards an explicit focus on learning knowledge and skills. They could vary the format of questions and, once they found topics that genuinely seemed to engage young people, frame cognitively-based questions around that topic, rather than 'learning to learn' or attitude-based questions. They could ask positive questions about motivation rather than reinforcing images of poor motivation, try not to presume automatic boredom and disaffection and not encourage young people to emphasize the quality of teaching and content as reasons for engagement or disengagement.

Nevertheless, technical changes to process and content cannot detract from questions about the educational value of e2e's assessment regime. Its roots in earlier outcome-based assessment regimes embody a liberal humanist ethos that, as Usher and Edwards argue, masks confession alongside self and external surveillance. This creates a pastoral form of governance which 'enables individuals to actively participate in disciplinary regimes through investing their own identities, subjectivities and desires with those ascribed to them by certain knowledgeable discourses' (1994: 215; see also Edwards and Usher 1994).

Although e2e can be seen as the latest manifestation of pastoral governance, a key difference is that older schemes, even the Youth Opportunities Programme and its successors, combined 'liberal humanist' ideas about student-centred teaching and assessment of subject and craft skills and knowledge, with personal development and self-assessment. In contrast, it might be argued that e2e combines powerful images of damaged and vulnerable young people with highly regulated and narrow targets that remove general subject knowledge. When formative assessment and teaching have no cognitive or subject focus, it is entirely rational to comply with targets that scrutinise the self and its attitudes in detail. e2e tutors in our project were responsible for translating the government's presentation of links between individuals' 'complex needs', their disengagement and associated problems, into disciplinary self-assessment. They were held responsible for failure and success, and their formative assessment strategy reinforced this.

The e2e assessment regime also reflects the politically successful deflection of attention from structural conditions on people's capacity for agency and political change. This demands that the education system enables individuals to adapt positively to social conditions and to take personal responsibility for their past and future.[8] The state of the employment market, the lack of opportunities available for young people who are notoriously difficult to engage in formal education, and the absence of resources such as time, facilities and specialist tutors, become invisible. Uncritical acceptance of this, together with lack of a clear subject focus and high levels of emotional labour, dominate the e2e learning culture.

In this context, a technical focus on changing a particular method reinforces exhausting demands on tutors and avoids difficult questions about what happens afterwards to young people, many of whom are destined to go in and out of similar schemes with no meaningful progression at all.[9] In this context, humanist goals for education are turned into *humanitarian* forms of support for vulnerable people.

Perhaps even more than other case studies in this book, e2e raises perennial questions about what might count as worthwhile subject content, teaching and assessment. Although we saw glimpses of possible change, and although some young people did benefit from e2e, intractable questions about the educational value of programmes for those at the very bottom of the education and training system and outside the labour market, continue to dog the FE system. Questions about what might be educationally worthwhile for these young people become even more pressing in the current economic recession. While probably everyone agrees that we cannot avoid addressing them, an intense focus on the vulnerable, demotivated self as the subject for learning and assessment enables everyone involved to do just that.

Notes

1. Award Scheme Development and Accreditation Network, which offers customized programmes and certificates of achievement for individual young people.
2. See Chapter 1 of this book for discussion.

3. Louise had not actually acquired any grades at school. She was referring here to progressing from her current Entry Level 3 to Level 1.
4. This internalization of official assessment language is very evident in other assessment regimes in FE, where young people can repeat verbatim the official criteria (see Ecclestone (2002); Torrance et al. (2005)).
5. This was another example of a term used often in policy texts, added to the list that tutors already used about 'vulnerable' young people, discussed in Section One.
6. It is important to note here that this checklist mixes up questions that require young people to evaluate the teaching, their tutors, programme content, themselves and their responses. In the chapter on BTEC National Public Services, the same confusing elision of evaluation and self-assessment questions is also apparent, as is the disaffected response of the participants.
7. See Chapter 1 of this book for discussion.
8. For critique of this shift, epitomized in social policy between 1997 and 2010, see Colley and Hodkinson (2001), Turner (2007).
9. For discussion of the fate of similar young people, see also Lawy et al. (2009).

7 Self-assessment and feedback in BTEC National Diploma Public Services

Introduction

Amidst the chaotic policy changes to the vocational curriculum over the past 30 years, the BTEC National Diploma has had a relatively long shelf-life. It has survived numerous attempts to rationalize the general vocational track to maintain its reputation as a well-known, respected Level 3 qualification, with a clear progression route to higher education. Offered in further education colleges, BTECs provide a mixture of general education, preparation for occupational roles in broad areas across a range of subjects, and opportunities to decide which courses or jobs to pursue afterwords. 'BTEC Nationals'[1] are a popular 'brand' within the EdExcel awarding body's extensive range of academic, vocational and work-based qualifications.

Yet, as this chapter shows, its assessment regime has been influenced adversely by the outcome-based systems of GNVQ and AVCE, and by the parallel introduction of target-led accountability systems in FE colleges. This, together with increasingly diffuse and uncertain meanings of 'vocational education', creates numerous pressures on lecturers' formative and summative assessment practices. As the two learning sites show in this chapter, the prevailing cultures of FE colleges, together with lecturers' and students' expectations and dispositions, exacerbate pressures for high levels of instrumentalism.

Differences in institutional ethos were strong influences on ideas and practices in formative assessment. Oldminster College had a new principal and a confident, upbeat ethos. Our two sites, Oldminster and Mid-Counties Colleges, were both large city colleges of further education, but each with a very different ethos and intake. Oldminster was the region's tertiary college, seen predominantly as the 'sixth form college' for a pleasant cathedral city with a mixture of prosperous and deprived areas, and a predominantly white population. Mid-Counties was more obviously employment-focused and competing with local schools and sixth form colleges for advanced level students in an industrial city with large ethnic populations: during our project, 45% of Mid-Counties' students were from ethnic minorities and 47% from disadvantaged backgrounds or living in areas of deprivation.

Oldminster College conveyed positive messages about both vocational education and the college's confident identity through the location of the National Diploma in Public Services (NDPS) in a new, prominently sited flagship building, together with sensitive renovations of old architecturally interesting buildings on the same site and another striking new building nearby for creative arts and drama. The high status of the premises signalled the equivalence of this vocational Level 3 course with general A-levels, a message which students' schools had often seemed reluctant to give (see also discussion of AVCE Science in this volume). It was presented as more of a direct equivalent to A-levels than it was at Mid-Counties, targeted primarily at those already interested in pursuing a career in the Police, Fire Service, Ambulance Service, Armed Forces, Prison Service, Customs and Excise, as well as community services such as Probation and Social Services, but also suitable for progression to higher education.

The year before our project, Mid-Counties College, a much larger inner-city institution undergoing refurbishment, had received a poor inspection report and, in response, lecturers had adopted strict targets to raise student achievement. At the time of our fieldwork, the NDPS at Mid-Counties was taught in a recently upgraded building but had not yet moved to a new state-of-the-art campus due to open a year later. Entry requirements were slightly lower than at Oldminster and another difference in status was that students without GCSEs in English and Maths were taught Key Skills in literacy and numeracy by members of the course team. At Oldminster, students without a GCSE grade C in English and Maths were strongly encouraged to re-take those subjects in their first year and all students took Key Skills IT as a discrete course in their first year. There was more emphasis on the 'practical' at Mid-Counties, with classes to develop skills related to job requirements and to develop fitness levels for physical selection tests. Students took part in specific Fire Service, Police Service and Army-based testing procedures, including some martial arts training. The division between theory and practical (i.e. a tough physical training regime) seemed to be embedded in the course which, unlike the NDPS at Oldminster, included a work placement.

The NDPS comprises 18 units assessed through a coursework assignment on each unit (divided into specific tasks with detailed criteria), and each assignment is graded Pass, Merit or Distinction. Students receive three final grades for the course at these levels, and there are no external examinations. The case studies focus on lecturers Sarah, Ben, David and Paul and students, Alexander, Anna, Dan and Tina at Oldminster, and lecturers Frank and Alan and students John, Jeff and Manisha at Mid-Counties. In the first section, we highlight students' and lecturers' expectations and aspirations for vocational education in a context where more and more purposes are added to the goals of courses such as BTEC National, and we draw out the tensions for pedagogy and assessment that multiple purposes create. In the second section, we show how these tensions led lecturers to downplay perceived pressures on students. In the third section, we outline lecturers' strategies for our project in two areas: self-assessment at Oldminster and feedback on students' work at Mid-Counties. In the final section, we show the profound pressures towards instrumentalism and its implications for an increasingly restrictive education for this age group.

1. Expanding the purposes of vocational education

Diverse aspirations

Despite a strong occupational focus on different public services, the NDPS reflected the expanding interpretations of 'vocational education' seen in other research and in the case studies of GCSE courses. The practical side, namely fitness training, was not really vocational, nor did the course encompass any sense of 'doing the job', not least because it was difficult for students to experience real-life situations with the uniformed services. Instead, 'vocational' encompassed various meanings. First, it included talks from professionals:

> It brings [the job] out of the book ... it puts it in context ... from the point of view of assessment there needs to be far more *specialist* input to help the learner understand how the *theory fits the practical*. So if you're talking about motivational theories ... we need to be out there seeing these principles in action and listening to stories from people who have done the job.
>
> (Alan, NDPS lecturer, Mid-Counties)

Second, students could consider future careers although, typically of vocational students, their views broadened out as the course progressed. Third, and more influential, was a view that transition to maturity was vocationally related:

> I want them to gain an understanding that the services they are going into require maturity, discipline and knowledge as well, subject knowledge. Hopefully if I'm doing my job by the time they leave here ... they will have a job advantage ... 'cos they can

talk at a more eloquent level than the person that has not done the Public Services course.

(Frank, NDPS course leader, Mid-Counties)

Fourth, perhaps the most dominant meaning was that 'vocational' encompassed generic, life-related 'skills' and dispositions, such as teamwork, personal and social attributes, and general motivation for learning. For example, Sara's background in teaching mathematics in secondary schools, and advisory and counselling work, led her to see a desire to want to continue learning, and to develop 'learning to learn' 'skills,' as all-important:

If they go away at the end of the two years...feeling that they want to carry on learning...that whatever subject...they've... got a sense that education is worthwhile...I'd want them to go away with the feeling that they'd achieved some really good things...or got really good grades and they'd learned skills and qualities [and] knowledge...that...they'll be able to transfer either into higher education or the work place or their personal life.

(Sara, NDPS course leader, Oldminster)

Yet, despite a strong tradition in BTEC Nationals of broader, more liberal meanings of vocational education, these were very fleeting at Oldminster and not espoused at all at Mid-Counties:

I think if you were to say, 'How will this *benefit* you?' you might get from some people an answer that...gives you a greater appreciation of what's happening in the world or the complex issues of the public sector.

(Neil, NDPS lecturer, Oldminster, original emphasis)

Finally, and again typical of many lecturers and students on such courses, our sample saw the course as 'vocational' because it had no examination-based assessment. This created what lecturers saw as too many criteria, of 'just trying to get all the knowledge in', eroding time to develop skills such as evaluation or learning from discussion:

I want them to be able to think. You know, to be able to question and to think about things really and not sort of just *know* stuff...'cos they're not asked to regurgitate stuff in an exam. I want them to be able to *use* information really.

(Sara, NDPS course leader, Oldminster, original emphases)

From a military background, Neil had been teaching for three years when he joined the project. Like Sara, he believed in skills that made students more 'rounded', stressing 'transferable skills' such as time organization and working under pressure. He saw his role as 'nurturing' students, developing them as whole people. All the Oldminster lecturers believed the course was as much about learning personal skills as gaining new information. David had a background in sport and the armed services and said he had a strong competitive and perfectionist drive. His ideas were marked by extremely frequent use of 'delivery'/'deliver' and a lament that time constraints reduced teaching to fulfilling the criteria: 'we have got such a vast range of units to deliver and so you are ... hitting what is asked from the criteria' where there was 'too much spoon-feeding ... basically doing too much of the task *for* them'.

In contrast to his colleagues, Ben's academic background led to an espoused theory of learning marked by high ideals and a holistic philosophy of education. In a similar vein to Derek in AVCE Science in this book, Ben never used instrumental vocabulary such as 'delivery', 'learning styles' or 'ticking boxes'. With an active interest in education from adolescence (he had taught a group of his classmates in another European country at the age of 16), he had subsequently gained several degrees, including two Master's degrees and a PhD. His appointment at Oldminster was his first FE post.

He presented teaching and learning as a moral and ethical matter: not only did everybody have a right to learn but also a 'duty to learn because unless you learn you can't become a responsible person', which, for him, was the overall goal of education. He was highly critical of a 'functionalist' educational system:

> It is there to offer a kind of false hope ... that, 'Yes, it is possible to compress things, it is possible to minimize things and that's how we can scrape through and survive.' But I'm afraid life is not like that ... I do insist that people who want to go on to do a merit or a distinction, because usually an analysis or a comparison or an evaluation is required, I try to say from the very beginning that it's not enough reading a book or researching, it's also important to think about things and to write down our ideas, to evaluate things as we go along, to have an opinion without being opinionated.
>
> (Ben, NPDS lecturer, Oldminster)

Instrumentalism and enjoyment

There was strong synergy between lecturers' and students' expectations and aspirations. Most students arrived with the aim of a career with a particular public service (joining the police was especially popular) but by the second year many had changed, some wanting to progress to higher education, some to employment in, for example, banks. For some, the shift to considering higher education was largely due to perception of an over-subscribed job market, but others had gained a broader awareness of job opportunities and a greater belief in their own abilities. Typically of vocational students at this level, aspirations sometimes remained stable, sometimes changed within the vocational area, and sometimes bore no relation to initially strongly held aspirations. Courses like NDPS gave young people time to decide:

> I find it hard for someone of my age to make a decision about what they want to do for the rest of their life . . . It doesn't have to be for the rest of your life but . . . public services [are] very much a kind of career thing. You can't go into it for a year or so, you have to do a minimum service or whatever.
>
> (John, NDPS student, Mid-Counties)

For others, a vocational course eased the transition to adulthood:

> At school I was always someone that lacked motivation. I struggled to get interested in the topics we were doing . . . and lost interest. But . . . I've realized, now I'm older, that you've got to work for something if you want it and . . . I do want to be a fire fighter . . . obviously it doesn't guarantee, but it will be a big help towards it . . . you've just got to . . . think to yourself, if that's what you want to do, this is what you've got to do.
>
> (Jeff, NDPS student, Mid-Counties)

Again typical of vocational students,[2] their enthusiasm was tempered by recognition of the lower status of the course compared to A-levels, partly because entry requirements were lower and because, in terms of contact time, 'compared to an AS course, it's nothing' (Dan, NDPS student, Oldminster). Alexander also commented obliquely on the status of the course:

> I was a little bit wary. Because it was a BTEC, I was worried about the level of what work was running at, I mean, like, intelligence-wise. I didn't want it to be too easy.
>
> (Alexander, NDPS student, Oldminster)

In their antipathy to academic work, students also had strong images of themselves as 'practical', where practical, simultaneously, was a counter to academic work and being out of the classroom: Dan much preferred the ND to school, describing himself as 'not really an academic kind of person. I'm more kind of hands-on . . . I like to be outdoors doing stuff.'

Although students saw themselves as less capable than peers taking single-subject A-levels, this self-perception changed and for two, motivation to achieve high grades acted as a springboard to work harder. The mixture of specific and more general vocational aspects meant that, as Tina described, the course was 'a window of opportunity... you could go on... to social work, anything, because it's all kind of related' (Tina, NDPS student, Oldminster).

2. Assignment-driven teaching and assessment

Feedback as pedagogy

Despite positive views about the course and its opportunities, motivation was highly instrumental and conditional. In both colleges, lecturers thought the curriculum was too crowded, and whether this was an excuse or not, our observations and interviews showed that most teaching began, progressed and ended with the current assignment, rather than being essentially topic-based, with the assignment requirements included within the topic. This was more marked at Mid-Counties where teaching, feedback and summative assessment were indistinguishable:

> [A]s they are going through the assessment, which is being marked all the time, I'm... trying to guide them, so if they make a mistake, I won't knock the grade off, I'll go up to them, stop the practical and say to them 'right, what did you do wrong then?... and then I'll say 'Think about this' and give them a scenario where this went wrong or that went wrong and hopefully they come across with the answer and then I can grade them... There is always some kind of assessment in normal lessons I think.
> (Frank, NDPS course leader, Mid-Counties)

Diagnostic assessment focused on students' difficulties with assignments:

> If it doesn't work, we get into groups, discuss it: 'Why don't you know the answer?, why don't you understand what I'm saying?'. We try and find out what the stumbling block is and I try and work another way around teaching it if I have to.
> (Frank, NDPS course leader, Mid-Counties)

Both Sara and Neil at Oldminster saw formative assessment as the formal requirement for feedback on assignments, helping students to complete each task for a unit satisfactorily, 'assessment as... they go along, so as they complete tasks' (Neil). He found the assessment criteria helpful both for the students and for himself and valued the objectivity they afforded:

> It's... clear what I need to mark against and it's also clear for them what they need to meet so... one does support the other.

The powerful trend in outcome-based assessment to become highly prescriptive, and to encourage students to demand ever-increasing transparency, was very evident:

> The students . . . said to me, 'We want it crystal-clear. P5, you need to do this, this and this. You've missed this, you haven't done that.' Crystal-clear, short comment, each criteria, not a holistic comment. Because they said . . . 'The holistic comment, if you're writing in that way, it can be misinterpreted and what I'm thinking might not be what the criteria's asking me to do.' So they want it crystal-clear.
>
> (David, NDPS lecturer, Oldminster)

Feedback was the core of assessment, understanding and learning:

> [Formative assessment] is where they . . . complete a piece of work and we . . . mark that, give it back to them and give them feedback . . . they're producing a piece of work that is being assessed but . . . that's not the final chance for them to be given the grades . . . they can go away and, perhaps improve that, add different things . . . then hopefully, improve what they're doing and improve their grade . . . obviously the feedback is a big part of that.
>
> (Sara, NDPS course leader, Oldminster)

'Unofficial' formative assessment underpinned the course, where oral feedback after giving back assignments, with written comments, was equally important: 'We're giving them verbal feedback all the time' (Neil, NDPS lecturer, Oldminster). Despite lamenting time constraints, lecturers were keen to develop skills of self-assessment. Neil was developing a form to encourage more thoughtful self-assessment that replaced what he described as the typical 'I did brilliant' comment with those that showed awareness of individual strengths and weaknesses and their effect on the team. He already encouraged self-assessment after presentations:

> I would normally get them to feed back to me verbally, how they thought they'd performed. Then . . . I'd get the class to feed back and then I would feed back.

Predictably, students appreciated all this feedback. Tina described how the lecturers 'write down little notes about what's missing, to what needs to be added, or what you could like improve on'. Dan explained: 'When you get it back they'll sit individual people down and talk through it . . . and say, "You did well here, you did not so well here."' They preferred this to the briefer, blunter feedback they'd had at school. For Anna, feedback was not only useful for gaining higher grades, but also had a broader life and work-related function, to develop the ability to be self-critical:

> You can see from like grades and feedback you get, what you're good at and what you're not good at, and what you can improve. It's important really, I think, in Public Services to be critical of yourself, to improve how you perform.
>
> (Anna, NDPS student, Oldminster)

Similar to students in earlier studies, they had internalized the language of assessment criteria, such as the need to 'analyse' and 'evaluate' for the higher grades.[3] They expected to target a particular grade for each assignment but were much more strategic than students in earlier studies:

> You've got to work to the grades you want to get and then finish off getting that grade in the two weeks [i.e. after the feedback and before the final submission date]. If...you want to aim for distinction but just do the passes the first time, then you can't go on and do the merit and distinction part in the two weeks, because you haven't aimed to do it before.
>
> (Anna, NDPS student, Oldminster)

Despite the highly instrumental learning culture of Mid-Counties, Jeff's observation indicated the contrast between an easy process of 'correcting mistakes' and potential for more holistic engagement:

> The first two assignments...if I got A's on them...I think maybe I wouldn't be as willing to push myself as hard for the next assignment, cause I would think 'Well, I've already got a couple of A's so I don't need to work as hard'...Whereas just with the comments...that helps 'cos...if you just keep improving it and not find out what you're getting, all you know is that you needed to improve it 'cos you had something wrong.
>
> (Jeff, NDPS student, Mid-Counties)

Negative comments could also be motivating:

> You think you've tried really hard and you get a negative comment and it can set you back miles...But at times negative comments have helped me more than positive ones. If it sort of says 'Oh, you can't do that', well you think 'Yes I can!'...then you...try and do it, to try and prove them wrong.
>
> (Jeff, NDPS student, Mid-Counties)

Only Ben emphasized the need for students to be involved actively, summarizing this as 'interactive formative assessment':

> I invite [individuals] to have a chat with me and give them feedback, and then I listen to their views. I explain of course where

things could be done and, if somebody has got strengths in certain areas, I point that out as well . . . they need to know this, not because they should sit back and relax, but because they could become equally strong in another area . . . it's part of learning, isn't it, and developing even.

(Ben, NDPS lecturer, Oldminster)

Downplaying the summative demands

Synergy between students and teachers around feedback to improve grades went hand in hand with downplaying the amount of studying required in a Level 3 course. This was reinforced by students' often strongly expressed preferences for 'learning styles', particularly at Mid-Counties:

Obviously, if you've got a bunch of students that learn best practically instead of sitting there doing book work and work sheets, try and get a few practical lessons in so they can actually interact with it.

(Jeff, NDPS student, Mid-Counties)

I enjoy discussions with either the lecturer or the group .. because I'm an auditory learner, I prefer talking about stuff, I also like . . . being shown what to do and . . . have a go . . . I don't particularly like writing notes and essays but obviously . . . you have to get on and do it but . . . if it's an essay and it's an assignment I won't particularly learn anything from it . . . I learn from doing other stuff and then I'll put it down on paper because I have to.

(John, NDPS student, Mid-Counties)

I'm a visual learner . . . I can't just read and get on with it . . . we all have different styles of learning and one of mine is visually, seeing things and even telling us what we have to do and then I can do it.

(Manisha, NDPS student, Mid-Counties)[4]

They particularly disliked copious amounts of writing:

[T]he first lesson we had of 'Understanding the Public Sector' was *completely* writing . . . hundreds of pages at once and . . . we were all nearly asleep . . . it was evil. But . . . [the observed lesson] was okay because we now do role group work which . . . makes it an activity.

(Alexander, NDPS student Oldminster, original emphasis)

Some of the lessons . . . can be pretty boring, but . . . they try their *best* by getting you . . . into groups or doing different things like presentations . . . but it still can be a bit boring . . . I don't really know how they can change that 'cos they do try [to make it enjoyable].

(Anna, NDPS student Oldminster, original emphasis)

In the face of expressed likes and dislikes, lecturers appeared defensive, inviting criticisms of methods while pre-empting complaints by telling students that 'boring' topics or methods could still develop broader skills:

And I would rather say, 'It may have been boring, but did you learn *anything* from that lesson?' . . . I mean, obviously we try and make it fun if we can but as I tried to say yesterday . . . the History and Development of the Public Sector *isn't* going to be *that* enthralling and . . . given the time-scale that you've got, you've got to try and *ram* that knowledge into them and . . . unfortunately you're going to end up taking notes . . . [but] at least you can refer back to them and when you get your assignment . . . as you're reading through . . . the learning will then come out because then you'll achieve . . . But in the lesson you may think, 'Oh God, this is *boring!*'

(Neil, NDPS lecturer, Oldminster, original emphases)

In contrast to his colleagues' somewhat pessimistic assumptions, Ben asserted strongly that good lecturers would always 'find a way' to go beyond a focus on grades and that covering the criteria did not necessarily mean an entirely instrumental approach:

The assignment's very specific, but the input can be of a nature that covers the criteria entirely and goes 'beyond' . . . The bad things begin when we . . . make them concentrate exclusively on what the assignment requires.

(Ben, NDPS lecturer Oldminster)

Glimpses of intrinsic motivation

A predominantly instrumental ethos led students to equate learning with gaining useful information from lecturers in order to complete their assignments. Yet, as a counter to lecturers' images of what students would or would not 'put up with', some saw wider value in learning new things. For example, Alexander at Oldminster praised what he had learnt about law in the Citizenship unit:

I've . . . picked up a fair amount of knowledge from it and . . . a lot of the stuff you see from TV . . . like politics, you can understand 'cos you'd never done anything on it. But now I know what it's about and what they're saying, it . . . makes everything a little bit more interesting . . . I will be in a world that is essentially a working world and I will be part of that now, so it's . . . important to me that I understand what I'm going to get myself into.

Some students appreciated wider knowledge, relevant to life in general such as human rights (Tina) and some spoke enthusiastically about topics they had enjoyed at school, as well as the variety of topics on the NDPS (Anna and Alexander).

There were also tiny, fleeting signs that students liked learning things for their own sake. Alexander's depiction of himself as a 'practical guy' had led him to abandon AS Philosophy at school, but he spoke eloquently about how he had 'loved the debate' and the challenge of 'intellectual discussion'. General education was also vocationally relevant, where learning about different religions would help him in his intended career in the police:

It allowed me, it broadened me, to understand, to respect everybody's individual need, and that way I could understand it.

Motivation was not therefore simply *external* (gaining grades for progression, whether employment or more education): it could also at times be *introjected* (they had internalized the detail of the criteria and their lecturers' goals) and *identified* (they saw the relevance and usefulness of the course). Occasionally, and perhaps more than lecturers realized, motivation included *intrinsic* elements, since students all professed interest in many of the topics. Again very fleetingly, there were signs of the deeper *interested* motivation, where Anna, for example, equated her intrinsic love of learning, both for school subjects and on the NDPS, as part of a desire to acquire 'knowledge' alongside her determination to do well in order to achieve her vocational goal.

Nevertheless, motivation depended greatly on constant oral and written feedback, so much so that it was a job-related goal in itself:

Seeing that I have managed to get good grades, I'm motivated to get good grades as well and want to keep that motivation. Sometimes it can get a bit boring – I'm not going to deny that – because sometimes I feel like I just can't be bothered to go in today, but I do.

(Anna, NDPS student, Oldminster)

But if you want a job you got to fight for it . . . at the end of the day, I'm here to get my qualification, I'm here to get my career.

(Alexander, NDPS student, Oldminster)

High grades proved at job selection procedures that one was capable of putting in a great deal of effort. 'Pushing yourself' was vital because 'that's what makes you stand out at the end of the day'.

3. Improving 'learning'

Introducing self-assessment diaries

At Oldminster, Sara and Neil introduced self-assessment of 'learning' by giving each student a notebook with a list of guideline questions[5] and asking students to complete an entry at the end of every session. The lecturers wanted to encourage students to think more about their learning by developing their capacity to be self-critical, to provide feedback on classroom activities and, through both, to increase motivation:

> I... presented it two ways. One is as a record for them, because there are certain parts of assignments where they need to go back and look at what particular skills they might have developed in certain areas, and also when they're doing application forms and CVs, they... need to look back at some of the topics that they've studied and... what they learned as well... but also for us as lecturers to try and get an idea of some of the things that they were enjoying or not enjoying, some of the activities that go well... what they were *learning* really in terms of content as well.
> (Sara, NDPS course leader, Oldminster, original emphasis)

Neil emphasized that the purpose was for lecturers to see how students 'were learning', but also to provide a space where students could be open about any difficulties they had 'with their learning'.

The strategy continued for four weeks, at which stage, lesson observations and interviews took place for our project. At the end of the observed lessons, students completed the diary task in the shortest possible time (always less than 5 minutes, sometimes barely a minute, depending on the student).[6] There were few thoughtful or detailed responses; the majority were superficial, sometimes flippant. Frequent diary-keeping was a boring task, with students unsure of what to write, and with little understanding of what a useful self-assessment response would be like. Unsurprisingly, popular, everyday associations of diaries with personal matters were also evident:

> Some of them... find it a little bit hard to know quite what to say and therefore they can then... lapse into just writing something silly or nothing at all, really... they're not writing anything

> amazingly productive . . . They're . . . focusing much more on how
> they're feeling and what's going on in their lives.
>
> (Sara, NDPS course leader, Oldminster)

Understandably, given lecturers' initial explanation, students tended to
opt for either a personal comment or a general summary of the lesson
along a continuum between 'boring' and 'interesting'. All the feedback
was on teaching techniques; as Neil expressed it, 'They're critiquing the
lesson . . . not critiquing themselves.' Rather than the 'reflective' activity he
had hoped, it was 'hitting all the wrong targets' with 'random comments'.

The ubiquitous term 'learning' was at the root of an inherent confusion
of purpose since it meant, variously: grade achievement, enjoyment of activities and behaviours and attitudes in response to activities. A particular
confusion was to elide formative assessment with evaluation, conflating
'learning' with judgements about teaching, as comments from Anna at
Oldminster show:

> [The lecturers] can take ideas without just asking us what we think.
> They can just read what we put down 'cos we'll put down what we
> think and so they'll get a better understanding, and then they can
> just try and make it a bit more interesting if we found it boring
> or this and that.
>
> (Anna, NDPS student, Oldminster)

Some thought it was an official requirement:

> What the College . . . wanted . . . [was] feedback from the students
> about how they were finding lessons, [to] see if they actually were
> learning anything and also what they were finding about lectur-
> ers' teaching methods.
>
> (Alexander, NDPS student, Oldminster)

> I see it as a kind of way to get feedback from us to them . . . just
> a way to change the lesson plans or how they teach or stuff like
> that.
>
> (Dan, NDPS student, Oldminster)

Useful for lecturers, but 'pointless' for the students was Alexander's sum-
ming up. Students saw it as just another task:

> a new thing we had to do after every lesson . . . just fill them
> out . . . what we thought of the lesson and just put down what
> we were thinking about it.
>
> (Anna, NDPS student, Oldminster)

The diaries were therefore used solely in the 'letter' of formative assessment, and the hope that students might gain a deeper 'understanding of their learning' fell by the wayside. With increasing resentment from students, lecturers decided to ask for less frequent entries for the remainder of the academic year.

Nevertheless, there were occasional benefits. David thought some comments enabled him to re-focus his teaching, while the open approach elicited feedback from some students who had never revealed anything before, and this, in turn, highlighted the importance of individual tutorials. During one such tutorial, Sara had gained particular insight into one student's difficulties; he had been criticized at school for writing how he spoke and told he had to find a different way to express what he wanted to say.

> I suddenly realized that he was desperately sitting there, coming up with things to write down, but thinking that they weren't okay... And I saw him today and he was writing loads and... I said, 'Oh that's really good,'... and... suddenly we'd worked out what was wrong.

Equally importantly, in a project where lecturers had time to evaluate practice, the strategy provoked important questions about self-assessment. A tension had emerged between open – endedness and focus, raising questions about how open guidelines should be, whether more specific questions or more structure helped students focus better on what self-assessment meant. Furthermore, lecturers started to question how far it was realistic to expect students to distinguish between teaching and learning, or even to assess their own learning at all. They decided that key formative questions for students could be: What else do I need to know? What don't I know?

Yet, lecturers' view that their strategy showed the need to develop understanding and skills in self-assessment as relevant for job applications, work and studying, moved self-assessment even further away from subject content, to become just another life-related skill: 'I think we didn't get over to them the importance of the skill itself' (Sara, NDPS course leader, Oldminster). They therefore also decided to build in self-assessment at certain points in the future: at the end of a unit or task or after a trip, and when writing a CV. At such points, they hoped it would appear more meaningful than after every teaching session.

Making feedback more focused and manageable

At Mid-Counties, lecturers adopted an 'integrated approach', dividing assessment tasks into smaller individual 'chunks' that could, as Frank described, be 'delivered independently', where students could be more involved in deciding how best to fulfil the criteria, where lecturers could make explicit links between grade criteria and the language used, and provide more regular feedback in individual tutorials. This made assignment-driven teaching more 'efficient', with classroom activity based on assessment tasks and 'quick' oral and written feedback to encourage students to develop their own strategy for carrying them out.

Lecturers hoped that this would enable students to raise concerns at strategic times as the basis for more 'nuanced' feedback. The aim was to raise grade levels based on more accurate understanding of individual 'grade capabilities', and to adapt the language of feedback to be 'less academic and more accessible':

> Whereas I would normally give them very formal written feedback, I've now tried to 'street wise' my feedback . . . in a language they will understand . . . put it in my words rather than these fancy academic words; they seem to get what we're on about.
>
> (Frank, NDPS course leader, Mid-Counties)

The strategy was successful, reinforcing Frank's initial view in our project that formative assessment comprised interim tasks towards summative outcomes. Breaking the process into smaller elements helped students understand how to satisfy the criteria 'more effectively'. Instructions therefore 'worked better [because] students come back for more help less often now'. In parallel, feedback became more 'strategic' through 'constructive' (as opposed to 'negative') comments around each criterion, while pre-typed marks on assignment specifications indicated each criterion within grade bands:

> A Pass 1 [criterion] is a normal task . . . 'identify 4 structures in the cardiovascular system', just identify them, whereas the Merit would ask them to 'analyze' and the Distinction would ask them to 'critically evaluate' those systems.
>
> (Frank, NDPS course leader, Mid-Counties)

Organizing everything around the criteria took 'ability grouping' or 'differentiation' to a new level: lecturers either grouped by criterion-based task to cover the range of grades, or by precise grades attached to individual criteria such as all P1, all P2, etc., across the topic range. The language of teaching and learning became surreally technical and incomprehensible to outsiders:

> If, for instance, there is sometimes a difference between the Pass, Merit and Distinction, so [that] maybe that [individual criteria of] D1, M1 and P1 all link together, we still treat them separately and then in a group as its own. If D1, M1 and PI and P2 are all linked,

and M2 and D2 are different subjects, we will concentrate on that one completely before we move on, so that they are not doing a mishmash of different things, so we can get all of the bits that relate to each other and then go on to the next bit.

(Alan, NDPS lecturer, Mid-Counties)

In a seamless logic, marking assignments was aligned:

There could be an assignment [with] P1, M1 and D1 ... so if they get the P1 they will get constructive feedback 'you got this because' ... Say they miss the M1 and the D1, we will give proper feedback on how they can achieve that – some people call that spoon-feeding, but, to be honest, we don't give them a method or recipe for writing that essay ... we give them as much as we can without actually writing the essay for them – so we hope they are learning rather than being spoon-fed.

(Frank, NDPS course leader, Mid-Counties)

Unsurprisingly, the strategy made the language of teaching, learning and assessment even more modular and bureaucratic than it had been before. It also made the strategy easier to 'sell':

The way I told it to them is, 'The way we're doing it now, you are guaranteed a distinction at the end of the 8-week period', or whatever period we use. So I sold it to the more obstinate students as being a better way of getting a distinction grade, whereas the old way, they may not have got the grade they wanted. To the lecturers I originally sold it to them as less marking for you, but I was wrong!

(Frank, NDPS course leader, Mid-Counties)

Students appreciated this more focused approach:

[Lecturers] go through things with us individually, making sure we have the right sections, going through the right stages of the work and if we haven't, he can make it clear that we've missed this and that, and get ... back to it, and go through it again ... that gives us more confidence and we can see we're on the right lines.

(Manisha, NDPS student, Mid-Counties)

Unsurprisingly, the strategy exacerbated a discrepancy between how students performed in class and how they did their assignments:

They sit in class and come up with great answers but a lot of them are not taking it down because when they go to do the assignment they can't remember what was discussed and automatically go and look it up on the internet.

(Alan, NDPS lecturer, Mid-Counties)

4. A parodox of professionalism

Unmanageable tensions?

Instrumentalism dominated the two strategies in both colleges, although it was both much more entrenched and seen positively at Mid-Counties. It was rooted in powerful stereotypes about appropriate teaching activities and about what students would and would not tolerate, but was also integral to the assessment regime itself. In learning cultures where 'achievement' and 'learning' are synonymous, the often-mentioned goal of encouraging students to have more of 'a say in their learning' through enhanced feedback transmogrified rapidly into helping students understand the difference between grades in terms of skills that needed to be 'evidenced'.

In spite of similar pressures, there were differences between the two learning cultures. At Oldminster, it seemed that assignment criteria and grades were used both in the letter and the spirit of formative assessment: although oral and written feedback referred constantly to the criteria, feedback also provided opportunities for deeper engagement by encouraging the skills of analysis and evaluation. Focus on the grades seemed to be highly motivating for students and so an instrumental starting point led to wider learning, at least for some students.

Consequently, the learning culture appeared to veer between restriction and possible expansion. Lecturers wanted the opportunity to break away from the syllabus restrictions but found themselves unable to do so because of the relentless number of units. To some extent, therefore, espoused theories of learning that were more liberal did not appear to be theories-in-use.

A 'paradox of professionalism', noted also in our case studies of GCSE Business and AVCE Science at Moorview, was emerging where professionalism marked by interest in students' progress, and by concern for developing interest in a subject, competed with a prescriptive, grade-dominated system that formalized and embraced instrumentalism. This raises the question of how broader professional values can co-exist with instrumentalism without producing unmanageable tension.

At Oldminster, students' responses to self-assessment arose in part because this paradox produced well-intentioned but muddled messages about the aims of the diaries as both a source of quick feedback on which teaching techniques 'worked' best and a way of encouraging students to become more self-critical. Students' responses were also a logical outcome of a learning and assessment culture where they were dependent on feedback, and pressurized lecturers about 'boring' or 'irrelevant' teaching. This encouraged students to equate self-assessment of learning with evaluation of teaching.

Lecturers also seemed to have an unacknowledged struggle between what they wanted to achieve philosophically and what the constraints of the course enabled them to achieve in practice. Neil and Sara used language that denoted a holistic approach to teaching and learning, but they also referred to 'delivering' the syllabus, and there was evidence of discrepancy between espoused theory and practice with both lecturers.

The drive for clarity

There did not seem to be any paradox of professionalism, or any expressions of these tensions at Mid-Counties. Although they espoused a less grade dominated view, lecturers' language and practice indicated the opposite:

> If I can find a way to pull a grade out of a student, I'll pull the grade out...[even if] it's like pulling teeth out...Whereas some of my colleagues might say 'Ok, well they haven't done that then I'm going to fail them', I try to pull them through as much as I can 'cos I don't think we're here to trip them up, we're here to guide them through.
>
> (Frank, NDPS course leader, Mid-Counties)

Yet, this summary should not suggest lack of critical perspective: lecturers were all highly cynical about what they saw as a bureaucratic, officious culture that did not care about how they got results this affected their own motivation and sense of professionalism.

In both learning cultures, there was synergy between students and lecturers around expectations of being given 'clear criteria', coaching to those criteria, grade achievement, and constant feedback. There was some potential for this to be a springboard for deeper engagement at Oldminster, but seemingly much less at Mid-Counties. Despite fleeting glimpses of intrinsic motivation and broader educational goals among some students in both colleges, lecturers appeared to have few expectations for intrinsic motivation or of being able to engage students with apparently 'boring' or 'irrelevant' topics. In parallel, students expected lecturers to teach to a particular 'style' that fitted stereotypes of 'vocational learning'.

These factors led lecturers to undermine their own confidence and authority, allowing students to pressurize them about teaching styles, to demand 'crystal-clear criteria,' and to criticize some teaching methods as not 'vocational' or some content as 'boring'. In this learning culture, giving students 'a voice' reinforced instrumental tendencies.

Conclusion

The NDPS case study shows just how far the activities and goals of assessment, teaching and learning have merged in vocational education. Despite variation between lecturers' beliefs and values in the two colleges, and indications that individuals could affect motivation adversely by very instrumental expectations, or positively by a more confident, optimistic view, instrumentalism was very marked in both learning cultures.

These factors, together with prescriptive criteria, have homogenized assessment practices, reinforced by the ubiquitous, empty language of 'learning'. The optimism of democratic clarity, promised by the introduction of outcome-based assessment in the 1980s, has produced strong student expectations of, and demands for, 'crystal clarity'. The overall effect is that the precision of line-by-line coaching to each grade criterion is now built into courses like BTEC National.

For Oldminster lecturers, involvement in the project highlighted tensions between espoused theories and theories-in-use, especially in relation to instrumentalism and broader ideas about education and learning. At Mid-Counties, the project enabled lecturers to introduce a new approach to formative assessment that enabled them to embed even stronger forms of instrumentalism, thereby responding effectively to pressures to generate better grade achievement. Lecturers recognized tensions but seemed resigned to a strategy that worked, and which students liked because it showed lecturers taking more interest in them than they had before, and because they were clearer about their progress.

Yet, prescriptive criteria and compliant college cultures are not solely to blame for instrumentalism. Although assessment dominates teaching and learning, and changes the role of the lecturer in very profound ways, the project also highlighted the extent to which subject knowledge and teaching have been integrated with the assessment criteria. This has diluted meanings of 'vocational' to general life skills and dispositions. These now include the life and work skills of discipline, motivation and engagement with the assessment regime itself.

The NPDS case study shows how this combination of factors has undermined teachers' own confidence in their ability to motivate students to learn content, and to allow teaching and learning relationships to be highly conditional. We return to broader implications for the content and purpose of vocational education in the final chapter of the book.

Notes

1. Before being merged with the University of London's examination board in 1997, BTEC was the Business and Technology Council,

offering a range of vocational education qualifications in subjects such as Performing Arts, Media, Business, Engineering. BTEC is now a brand name for those qualifications, familiar to employers and higher education institutions.

2. See Ecclestone (2002; 2006; 2007); Bathmaker (2002); Torrance et al. (2005); and Chapter 3 in this volume.
3. See Chapter 1 of this book for discussion, and note above.
4. For detailed analysis and a strong critique of the orthodoxy of learning styles in further education, see Coffield et al. (2008).
5. See Appendix A below.
6. See Chapter 6 on 'Entry to Employment' for almost identical goals, approaches and responses to self-assessment.

APPENDIX A

Ideas to help you evaluate your learning

- ➢ What facts/information did you learn in this lesson?
- ➢ What skills did you practise in this session? (e.g. listening, presenting, writing, analysing, problem solving, etc.)
- ➢ How did you contribute to the lesson? (helping others, asking questions, etc.)
- ➢ What did you find interesting about today's lesson?
- ➢ How well did you perform in the tasks?
- ➢ What would you do differently if you had the lesson all over again?
- ➢ Did you find anything difficult in today's lesson?
- ➢ Do you need extra help with any topics/issues?
- ➢ What sort of mood were you in, in today's lesson, how do you feel?
- ➢ What was your favourite/least favourite part of the lesson?
- ➢ Did you learn anything about yourself in the lesson today?
- ➢ Did you learn something from any of the other students in the group?
- ➢ Did anything prevent you from learning something today?

8   Reviews of progress and individual learning plans in adult literacy and numeracy classes

Introduction

As our case studies have shown so far, the widespread merging of teaching, formative and summative assessment in order to meet narrow targets is caused by diverse political, social and educational pressures. In adult education, the marginal, part-time and often isolated conditions of teachers may make similar pressures both more pronounced and more difficult to resist than in other sectors. In addition, the introduction of highly prescriptive Skills for Life tests, alongside funding-linked targets for achievement and progression to other courses, are very recent. They run up against a history in adult education of professional autonomy, lack of regulation and a strong public service ethos. This tension is particularly evident in courses run by separate adult and community education centres rather than further education colleges or workplaces.

Another dimension to such tensions, illuminated by our project, is the view of these adults as 'vulnerable', lacking in confidence and self-esteem, managing very difficult and constrained domestic lives, and preferring one-to-one, personalized diagnostic assessment and individual approaches to teaching. In a context of intensive targets and extremely diverse learning groups, with 'roll-on, roll off' recruitment and progression, such images require teachers to navigate the line between creating comfortable, 'safe spaces' to learn and challenging adults to overcome fears of literacy and numeracy and, crucially, to progress out of their classes. In some ways, these pressures are very similar to those facing teachers in Entry to Employment programmes, discussed in Chapter 6.

As we show here, the special features of an adult education learning culture affect teachers' uses of tutorials, limiting the very real potential that exists for those activities to be educationally productive. Yet, perhaps more positively than in other learning cultures, our ALLN case studies also show how teachers might capitalize on that potential. Discussion draws on in-depth research with teachers and learners in Larkshire Adult Education centre, based in a small Midland town, and owned by the County

Council, which runs a large adult education service covering a mainly rural area. The centre offered humanities, arts and crafts and independent living programmes, as well as adult literacy and numeracy. It was a clean and bright environment, served well by administrative and premises management staff, who are almost always the first point of contact with students. There was a palpable ethos of friendliness and support, deeply rooted in and respected by the local community.

We focus here on teachers from two adult literacy classes, Alice Jones and Holly Bates (one working at levels E2–L1 and the other at levels L1–L2), a numeracy teacher, Sarah Robinson, (working at levels between E3 and L2), and four students: Summer Harrison, Abigail Compton, Elena Maria Atkins and Rachel Blythe. During our project, each group met for two hours per week over 30 weeks, operating roll-on, roll-off enrolment where new students might join the class at any time during the year and where the teacher might/could have to cover topics already covered for the others. The teachers are part-time, teach at different times, and are only paid for the hours they teach. However, all the teachers and staff at the Larkshire centre belong to a regular Thursday lunch club, bringing food to share, even if they have to come in specially. This informal event helps them to stay in touch and feel like colleagues, though work concerns are often not the subject of conversation! While the management style in the county service was, in principle, very enabling, in practice, the service was thinly spread so that County Hall was felt to be distant. Nevertheless, the curriculum manager on site was very much a colleague of the teachers.

In this chapter, we first evaluate tensions between teachers' and their students' expectations of teaching and learning and, in particular, their previous experiences of trying to learn numeracy and literacy, and the demand for highly personalized diagnoses of their needs, and approaches to teaching and assessment. In the second section, we explore how personalization affects pedagogy and assessment, and the ways in which a public sector ethos counters potentially diminished expectations. In the third section, we analyse the goals and uses of formal reviews of progress introduced by teachers for our project. In the final section, we evaluate the ways in which teachers might use the strong potential evident in the Larkshire learning culture for tutorials to be more challenging and educationally focused.

1. Juggling fragmented circumstances

The failure of schooling

A powerful factor shaping the learning culture of all adult literacy and numeracy classes to a greater or lesser extent was convergence between teachers and students around certain images of dispositions, previous educational experiences and attitudes to learning. The idea that adults doing basic skills have been 'failed' by compulsory schooling was a deeply-held belief among teachers. It was reinforced by sensitivity to the very real feelings of shame and embarrassment of being poor at numeracy and literacy, (and in some cases, innumerate or illiterate) among many, but not all, of their students.

Students had different reasons for attending the classes, but most common were wanting to help children with their schooling, to improve employment opportunities (Level 2 qualifications in English and Maths are now a requirement for entry into any professional training pathway), or simply, yet powerfully, to prove something to themselves or others after an unsuccessful school career. A significant factor shaping this particular learning culture, but also evident in our other adult language, literacy and numeracy case studies, was a negative experience of school:

> When I was at school, we...had a teacher who used to tell us quickly what sort of thing we was actually doing...you couldn't ask him anything, even if sometimes he would say, 'Any questions?'...you think, 'If I put my hand up they are going to turn round and say you are thick' or something, I didn't want to be ridiculed...I used to think it was my fault all the time but now...I think it was actually teacher's fault...I just sort of struggled and pretended I understood when in fact I didn't...I don't think they was interested...they didn't have the time...they wouldn't give a one-to-one like Sarah does, explaining to you even if it takes about 10 to 20 minutes...getting it to sink in...they wouldn't have took that time anyway.
>
> (Summer, numeracy student)

Students had a wide range of different ideas and feelings about learning, based on previous experiences. These affected how they approach the teacher, the content and other participants and shaped their levels of resilience, motivation and confidence:

> I'm probably not the brainboxiest person...but if...somebody gives me instructions it takes me ages to work them out, but if I'm shown, I'm actually better at doing stuff that way...that's how you learn in life, it's the same with the English course, you make so many mistakes on work, and sometimes you go on a bit of a downer some days, thinking 'Oh no, I'm not very good' but then you'll get it right another time and that's how, you're learning from your mistakes.
>
> (Abigail, literacy student)

In contrast, other students were much less keen to take risks and expose themselves by making mistakes, or saw the teacher as solely responsible for their achievement. For example, Elena Maria was relatively new to the classes, with very little experience of schooling. From a traveller family, now settled, her aims were connected with being bored at home and feeling she would like to have a job, now that her children were growing up. This would be a big change for her and, like significant numbers of women in adult education, she was not supported in her ambitions by her husband, who did not understand why she wasn't satisfied to be at home all day, and expressed embarrassment if she wanted to go out to work. For her, going to work was not based on financial considerations, but simply wanting to broaden her experience. Even coming to the class was a significant act for her; her friends and family did not understand her and were not supportive. Yet, in spite of her lack of schooling, she described herself as a good reader: her problems were with accurate spelling and writing. She was also doing the same maths class as Summer. In this context, she was very cautious about getting personally involved with her learning, preferring to see it as a process similar to learning a handicraft, interesting rather than emotionally demanding. She was only provisionally committed to the class and seemed still to be afraid of failing, or that she might not, after all, improve.

Friends and helpers, or teachers?

For most if not all teachers in ALLN, these observations will be unsurprising. None of the 18 ALLN classes in our project revealed anything other than the typical range of highly diverse and idiosyncratic beliefs, attitudes and responses which shape relationships, activities and outcomes throughout adult basic education. Yet, while teachers at Larkshire believed that past experiences of school were entirely negative and damaging, they had to work out, often informally and almost tacitly, how past experience affected each individual's motivation and attitude to trying to learn literacy and numeracy in formal classes perhaps for a second or third time, often as part of a lifetime of doing so. Nevertheless, although considered either onerous or challenging, and while recognizing that many ALLN students were not going to become completely fluent in reading or writing, or become completely numerate, few regarded this as a negative struggle.

One effect was to place a premium constantly on good personal relationships between teacher and student, and between the students themselves; and on rich communicative dialogue between learners and a teacher who was seen more as a relatively expert friend and helper rather than a figure of authority:

> the atmosphere definitely . . . helps, it's not just sat in silence for a couple of hours, but we talk and we have a laugh.
>
> (Rachel, numeracy student, Larkshire)

> I like to work with the students as opposed to working against them, I know that sounds a bit odd, that does, but I would rather us all be together as one, so to speak, rather than me being apart; I like to keep working totally with the students.
>
> (Holly, literacy teacher, Larkshire)

Individual working in classes was the predominant mode, particularly at the beginning of the year. For most students this was congenial since they did not want the experience to remind them of school. Teachers were aware that many students resist a group orientation, depending on their espoused ideas about how learning takes place and therefore about the 'proper' role of the teacher. Some students felt that success was mainly about hard work and concentration on individual skills acquisition and, as a result, saw co-operation, discussion and conversations about learning as pleasant but actually a waste of valuable time. In part, such views may be associated with a more instrumental perspective on learning, but not exclusively; they are also related to images of 'typical' adult education classes, antipathy to past experiences and teachers' own expectations and preferences.

The respect of all three teachers for the equal status of the learners as other adults, as well as their natural concern not to undermine confidence, often inhibited the need for more teacher-directed and challenging approaches, particularly in the two literacy classes. Yet, as Alice's somewhat apologetic acknowledgement of the tension shows, teachers need a strong sense of their own ethos and preferred way of working:

> I don't want them to feel like I'm being superior but at the same time I do want them to feel that I'm in control of what's going on in the class. I think there's nothing worse than feeling like you're on a ship with no captain when you come into a classroom. So in that sense I will have some degree of formality, I might as well say it, I like to 'have a desk'! Some people don't 'have a desk' and it just works like that, but I think they value that someone's got something there, and got things set out, even if they don't sit behind the desk all the time, knowing that.
>
> (Alice, literacy teacher, Larkshire)

2. Personalized teaching, tutoring and assessment

As we showed in Chapter 1, the Skills for Life initiative introduced new forms of accreditation for adult literacy, language and numeracy. One of its goals was to break a strong tradition of students attending classes year after year, with no wish to 'move on' (or 'progress' as the policy term puts it). However, unlike the more homogenized learning cultures of vocational education classes which are geared heavily to getting students through the same summative assignments, a significant number of participants in literacy and numeracy classes do not want the qualification.

The differences in focus of accredited and non-accredited courses can lead to considerable variations in teachers' purposes for dialogue and communication with individuals. On an accredited course, teachers tailor their styles of communication and topics for dialogue for individuals in a constant diagnosis and re-diagnosis, moving from one person to the next, with the additional pressure of getting students through the Skills for Life tests. Communication is often about subject knowledge (such as the correct use of apostrophes, or an appropriate methodology for calculating percentages), or it may be concerned with practical questions about 'how to learn' more effectively (for example, through practice, homework, or talking to others), or it may be about what is meant by achievement (recognizing the connection between classroom activity and improved effectiveness in everyday tasks, or the success criteria in an external assessment process). Discussions may be triggered by the externally-driven focus on summative assessment which may or may not be of primary concern to the students, but cannot be ignored because of institutional requirements. The limiting factor that dogs all interactions, however, is lack of time for discussions to develop, either because the teacher has to get round to another student, or because it is the end of the two-hour class period and the teacher or the student has to leave.

These circumstances are exacerbated by the tendency for each teacher to be working with numerous part-time students in different groups at any one time. It was therefore unsurprising that new forms of paperwork, such as the Individual Learning Plan (ILP) and diagnostic tools such as the 'spiky profile' chart,[1] are often used administratively rather than for meaningful diagnostic assessment and for more focused teaching and support for individuals or the group as a whole. In ALLN programmes, there are simply fewer formal resources with which a part-time teacher can support a sustained formative approach.

It was therefore difficult for teachers simply to make plans for their lessons and carry them out. The numeracy teacher could be describing any of the classes here:

> Because I have got a core of people who were here last year, I am able to get them to do things together; like this morning, we would do a subject that they are all going to be learning together, then give them some work to get on with, but they will all be working at completely different paces so I can't keep it together – this

morning there were one or two glazed looks...but more often they will all be working on their own...and I will be going round to each one seeing how they are doing, getting them more work to do, explaining things, coming round if they need assistance.

(Sarah, numeracy teacher, Larkshire)

In addition to this highly individualized approach, teachers are constantly mindful of the vagaries and variations of each individual's motivation:

If they really are struggling sometimes it may be, 'Well, OK, let's leave it for this week' because they can get a bit distressed...and sometimes they get too comfortable, they know that they can do it, and they need pushing on.

(Sarah, numeracy teacher, Larkshire)

A public service ethos

ALLN teachers place much emphasis on developing and maintaining a culture in the class that creates the best chance for students to develop their capacities, confidence and skills in limited time. It follows that other factors in their lives such as family support, or work circumstances, as well as their own beliefs and feelings about learning, play a proportionately greater role for better or worse in this process. Sometimes these factors combine with the teacher's efforts and make a significant difference. At other times they undermine teachers' and students' efforts to improve learning, by questioning confidence or preventing students from attending the class regularly.

Yet, images of fragility and uncertainty, and a tradition that privileges highly personalized approaches, that might, in other learning cultures, lead to diminished expectations and hesitant approaches to teaching and assessment were balanced in Larkshire by a wider local authority public service ethos. This was reproduced primarily through social interactions in the centre and its strong place in the local community. All teachers passionately espoused a view that their role was to widen access to learning of all kinds, based on awareness that education had a marginal place in many students' busy lives and that they often experienced difficulties in enrolling and attending regularly. The learning culture was also affected by teachers' deeply held belief in all students' potential to learn successfully, their awareness that students were likely to have low levels of confidence, and an emphasis on establishing trust and co-operation. Achievement measured by qualifications was valued, but good relationships and the students' own learning objectives, whatever they might be, are valued more highly.

3. Introducing a formal tutorial

Multiple purposes

All three teachers in our project in Larkshire chose to adopt the same new approach to their formative assessment, namely to implement short one-to-one tutorials in order to formalize their discussions with students about progress and their motivation. This might seem a somewhat mundane change, but in a part-time, roll-on, roll-off course and on hourly paid contracts, teachers either had to put in their own time to allow tutorials to happen or find funding: in this case, the manager of the centre found a small fund to pay for the extra time involved. The tutorials mostly took place once each term for each student, and lasted between 15 minutes and half an hour. They usually took place during the coffee break, or after the end of a class, depending on the availability of both the teacher and the student.

Teachers' motives and approaches varied, but there was a tendency to try to encompass a range of purposes in one method and in the very short space of time made possible in a part-time course with diverse individuals:

> I have introduced tutorials as a way of improving communication with the students in a private and confidential manner. They were encouraged to complete a spiky profile relating to their skills near to the start of term and completed another towards the end of the summer term . . . during the tutorial they were also encouraged to discuss any other issues surrounding the course, e.g. relationships with other students, the learning environment, qualifications/ accreditation, etc.
>
> (Holly, literacy teacher, Larkshire)

Sarah's main concern was to have an opportunity to speak privately with students, so as to avoid students comparing each other's progress directly, but she also had other aims, such as encouraging students to assess their own progress, using and updating the spiky profile chart, and using insights to help with planning through detailed information about the students' understanding and purpose and, finally, checking that things agreed were acted on:

> I produce a 'spiky profile' for them to work on . . . they have to have a 10 and 0 was at the bottom so they have to start at 1. This was the basis for the tutorial . . . 'has anything changed on here?' and this has brought out some very interesting things, e.g. some have said their tables were low and it was hindering their progress and I hadn't thought of that, and so I have focused on

this whereas if I'd introduced it, they'd have thought it wasn't relevant at the beginning. This informs my action plans and shows improvement.

(Sarah, numeracy teacher, Larkshire)

Holly's aims and expectations varied for each student, adapting to the extent of her knowledge about individuals. For example, Abigail had been a student in the centre for four years, and so the main purpose was to find out how she felt about taking the national literacy test for the second time: 'I mean, I did know, I have a good idea about why she is worried about it, but I wanted to just have a quiet time [with her]' (Holly, literacy teacher). In the tutorial, her aim translated through the formal structure of looking at the spiky profile chart and ILP which provided a framework to make discussion about the test less potentially threatening. Different expectations applied to Elena Maria's tutorial since she was new to the course, and here, the ILP provided a focus for confidential discussion about the class, the teaching approach, Elena's experience of schooling, or lack of it, and her relationships with other students.

Tracking and checking progress

In practice, getting through the process was paramount and many students thought the main purpose was for the teacher: 'to find out whereabouts I am on the maths, if I am comfortable with what I am doing, whereabouts I am heading' (Summer, numeracy student, Larkshire). In addition, although teachers thought students needed private space to talk, this was not always the case. Nevertheless, it enabled them to discuss particular points and to build confidence with the teacher.

Sarah focused her approach primarily on topic headings, and how the student 'felt' about each one, and, despite self-assessment, there was little discussion about its outcomes:

Sarah: Are you happier with that now?
Summer: Yes, I have cracked it . . . it is still a bit hit and miss sometimes, but especially if I try and rush them, I can be quite impatient and you can guarantee if I can't do something, I will damn well make sure I can do it.
Sarah: Percentages, still OK with those?
Summer: Alright, yes.
Sarah: No, metric measures, you have done quite a lot of work on, is there anything on that you are still struggling with?
Summer: Conversion (Imperial and metric), we will look at that, it will come in through GCSEs as well.

Sarah:	Area, perimeter, volume?
Summer:	I could do a lot of improvement on that, I am still a bit rubbish on them.
Sarah:	Have you got the formulae written out somewhere?
Summer:	Probably somewhere, because they are all over the place.
Sarah:	You need to get a little notebook and write it in.
Summer:	I have got a notebook and I will write it in.
Sarah:	Some people spend ages rewriting everything, getting it all neat and tidy but that is a waste of time, it is better to get on and do the work like you are doing.

Practical advice based on checking and recording was accompanied by general encouraging feedback that Summer had improved 'in leaps and bounds' since she started, a verdict with which Summer agreed: 'Yes, it does look like I have a got a brain in there somewhere.'

Despite the rather mechanistic approach, Summer told Sarah how the positive relationship with her was essential for motivation and confidence:

> Like when I was at school . . . I didn't get feedback and now I have been coming here and I am dead comfortable with you and I am like myself, getting on with my work. And it has got me thinking I want to do the maths, and if I do pass my GCSE then I am thinking about A level, then I will do that, and become a teacher as well.
>
> (Summer, numeracy student, Larkshire)

All students appreciated the personal attention of a tutorial. Abigail's explanation was typical:

> She wanted to find out how well I have been doing personally you know, . . . how I feel about what she was doing, so she has got an idea then of how she can lay her work out as well, and also, around me, what I need to improve on.
>
> (Abigail, literacy student, Larkshire)

For students gaining a sense of their own agency in learning, and recognizing the value of detailed and ongoing communication between themselves and a teacher, teachers were, in a very real sense, partners in learning:

> She thinks I am doing a lot more better than probably I thought. Some areas I know I am alright with, and then there are others she pointed out, you are doing really well with that, you know, and gave me confidence; but there are not many other areas that I struggle with because I have been here a long while . . . I can talk to her now and say I do struggle with the exams . . . I think [the tutorial] has been good because it has been making me think, like,

> I say I forgot what [to do] with the nouns and the adjectives and
> she will go through it again.
>
> (Abigail, literacy student, Larkshire)

The tutorial helped Abigail to get a realistic, honest assessment:

> In the past . . . you didn't know whether you had really done well
> or not, you know, you are thinking, 'Well, I think I have done well
> this term.' You just went by what work you had done. I hadn't got
> to see the teacher to say I am doing really well, but just while you
> are in a classroom situation they say that to most people, so you
> don't think much of it.

In contrast, Elena Maria had very different expectations and responses.
She was happy to 'go along with' whatever the teacher prepared for her,
but without great expectations of success. For her, improvement was based
on gaining confidence in attending classes: 'Sometimes I feel a lot better,
it was getting my head round it . . . [I feel] more confident, I don't worry
about coming every morning' (Elena Maria, literacy student, Larkshire).

She thought the tutorial activities were useful up to a point, but more
useful for the teacher: 'It is more useful for Holly than me really, I mean,
I know where I am going with it but that is really there for reference.'

These positive responses and powerful motivation were much less evident in other learning cultures in our study. Yet, teachers did not ex-
ploit the potential offered by these powerful factors to do more than track
progress and affirm confidence. For example, Summer's animated discussion of her son who was about to be put into the lower tier GCSE Maths
exam at school, and her view that it was unfair that students in the lower
tier cannot ever get an A, showed a potentially sophisticated understanding of assessment. Even though she saw the relevance of this discussion,
Sarah thought it was 'probably a waste of time' because it was not focused
on Summer herself, and because the formal agenda did not include discussions of grade criteria and assessment systems. Instead, valuable and
constrained tutorial time had to focus on topics of study, progress towards
the official learning goals of the course, and information needed for planning. Although part of the tutorial's purpose was to get students to assess
themselves, there did not seem to be time to explore the thought processes
Summer went through to do that and to relate it to her son's experience.

In the literacy class, Alice's goals and approach were influenced by her
emphasis on a lively atmosphere in the group as a way of countering tendencies among many literacy students to be nervous, diffident and quiet,
even when they have been attending for some time. The tutorial helped
to achieve this atmosphere, and also encouraged students to participate
pro-actively in self-assessment. However, despite good intentions, and,
like her colleagues, with a very positive relationship with students, Alice's

focus for participation was mostly on feelings about how students were doing in relation to particular topics and checking in broad terms that they were happy with the group dynamics. Although specific suggestions made by students were implemented, increasing their motivation, the tutorials did not enable deeper level discussions about literacy and numeracy to take place. Interviews with the students suggested that each of them would have been willing and able to talk about subject content more deeply, had there been more time, and had the teacher felt able to follow up these issues.

Changing teaching and assessment

Partly as a result of tutorials, all three teachers began to increase the amount of whole class teaching and group activities:

> What was interesting was that [in the tutorials] they particularly emphasized the group and discussion work as something that they really enjoyed doing, I have been doing more of that...and it seems to benefit everybody so that has worked out really well...it was something that I might have done once every few weeks instead of every week as I do now.
>
> (Holly, literacy teacher, Larkshire)

There was a strong view that tutorials had worked well:

> Having individual time for everyone...I would love to do it in every class with every learner every month, but you haven't got the time to spend with individuals, no...After their introductions we never really get to sit and talk to them about what they want to learn, it was an odd minute or two grabbed here and there, so it was very different – [this] gives us an actual chance to talk to them and a chance for them to raise concerns.
>
> (Sarah, numeracy teacher, Larkshire)

Both students and teachers welcomed tutorials because they improved communication between them, by being one-to-one, and by being private (although privacy did not seem to be of major concern to students). Although the time involved was very short, the tutorial was organized fairly formally, around the self-assessment spiky profile chart, and the teacher's agenda of checking how students felt about topics, the environment of the class, and purposes and aspirations. Teachers valued these aspects because they helped with planning.

Yet, despite good relationships and positive motivation, there was much more potential to discuss how students made judgements about their skills and understanding, even when, occasionally, either the teacher or the student was surprised by what the other was saying. There appeared to be a reluctance to 'challenge' the other, or to ask students to explain the basis of their judgements in more detail. Teachers argued that such a challenging mode of discourse might undermine the student's sense of comfort, which was the other main focus of the tutorial. It was also a practical recognition that the time for tutorial was very short.

Nevertheless, in-depth knowledge of individuals that teachers sought and valued so highly was not always exploited. For example, even when the topic of discussion was the student's state of readiness to undertake the national test (and, in the case of Abigail, this was a sensitive subject as she had failed it the last time), the opportunity to look at deeper aspects was not taken up, in spite of Abigail's clear awareness and willingness to talk about the difference between her exam performance and her actual skills. In contrast, Elena Maria, who was still cautious about her commitment to the challenge of learning, presented a different task for the teacher, as she was much more resistant to anything more than purely instrumental discussions about her learning. In her case, the focus on ensuring that she was 'satisfied' with the class in this instrumental sense was probably appropriate at the stage we observed her.

Finally, there was little discussion aimed at deepening understanding, so that apparently disconnected concerns closely related to questions of formative assessment and motivation were not seen as high priority, and so were not pursued. Instead, the tutorials in all cases tended to be used for additional intensive encouragement and confidence-boosting. Teaching and feedback on specific practical maths or literacy issues were seen as something that happened in classroom time.

4. Reinforcing comfort zones or encouraging challenge?

In the learning cultures discussed here, group activities were the exception rather than the rule and the introduction of individual tutorials fitted that ethos. This hindered an expansive approach to formative assessment that promoted deep engagement with both subject content and learning processes because this required group rather than individual participation. We therefore saw the 'spirit' less frequently than the 'letter' of formative assessment.

Nevertheless, there were very strong constraining factors that had direct and indirect effects on the learning culture at Larkshire. First, there was the very limited teaching time, together with participants' varied dispositions and purposes, and the roll-on, roll-off individual enrolment. Second, for these part-time students who attended only two hours a week, family or work circumstances and their own dispositions to learning generally, as opposed to more specific responses to individual subject topics, were central to their attitudes and responses. Sometimes external factors combined with the efforts of the teacher and the student to make a significant difference. At other times, they undermined confidence or prevented regular attendance. Third, these part-time teachers often worked with greater absolute numbers in different classes and in different centres. In addition to being part-time, three of our sample at Larkshire were on temporary contracts of employment. Although teachers did not raise this explicitly in accounting for their approaches to assessment, we argue that it had important indirect effects on the institutional and professional culture teachers felt they were part of.

In this context, then, it was not surprising that administrative support structures and tools, such as the Individual Learning Plan or the diagnostic instrument of the 'spiky profile' tended to be used bureaucratically, or as another communication mechanism that focused on process rather than content. One outcome was that teachers' overall strategies prioritized developing and supporting an atmosphere conducive to learning together with providing learners with learning materials and workshop support on a largely individual basis.

Notwithstanding these constraints and although the focus on tests in recent policy has been controversial, it does seem that summative Skills for Life tests, and the new focus on measurable outcomes, have served in some respects to move the learning cultures of many ALLN teaching and learning situations from a relatively cosy stability in which teachers were under little pressure to challenge students (particularly those seen to be vulnerable), to a more dynamic and expansive culture, albeit one in which the teachers have less control, but much more demanded of them. This was particularly true at the Larkshire site. Despite making the process more pressurized for the teachers, reinforcing their concerns about adults' lack of confidence and potential fear of tests, it also opened up the possibility of more meaningful dialogue about educational content and outcomes.

As with other teachers in our adult education case studies, teachers at Larkshire had an intuitive affinity with some principles and practices of formative assessment, based on their view that the needs and feelings of their students, as they saw them, were central. This was strongly reinforced by the organizational culture. However, Larkshire teachers did not see clearly how to translate a 'learner-centred' personal and cultural orientation into specific, effective approaches in the 'spirit' of formative assessment. Although surprised that in the first tutorials learners asked for more group work activities, to which they responded positively, nevertheless, they saw it primarily as a variation of their existing practice rather than a fundamental change in approach.

In general, the learning culture emphasized participation and positive engagement in the processes and activities of classes more strongly than achievement and progression in particular subject content. It prevented teachers from seeing ways in which they might change this perspective towards aims and activities more in the 'spirit' of formative assessment.

Conclusion

The tutorial was intended to provide quality time between the teacher and individual student and the particular learning culture of Larkshire encouraged transactions about targets and feelings about individual topics rather than about deeper understanding of the topics and concepts.

The Larkshire case study also shows how factors in the learning culture of adult basic education affect teachers' ability to change practice towards the 'spirit' of formative assessment, and how a particularly strong local, community centre can reinforce certain approaches, expectations and beliefs, for good or bad. Our teachers adopted almost identical approaches, rooted in very similar beliefs and expectations. Compounded by pressures on time, without extra funding, the temptation was to use a tutorial, however short, as a means of enhancing the existing pedagogic plans and imperatives. In this case, the overriding imperative was to support the process of target setting and formal achievement, and to focus more on individual's responses to these, rather than intellectual excitement and challenge with group activities.

The problem for any teacher is to see a way to give time to approaches more in the 'spirit' of formative assessment. In addition, the benefits of the kind of formative assessment that engages students deeply with the content of a subject are not possible unless teachers recognize the pressures on them to implement more instrumental practices.

Yet, unlike other learning cultures in our study, and despite very formidable barriers, the culture at Larkshire, as with others in our ALLN case studies, provided huge potential to use these processes and the positive relationships that underpinned them, as a springboard to more meaningful, deeper engagement, even in 15-minute tutorials! This potential was much stronger in ALLN classes than it was in vocational education. We return to practical suggestions for developing this potential further in Section Three of the book.

Note

1. A 'spiky profile' is a form of self-assessment that shows a student's perceptions of her or his literacy and/or numeracy competencies on a

numerical scale of 1–10 for each one. An Individual Learning Plan is a formal requirement on all SfL courses, and many others, for initial diagnostic assessment and target setting (see Hamilton 2009). In some institutions, teachers can design their own but in growing numbers, they must conform to a particular format.

9   Self- and peer assessment in part-time ESOL classes

Introduction

Although English for Speakers of Other Languages (ESOL) provision is included with adult literacy and numeracy within the government's flagship Skills for Life initiative, from the perspective of learning cultures, it is quite distinct. Even within the same group and working at the same level, ESOL students are likely to have had widely differing life histories and educational backgrounds, in terms of linguistic culture, migration narratives, years of schooling, the features of their home country's schooling system, and levels of educational achievement. Many ESOL students have had little experience of schooling at all, and may not have literacy in their first language. Others are highly literate and qualified in their mother tongue and other languages, with high levels of confidence and autonomy as students. Many, whatever their experience of schooling, have had traumatic and tragic experiences of war, forced migration, family dispersal and cultural dislocation.

The fact that ESOL students may have little in common apart from their need to improve their speaking, listening, reading and writing of English creates high demands on teachers' subject knowledge, empathy and communication skills. However, a common aim provides an unambiguous learning goal understood in principle by everyone, whatever their starting point or their history: both sets of students in the groups that are the focus of this chapter, although working at very different levels, understood in general terms what was meant by proficiency in English. They also knew that their general objectives were shared by their teachers.

This means that the complexity of the different types of positive and negative motivation discernible in literacy and numeracy classes are not as significant in ESOL classes. Of course there are important differences; some students, for example, can present difficulties because they might be overconfident and expect their learning to happen more or less effortlessly, while others seem initially to be overwhelmed by the challenge facing them. But these ideas about learning are not generally associated with negative previous experiences of education: as we see in the two learning sites that are the focus of this chapter, images of 'vulnerable' adults with fragile or damaged motivation were non-existent.

In these important characteristics, ESOL can be said to be a 'strong' subject and this was central to the assessment strategies adopted by the two teachers discussed in this chapter. Our evaluation of formative assessment in two part-time ESOL classes draws on fieldwork in programmes provided by City of Westhampton College, where a series of mergers between smaller colleges has created one of the largest further education colleges in the country. Of 30,000 students, 8,000 were studying for Skills for Life qualifications. Each of the classes met once a week for three hours, from September to June. We focus here on two teachers and four students: Ruth Merchant whose class catered for students working at PE/E1, and her students Halima Jama and Bint Clark, and Allan Thompson taking a L1[1] class, and his students Ali Ahmed and Maria Zia. Both teachers were well-qualified, confident and experienced. At the time of our project, Ruth was studying for a teacher training qualification and was very interested in theories about how students learn.

The Bradwell Centre, where Ruth's PE/E1 level class took place, was a long-established college site in a mainly residential area. The centre was a little run-down with large, bright teaching rooms containing cupboards of learning resources and materials all around the walls, and displays of reading books and students' work. Allan's L1 ESOL evening class was in a community centre owned by the Westhampton Council, in an area close to the city centre with high numbers of ethnic minority residents and visibly poorer than many other parts of the city. The centre was built in the past five years, and was very modern, clean and cheerful. Like Larkshire in Chapter 8, it provided a range of community activities and classes, with a café, computers available for community use and art-works typically produced in the centre.

The chapter starts by outlining how, in different ways, the learning cultures of the two classes centred around high expectations among the two teachers and their students. The second section explores the changes to assessment that each teacher implemented in our project in order to enhance students' autonomy within the subject of ESOL. The third section shows how each teacher in different ways was able to resist pressures towards instrumentalism and diminished, short-term concepts of learning. Finally, we draw out contrasts with other areas of adult basic education.

1. Challenging comfort zones

A clear sense of autonomy

The 12 students in Ruth's class spoke 10 different first languages between them, including Italian, Polish, Gujarati, and Bengali. They were all very hesitant in speaking English, varied greatly in confidence, and in sensitivity to working in group situations such as listening to others and not interrupting. Two women from different regions of Italy sat together and retreated often into Italian between themselves. One or two students had to be coaxed to try to say anything in English. Allan described his students as falling into two broad groups: European students who were usually reasonably well educated, and students from other parts of the world, who had often left school at 12 or 13, or even earlier. Both groups tended to have respect for the teacher and to be highly motivated, but students in the second group often had very complicated lives and so, according to Allan, 'were not always as present as they might be'.

The level of study each group catered for affected the ways in which students contributed to classroom activities and the social atmosphere of the class, and influenced teachers' planning and approaches. Although the classes took place in different types of building in different parts of the city, this made no significant difference to the learning cultures: in each case the central determining element was the personality, skills and motivation of the teacher. Both teachers were conscious of their importance to their students and were willing to use this to persuade them to take on challenges in the interests of their learning.

Each explicitly saw a key part of their role as trying to get students out of their 'comfort zones'; that is, both were primarily subject- rather than student-focused. Within this goal, two aspects of autonomy were evident, both rooted in a sense of progression within subject knowledge and skills.[2]

Ruth's highest priority in her teaching was to help develop the personal and social autonomy of her students, who were at the lowest level of proficiency in speaking English and therefore experienced continuous difficulties in key aspects of their lives in Britain; for her, developing their personal and social autonomy in the group was a springboard for confidence in learning English, as a means to an end rather than an end in itself. Allan, teaching at a higher level to students, most of whom were also well-educated in their own countries, regarded autonomy as the ability to be more accurate in their use of English. For him, improving accuracy was the difference between students of English and effective users of it. In this sense, technical autonomy was a springboard to becoming more sophisticated in using English effectively. The main focus of his teaching was on generating opportunities for feedback, whereas Ruth's main objective was to create supported opportunities for students to assess their own and their co-students' work, through which she believed they would gain confidence and skills and increase their autonomy in an English-speaking culture.

In common also between the two classes was the clear feeling that the teachers were, in practice, also largely autonomous themselves, particularly in terms of their approach to supporting students. Skills for Life classes are subject to a firm regime of external assessment, but this was a low-key, rather than dominant aspect of each class. The students in the higher-level class were working towards the national Skills for Life tests in the summer term, but Allan was confident that his lessons would prepare his students properly for the national test without planning them around it, at least until the last few weeks: 'Summative assessment is something I don't really think about until after the Easter holidays – after that there will be more practice papers and that type of thing' (Allan, ESOL teacher, Westhampton). This helped him to keep the subject at the centre of his teaching, thereby giving him the authority to make challenging demands of his students based on what he saw as the requirements of the subject itself. Ruth was not under pressure to prepare students for national tests, because they were not applicable at level E1. There were alternative accountability requirements she had to satisfy,[3] however, which she appeared to manage 'invisibly', so that here too, the students were given a strong impression of the autonomy of the teacher. As we will see, each teacher used this apparent autonomy in different ways.

Thinking about learning

Before they took part in our project, both Allan and Ruth were concerned more with learning than with teaching:

> I'm not asking, 'Can I get through this?', or 'Can I survive?', or even 'Can I teach better?', but 'Is learning happening?'
> (Allan, ESOL teacher, Westhampton)

While Allan's view was that his role was to be highly directive, Ruth felt that she needed continually to be trying to give space to her students:

> I can be quite a controlling person. I have to work hard on giving them that space, so I worry then when I do start directing, I have got to decide to what extent is this bit of direction helping them and to what extent is this allowing them to get away with not doing it for themselves.
> (Ruth, ESOL teacher, Westhampton)

She was aware that her preferred approach was in tension with some of the prescriptive and restricting procedures required by her institution:

> We work within a structure which is driven by the scheme of work, you have to plan everything in advance and you have to save it to the shared drive.[4] I don't know how much people stick to them. But I like to go away at the end of a lesson and think 'OK, based on what happened in that lesson, what are we going to do next?', rather than just do the next thing on my scheme of

work . . . You can sometimes change a lesson completely because you realize for some reason what you have planned isn't going to work, or an idea comes up that you think is better. I call that 'seat-of-the-pants teaching', and often it goes really well.

(Ruth, ESOL teacher, Westhampton)

In keeping with the idea that diagnostic and formative feedback was integral to classroom teaching, she wanted the freedom to be able to 'go with the teachable moment'.[5] She believed this approach worked well with groups with a wide range of levels of need:

A lot of the literacy students have difficulties that are quite different from the difficulties of the ESOL students. I have taught medical people, anaesthetists and doctors and very highly educated people. C has been to university, and I have got other people in the class who never went to school: S, for example, started off illiterate. So we have got a very wide range of people but they haven't got the kinds of problems that (native) literacy or numeracy students in this country have.

(Ruth, ESOL teacher, Westhampton)

She thought that teachers needed to be aware that ESOL students might well not have study skills, but they did certainly have life skills, and these needed to be recognized, and built on. She tended not to give grades when marking, and preferred to indicate errors but for students to correct them on their own. She pointed out that oral feedback, rather than written, was easier for low-level ESOL students to understand.

For Allan, feedback had always been a central element of his teaching, but in the past he had seen it primarily as helping him plan, rather than as a tool for developing autonomy. His emphasis on practice, however, implicitly supported autonomy in the use of language skills, rather than just the acquisition of subject knowledge.

Rising to challenges

Interview data collected from ESOL students was problematic, particularly with the lower level students, due to potential misunderstandings of both questions and answers. The students had widely varying attitudes to learning and assessment, and perhaps varying degrees of understanding of the concepts in English. Bint described the way Ruth assesses her work:

When I bring my homework back, she checks it. If I do something wrong or spell something wrong, she will tell me check that again; she won't give me exactly what it is, she will say check it again.

(Bint, ESOL student, Westhampton)

She was not very interested in getting marks: 'all I'm interested in is learning and not an exam – the marks are not that important really' (Bint, ESOL student, Westhampton).

All the students interviewed were motivated by improving their job prospects, for which they saw improving their English as essential. Bint was strongly motivated to become more self-sufficient:

> [I want to] achieve something and be able to learn and to be able to read and write and to be able to do my own personal things, reading my letters, and all that... sometimes my children read letters for me or sometimes I need to find a friend to read the letter for me, or sometimes it can be a confidential letter that you don't want people to know about, so if you can't do it yourself then people know all your confidential and everything, and you've got no secrets to yourself so this is what is good about learning.
>
> (Bint, ESOL student, Westhampton)

Bint also wanted to learn more about computers when her English was better, and ultimately to get a job. She said she would be willing to study for more hours if that were possible.

Ali, a Somali student in Allan's class, was highly motivated by his own ambition 'to secure the life for my family'. He had a high opinion of his own abilities and felt that he was not able to make as much of a contribution at his work as he might, leading to arguments with the manager. Having gained a place at university, starting the next autumn, his sense of what he could achieve had increased. His learning identity was mainly based on a static concept of people's potential, that people are either clever or they are not. This led him to think and behave as if he spoke English better than in fact he did.

He thought that his learning would be based in equal parts on his own work, the work of his teacher, and the support of his family and his employer. He saw challenge as a double-edged sword:

> Challenge has one positive side and one negative side... the positive side is that if I'm challenging you and I succeed this may give me more motivation, [but] if I challenge you and I fail, this will make my motivation come down.
>
> (Ali, ESOL student, Westhampton)

For Ali, learning was a matter of determination and depended on a teacher who explained things well. He was highly motivated, and this was demonstrated in three different ways: he did not care about the other students, only about his own future; he thought that students should be given detailed information about the class so that he could start his learning at home, before he came to the class; and finally, he felt that his level of proficiency meant that he should really be a in a higher-level class. He felt strongly that taking parts of the test in pairs was unfair since he did not want his result to depend on someone else's performance. He particularly liked the fact that Allan taught students as individuals.

He admitted he has had difficulties doing his homework, but appreciated that Allan did not let up the pressure on him to do it:

> I hate to do the homework, but he tries many times. I don't have any time, I am working all the days and after I am playing with my daughter.
>
> (Ali, ESOL student, Westhampton)

Sometimes he came close to giving up, but Allan managed to make him change his mind:

> I wanted to do this reading exam for a higher level...we did it on the computer and I almost passed, and I was feeling so stupid...and he said to me, 'I know that you will do it', he gave me one more chance, but really I was so disappointed at the time...I said, 'OK that's it', but he changed my mind.
>
> (Ali, ESOL student, Westhampton)

He liked the self-assessment innovation that Allan introduced, discussed in the next section, particularly because it allowed students to make a private assessment, available only to the teacher: he said that he would be embarrassed to make a mistake publicly in front of other students. Yet, his instrumental approach meant that he was not interested in the meta-questions about his own learning, and he was largely frustrated by the slow process of having to improve his speaking and listening abilities in English.

Halima, in Ruth's class, was strongly focused on grades because she knew she had to achieve a formal qualification to realize her goal of becoming a nurse. She thought that any activity in which the group talked to each other in English would help to improve their language skills. She did not think that discussion of assessment was useful *per se*, though possibly there were problems of understanding about this point. She seemed to say that what was important was that the activity involved everyone in the group talking together, rather than that they were talking about assessment and learning. She was highly motivated, enjoyed group discussions, and believed that they were helping her improve her language skills and confidence.

2. Enhancing subject autonomy

Self- and peer assessment

Ruth's main objective was to create supported opportunities for students to assess their own and peers' work. She realized at the beginning of the year that this was a group of potentially dependent students, lacking in confidence, particularly in terms of their spoken English, and easily 'taking refuge' by retreating into their first language when they could, both inside and outside the class. When invited to become a participant in our project, she had already decided that over the teaching year, she would focus strongly on developing their autonomy and confidence, and an understanding of their learning:

> I had a class of ESOL beginners that believed they could only learn from the teacher . . . such dependence limits their learning to responding to direct inputs from the teacher, discourages critical thought, makes differentiation difficult and puts great pressure on the teacher.
>
> (Ruth, ESOL teacher, Westhampton)

For Ruth, autonomy was connected with her sense of the complexity of their lives:

> because they need to get by in English they need to be able to access services, use buses, go to the doctor's and do the shopping, that sort of thing . . . exam results are great, but it's the life skills that motivates me and really what motivates a lot of them.
>
> (Ruth, ESOL teacher, Westhampton)

She believed that using a different approach to formative assessment would enhance the quality of students' learning in the present, as well as their potential for learning in the future, while also addressing a number of difficult pedagogical problems facing any teacher of a large group of ESOL beginners.

Her intervention was to implement, over a period of many weeks, a staged programme of linked activities, starting with group discussions about appropriate assessment criteria for making a formal speech or presentation to the group. This required her to teach vocabulary connected with quality judgements, and to introduce a very highly-structured process through which possible quality criteria were discussed. These included such simple ideas as speaking loudly enough to be heard, speaking clearly with good pronunciation, and making it enjoyable for the listeners with interesting content, correct use of English, and so on. She spent significant amounts of time on this activity, emphasizing all the time the idea that the group should decide the criteria they were going to use, for themselves. At times it was a struggle, not least because one or two of the students were not used to participating in such activities.

Having agreed on assessment criteria, students then worked on their presentations. This stage of the process was also carefully planned and all students took part formally in the presentations and in the group assessments and self-assessments of them. Afterwards, Ruth produced sheets on which were recorded the results of each student's self-assessment, the others' assessments of them, and the teacher's assessments. The differences between these were then discussed. In keeping with typical responses to self-assessment, most students had assessed themselves at a lower level than their colleagues did. Ruth thought her staged approach had paid off:

> I started out with the intention that students would identify their own criteria and plan and design their own assessment procedures in full. I came to realize, however, that the teacher will probably need to suggest a range of strategies for the students to consider at first. Presenting, discussing or even implementing inappropriate strategies can be of great value as it forces the students to identify the criteria by which to plan and judge future assessments. This learner input appears to lead to increased motivation. It's easy when teaching low-level groups to forget that they are sophisticated thinking people. The focus on trust and respect worked: at the beginning of the year some of them wouldn't listen to each other, but now they are all happily doing self- and peer assessment.
>
> (Ruth, ESOL teacher, Westhampton)

The central aspect of Ruth's strategy was to carefully design tasks and activities that would force students to work as a group, creating a situation in which they needed to co-operate, thereby increasing 'their appreciation of each other, improve their confidence in group- and pair-work, and accept and value peer assessment and help'.

This meant explicit consideration of the affective dynamics within the learning culture, including, according to Ruth:

> a significant shift in power relationships within the classroom which would pose challenges for all concerned ... the students may feel uncomfortable and even resentful because the teacher is not fulfilling the expected role. They may not immediately understand what is expected of them or feel incapable of completing the task.
>
> (Ruth, ESOL teacher, Westhampton)

Ruth aimed to deal with these issues systematically by incorporating a sequence of classroom activities into an overall classroom project or scheme of work, designed around the activities themselves rather than elements of the ESOL curriculum, though covering these at the same time.

Through these activities students expanded basic English vocabulary, repeatedly practised language speaking and listening, reading and writing, in an unpressurized, encouraging environment, collaborated with peers in agreeing criteria and assessing each other's work, devised and gave formal presentations. Experience of an active rather than passive mode of classroom learning had directly supported their increased autonomy. Nevertheless, of course, other factors such as regular attendance also influenced the extent of their learning.

Enhancing feedback and dialogue

Like Ruth, Allan's teaching approach explicitly focused on increasing his students' autonomy, by helping them improve precision and accuracy in their use of English. His was a deliberately teacher-centred approach, based on the consensus in his class about the importance of the subject, about which he was seen as the expert. His approach had always had a strong emphasis on constructive and corrective feedback from himself to his students, particularly on written work:

> I regard what I'm doing as training rather than teaching – I feel like I'm training people to use a language not just teaching them a language. I try to get them writing most sessions; it gives me a chance to understand how much they've understood and to guide me and what we do the next session.
>
> (Allan, ESOL teacher, Westhampton)

Allan's chosen innovation was to implement a 'traffic light procedure', in which students regularly evaluated their learning of a particular topic, showing a green card if they felt they had learned it successfully, amber if they needed more help, and red if they felt they had not made any progress at all.[6] He provided them with a rubric for describing their self-assessments, using the terms 'emerging', 'consolidating', and 'established', terms recommended for this diagnostic and formative purpose by the Skills for Life support materials.

He thought that it worked well for him, though he was uncertain whether many of his students appreciated the purpose of the exercise, or whether it made any difference to the way they saw their own learning. He felt that it gave him important insights into the learning that was taking place, which he could use in an iterative way for his lesson planning. However, on reflection, and as a result of his participation in the project, he felt that there was more to the approach than merely carrying out a particular self-assessment exercise.

He saw this innovation as a development of his existing approach, in that it introduced a more explicit aspect of dialogue about assessment into his lessons which was diagnostic in aim and effect:

> I feel I am moving towards a position where we have much more dialogue, and my students are giving me feedback and I am forming lessons around what they are telling me, not just working through the curriculum – I don't see it as a radical step.
>
> (Allan, ESOL teacher, Westhampton)

His consistent emphasis on the demands of the subject meant that when necessary he could be very firm with some of his students, including one who:

> sat there and thought 'I know this already', but she didn't. When she finally did a piece of written work for me, I sat down with her with my red pen and I went through every single mistake. I said to her, 'Look, this is the kind of thing you did six months ago and you're still making the same silly mistakes.' That was quite a shock to her and it did motivate her to produce better work and more frequent, but it's not a tactic I enjoy.
>
> (Allan, ESOL teacher, Westhampton)

For Allan, then, the traffic light innovation did not represent a formal change in his approach, but enabled him to make his existing emphasis on feedback and an explicit message about high standards and hard work more effective: through it, he helped the students themselves 'own' the challenges they were setting themselves and to understand them in a more realistic light.

3. Resisting instrumentalism

High expectations and standards

Like Derek in our case study of AVCE Science, Ruth and Allan appeared to be consciously resisting the pressures of instrumentalism through improving their own skills and knowledge about teaching and assessing their subject. Both saw a key dimension of their role as finding ways to support the development of their students' autonomy, in terms of their ability to participate in work and their communities and society in general, and this required them to continuously 'go beyond' the relatively limited requirements of the formal qualification system.

From time to time, some of Ruth's group experienced real difficulties with their tasks, but they persevered with her support, confidence, and through collective effort. The culmination of the process was when students compared peer assessments with their own and the teacher's, all collected on the same pro-forma, and found that they had all scored themselves less well than their peers had. The longer the process continued, according to Ruth, the more all the students became more relaxed about it:

> It is getting a bit better each time, in that more people are getting involved with the speaking and most of them, even when not speaking, are listening and thinking more about how they learn. When a new student joined the class half-way through the term, a confident and vocal woman who said she didn't like the self-assessment activity because she thought it was the teacher's job to assess students, one of the other students said she was wrong, that they learned more through self-assessment.
> (Ruth, ESOL teacher, Westhampton)

This second student had been unable to speak a word of English when she first joined the class, bringing an interpreter to her interview. Although working through this process was at times a struggle for everyone in the class, Ruth believed that if she were to repeat it, students would be more used to it, they would know what to expect, and she would therefore have enhanced their perceptions and understanding of the learning process, as well as supporting them to take a more active role in it.

In another way as well, Allan was explicitly modelling to his students a pro-active approach to learning, and at the same time enriching his opportunities to give feedback to them. Consistent with his message about the importance of written work, he encouraged them to email him with work they had done, and with questions about their homework, and promised to respond to them within 12 hours with feedback. He believed that this had been highly motivational, partly because feedback can be motivational in itself, but also because of his willingness to offer this type of support. It meant that they could communicate with him when they needed to, not just during the weekly class. Although he admitted that most of his colleagues would not have encouraged this, being afraid of being inundated with emails, Allan's view was that 'It's crazy not to use technology in this way.'

This was far from being a supportive prop designed to counter poor motivation seen in other case studies in this book. Instead, he recognized that this approach would only work if people were intrinsically motivated and understood that learning requires work. He was therefore consistent in his expectations of high standards of commitment and motivation, and was offering extra support to those willing to work outside the class.

Improving professional skills and knowledge

Both teachers were highly committed to improving their practice. At the end of the project, Ruth firmly believed that effective formative assessment needed to be viewed as an integrated part of the teaching and learning process, given added potency by increased learner participation in the planning stages.

Critically, she learned to take a less idealistic perspective on introducing self- and peer assessment activities to low-level students. For Allan, involvement in the project appeared to move his thinking in the other direction, in which he began to see the value of more dialogue with his students about their learning, although he still saw the main purpose of this as enriching his feedback to them, both on the accuracy of their work and on their motivation and preparedness to provide him with regular written work:

> I've become much more focused on giving verbal feedback – it's something I've done before but I appreciate the value of it more.
> (Allan, ESOL teacher, Westhampton)

Allan felt that the innovative activity itself wasn't so much the cause of improvement in his self-awareness as a teacher, as the thinking engendered by his discussions with other teachers during the project development days, and since. He had always organized feedback around written work, not around activities in the classroom:

> When I trained to be a teacher I was told, don't ever ask students, 'Do you understand?' because they will all be nervous and say, 'Yes, I understand.' But the traffic light innovation gave the learner a chance to give three levels of response, and it helps that the information is not public – they are less likely to be inhibited by comparing themselves with their peers.
> (Allan, ESOL teacher, Westhampton)

He found the formative assessment approach useful, but observed that it was new to him in many ways:

> Until I started the formative assessment (project) I had always done feedback on written work, but I had never done feedback on 'how are you finding this activity?'
> (Allan, ESOL teacher, Westhampton)

So although Allan had always been focused strongly on the need for his students to be able to use language skills more fluently in real-life situations, rather than merely on passing formal assessments, for him this had become less of a technocratic process of development managed solely by himself as the expert teacher. As a result of being involved in the research and being encouraged to reassess his role as a teacher, he felt he had become more aware of the value of the students' own views about the learning process, both to themselves as students, and to him as the teacher:

> What I hope is that the students get the message that I am responsive to their needs and I hope that makes them more motivated to receive feedback but also to be involved in activities, as they learn that we are doing things not just because that is the next thing down on programme, but because I have seen that that is what they need.
>
> (Allan, ESOL teacher, Westhampton)

The authority of the teacher

On the face of it, Ruth and Allan's resistance to lower expectations and to instrumentalism is surprising, given what we observed in the adult literacy and numeracy classes discussed in Chapter 8. ESOL classes are located within the Skills for Life policy and regulation system, alongside literacy and numeracy programmes, and they take place in broadly similar organizations and under similar conditions.

Yet, there were important differences. In the literacy and numeracy classes discussed in Chapter 8, the learning cultures included factors such as a historic tendency for teachers in local authority centres to see students as potentially 'vulnerable' and needing protection and security, thereby inhibiting challenging approaches to learning, reinforced by a powerful awareness that students are very likely to have had negative, possibly humiliating, previous experiences of formal learning at school.

Adult literacy and numeracy teachers were continually managing the tension between the need to establish good relations and a relaxed atmosphere in their classes, with the need to be 'teacherly', to take the role of the expert, be directive and perhaps to challenge students in their learning. In this context, teachers' natural concern not to undermine students' confidence often inhibited the necessity for more teacher-led and challenging aspects of learning. In addition, the roll-on, roll-off aspect of the classes, in which students might start in the class at any time with little advance warning for the teacher, led in many situations to mainly individualized teaching and learning within the group, to enable the teacher to plan for and manage the uncertainty involved.

These tensions clearly existed also in the ESOL classes, but in a much less acute way. Of crucial importance was that the subject was strong enough to be an explicit, understood focus for both teacher and students. This diverted attention from students' 'vulnerability' and undermined any pressure the teachers might feel to focus primarily on it, thereby leaving them much freer to organize activities around the demands of the subject, even if these were likely to present challenges to the students. Second, while ESOL teachers need to be sensitive to the possibility that students may have had very difficult lives, possibly including traumatic experiences of war and family dispersal, as well as the problems involved in living in a different and sometimes hostile culture, they need not assume that these create negative feelings and attitudes to learning. There is no reason to suppose that the experiences of ESOL students include humiliating experiences of schooling – this may indeed have happened, but it is not a defining characteristic. On the contrary, ESOL students tend to be very positive indeed in their general attitudes to learning, and have a strong subject focus.

These factors meant that the teacher's role was different. Ruth needed to create a comfortable and relaxed learning environment that enabled students to overcome shyness in trying to speak English: as long as they understood her strategy and her instructions, they were quite happy to accept directions because her authority was not seen as conflicting with her support and commitment to them. Crucial to this was clear agreement about what they were all engaged in, governed by ESOL's strength as a subject. Allan, teaching at a higher level, had high expectations of his students' commitment to their own learning, and expressed this directly to them, even to the extent of being critical of their lack of effort where necessary. For him, the tension between being a friend and being a demanding and at times critical teacher did not really exist. ESOL as a subject demanded that his professionalism expressed itself through his high expectations, and his students recognized this, even when they were not doing very well.

Finally, these factors enabled teachers to put prescriptive requirements to one side. Even though they were subject to accountability and funding requirements and had to ensure that students formally achieved the relevant qualification aims, neither saw this as a major problem, or constraining factor. Ruth's class was 'internally accredited', meaning that individual, 'personalized' learning goals aligned to the national ESOL curriculum were set for each student as part of an auditable Individual Learning Plan, against which success would be measured and evidenced by Ruth herself. This created a certain amount of paperwork for her but did not constrain her approaches to teaching. Allan's students were going to be assessed during the summer term through the national tests, but he was happy to ignore the tests until much nearer the time, because he was confident that his preferred approaches would help them to pass, even though that wasn't his overriding objective. Again, the real learning objectives for all the students were determined by the demands of the subject.

Conclusion

This chapter demonstrates the central importance of the subject's own contribution to the learning culture of a particular class. In these ESOL classes, a strong sense of subject enabled the two teachers to exercise and develop their confidence and expertise in a way that put the formal requirements firmly in their bureaucratic place! As a further aspect of the same point, both teachers' approaches were based on continual demands on their students, either by making explicit the expectation to produce written homework assignments and to continue learning between the weekly class sessions, or, in the sessions themselves, supporting students to take part in complex and demanding learning activities which set challenges to their confidence and skills.

Crucially, Ruth and Allan did not merely reject stereotypes of fragile adults, seen in other classes in basic education; they did not subscribe to these images in the first place. This was enhanced by the way in which students' motivation appeared to be more homogeneous and much more strongly subject-focused than in other classes in our study. In spite of quite different perspectives and purposes among students, the subject itself was relatively unproblematic. The strong focus on the subject diverted attention away from emotional, personal aspects of the learning and assessment process which might lead to demotivation at times when the necessary challenges of learning were being experienced. For both teachers, this helped significantly in their overall aim to develop students' autonomy.

The contrast with the much more varied motivation seen in our case study of Larkshire adult literacy and numeracy classes, and in other ALLN sites in our project that are not included in this book, suggests that dealing with diverse motivation requires teachers to make their goals and ethos explicit, and to underpin their support and sensitivity with confidence and a sense of teacher authority rooted in a strong sense of subject knowledge and skills.

The other important feature of the two ESOL learning cultures was the willingness of the two teachers either to buck the system, or to play the game at one level while doing something different. Importantly, this was an empowered form of subversion based on a confident sense of subject knowledge and its centrality to teaching and assessment strategies.

Finally, this chapter shows the need to be clear about what autonomy really is: other case studies in the book show that the notion is both ubiquitous and bland, encompassing autonomy to navigate learning and assessment processes without help, working alone or without the teacher, or setting one's own targets. In both ESOL classes, autonomy was seen explicitly as a subject-based springboard for confidence in learning English. It was therefore a means to an end, rather than an end in itself. Inextricably linked to a sense of subject autonomy was the autonomy of the teachers. Despite the official requirements and possible adverse reactions from students, they both had the confidence to go ahead with strategies even when students might not like them, and to resist diminished images. Central to this autonomy was the teachers' enthusiasm for, and commitment to, critical evaluation of their own practice. Through this, they identified in the project aspects of their teaching and assessment they wanted to change for themselves.

Notes

1. ESOL provision at the time the research took place was funded by the government as part of the Skills for Life initiative, which encompassed literacy, ESOL and numeracy classes for adult students. Skills for Life specifies standards and offers qualifications for each subject at 6 levels: Pre-Entry (PE), Entry 1, 2 and 3 (E1, E2, and E3), Level 1 (L1) and Level 2 (L2). These levels fit within the overall National Qualifications Framework (NQF), but the Skills for Life subjects sub-divide NQF Entry level into three stages. A L2 Skills for Life qualification is therefore defined as being equivalent to a GCSE. In practice, many students need to work at different levels for different skills within their subject, so the level given for a particular class is a rough guide rather than a precise classification. The Skills for Life ESOL curriculum specifies skills and knowledge at these levels across the domains of Speaking and Listening, Reading and Writing.
2. See Chapter 2 for a detailed discussion of different types of 'autonomy'.
3. For Skills for Life courses at E3 and below, accountability takes the form of the setting of individual learning targets mapped to the national standards and recorded on Individual Learning Plans (ILPs). The setting of these individual targets is done as far as possible by the teacher and student working together, the idea being that it is in principle helpful if the student owns and understands their targets. If the students achieve their targets, these are counted towards the college's overall achievement rate just as if they had passed one of the national tests. For each student that achieves, funding is also released from the LSC.

Thus the ILP is an auditable document for students at these levels, in terms of funding and accountability.
4. This refers to the requirement in many colleges for teachers to place their plans on the college computer, so that any staff or managers can access them for internal and external inspections, or audits.
5. See Chapter 2, for discussion.
6. This well-known formative method of 'traffic lights' was outlined on the introductory development day for teachers participating in the project.

Section 3

Transforming formative assessment

10 Changing teachers' assessment practices

The prognosis for professional development

Introduction

Changes to teaching and assessment practices are notoriously difficult to bring about in the British education system. One of the most systematic, large-scale attempts to do this has been the ten-year £50 million Teaching and Learning Research Programme (TLRP), which began in 1999, with projects encompassing early years, primary, secondary, further and higher education, workplace and professional learning. The TLRP set out to provide what policy-makers hoped would be 'robust evidence' on which good, 'effective' teaching and assessment practices might be based.[1]

As that programme showed, and our own research confirms, it is possible to provide rich, sometimes insightful analyses of the factors that support or militate against change, but impossible to offer 'blue prints' for good practice or even to agree what it is! In addition to huge investments in programmes like the TLRP, the post-compulsory sector has also seen significant expenditure on teaching and assessment through the work of the DfES Standards Unit, the Learning and Skills Development Agency and the National Research Centre for Adult Literacy and Numeracy, to name but a few. In the more specific area of formative assessment, our own project built upon work by researchers working with school teachers to evaluate changes to formative assessment practices.[2]

In different ways, policy-initiated programmes of research and development aim to identify factors affecting change, provide evidence of 'what works' and to offer advice about how to 'scale up' good practice and 'roll it out' more widely. Yet, not only are there very difficult questions about what counts as 'good practice' and the 'evidence' upon which we might infer it or characterize it, but the problem of extending understanding, skills and knowledge beyond the teachers taking part in research and development projects is notoriously hard to solve.[3] Instead, the teaching profession in all sectors of the British education system, particularly in England, is increasingly subject to patronising, simplistic and ineffective guidance that undermines teachers' professional independence.

Nevertheless, research can generate insights that are hopefully useful. Our project and other studies show that a socio-cultural approach offers a useful way of understanding how and why some teaching and assessment methods take on different forms, have different beliefs and educational values, usually implicitly, and produce different educational effects. Despite all the caveats about defining and agreeing what good practice is, and about how to work with teachers to develop it, the concept of 'learning cultures' has helped us go some way towards suggesting what educationally worthwhile formative assessment is, and which factors make it more possible in some contexts than others. In part, this is because we adopted a strong normative stance from the outset about the need to resist instrumentalism in vocational education and ALLN, even if we understand why it is an entirely rational response in most of the learning cultures of our case studies.

Although our approach and analysis cannot provide easy answers for resisting instrumentalism, we highlight here how a problem-based approach to professional development can help teachers raise questions about their practice and seek to answer them. In this chapter, we summarize some problems with typical approaches to bringing about change to teaching and assessment methods in post-compulsory education. We also describe our own approach in detail and evaluate its pros and cons in the light of teachers' responses to it in our project. Finally, we evaluate the prognosis for extending some of its implications to other teachers.

1. Typical approaches to professional change

Models of change

Box 10.1   Models of change

The project 'Transforming Learning Cultures in Further Education' worked intensively in four colleges and identified four broad models of change that teachers experience, either explicitly or implicitly:

- A *technical* view of how change happens, where bringing about change was seen as a rational process of finding and building up knowledge about 'what works', communicating this to tutors in the form of recipes for action, and expecting that once tutors adopt these recipes, improvement will follow.

- A *professional* model of change. Central to this view is the idea of tutors who, based upon their knowledge and understanding and informed by their professional values and orientations, make judgements about the most appropriate course of action and, through acting upon their judgements, bring about change.
- A model of change closely connected to *market needs*. In this case, tutors and managers need to find out what the market of students, employers or others wants and then change the college structures and teaching provision so as to provide this. The college should not try to judge whether the change is 'for the good', as the market will soon say if they have got it wrong.
- A fourth model is focused on *power*. From this perspective, change in colleges happens because managers are constantly manoeuvring in order to retain their power in a sea of shifting sands. The managers adopt the language of whatever idea is in fashion at the moment and use it in order to retain their position, and that of the college.

The authors identify fundamental problems with a technical approach: first, it oversimplifies the social reality of a complex, dynamic activity; second, it assumes that teaching and learning are essentially the same everywhere; third, it usually seems to presume that it is *teachers and their teaching* that need improvement, when there are many other factors and issues involved. This reveals that it is not only the *content* of change that has implications for the power relations in FE, but also the *method* that is used, and how that is thought about. Models of change are not just value-free techniques.

Source: James and Biesta (2007: 121)

We can add another, more sophisticated version of professional change that combines technical and professional models. Used by academic researchers working intensively with school teachers to develop formative assessment practices, over a relatively long period, it employs intensive development sessions or 'workshops', interviews, observations and other forms of data collection and inputs. These approaches to developing teachers' understanding and practice also offered teachers 'a variety of living examples of implementation, by teachers with whom they can identify and from whom they can both derive conviction and confidence that they can do better, and see concrete examples of what doing better means in practice' (Black and Wiliam 1998: 16). A similar approach was used in the TLRP project 'Learning how to Learn'.[4]

Initial teacher education and professional development

The lead author and two of the collaborating authors for this book teach regularly on courses for further and adult education tutors, at all levels from introductory short courses to the full post-graduate certificate. Our experience and our insights from this project lead us to suggest that, when it comes to educating and training new teachers to understand and implement good formative assessment, many teacher education programmes are an inadequate preparation for developing the sound theoretical and practical basis necessary to address or even to recognize the problems we identify in this book.

The 'standards of competence' on which such courses are based convey the right messages about formative and summative assessment. Yet, they also embody much of the general rhetoric about learning and autonomy that we saw in our case studies, confusion between evaluation and self-assessment, the elision of formative assessment, continuous summative assessment and 'learning', and encourage instrumental practices and content. In addition, the teacher education 'curriculum' is over-crowded with complex 'standards of competence' for teachers to achieve, and therefore lacks theoretical depth. For example, there is rarely time to explore fundamental meanings of formative, diagnostic and summative assessment, and differences and overlaps between them, let alone the detail of how to use methods or approaches for transforming learning rather than for getting students through the summative targets. To make matters worse, highly constrained conditions of service and poor resourcing prevent new teachers spending proper time on their training and teacher educators from doing their own scholarly updating. These factors conspire to make many trainees and their tutors as instrumental as some of our examples in the book!

Arguably, the state of continuing professional development (CPD) in relation to enhancing and renewing understanding and practice is equally lamentable. Although there are requirements for tutors in further and adult education to participate in at least 30 days of CPD have been introduced, there are far too many examples where this target is 'ticked off' instrumentally, through certificates issued at conferences, courses and seminars which contribute to the formal 30-day requirement, regardless of quality and impact on practice. In addition, many of these of courses are exercises in compliance with the latest policy initiative.

Growing numbers of teachers therefore learn for themselves the ethos of instrumental compliance with externally defined criteria, as a form of socialization into the practices we saw in many of our case studies. Nevertheless, despite these constraints, and our rather negative picture of them here, there are examples of excellence in various aspects of teaching and learning, including assessment. For example, some courses have whole modules on the policy and practice of assessment taught by enthusiastic experts, and there are excellent short courses, conferences and seminars devoted to formative assessment, some based directly on findings and insights from research.

A problem-based approach to professional development

In response to the shortcomings of existing models and approaches to professional development, and recognizing that we did not have the resources to replicate the intensive research and development projects (supported enthusiastically by local authorities and institutional managers) in earlier studies, we adopted a specific problem-based methodology (PBM) to support the improvement of teachers' professional practice. The PBM had already been used successfully in a number of small-scale projects.[5] It was known to function without intensive and prolonged input from researchers or professional development staff, and found to be effective in terms of enhancing teacher thinking, understanding and practice.

These earlier trials of the PBM with lecturers in further and higher education, and with early years teachers, seemed effective as a method of shifting the position of teachers from a typical professional development process of merely reflecting on an input, to conceiving areas for development and strategies for improvement and perhaps, but not always, implementing them. This contrasts with the use of objectives or, to use current terminology, targets. The PBM can be adapted for different circumstances and can be used by groups or individuals. The focus of the PBM is very practical and the team-based nature of the activities provides further impetus to implement formulated strategies. The explicit link between new learning, in relation to material from the method's introductory workshop, together with developments in teachers' practice, is intended to foster continuing learning that leads to deeper understanding.

We also adopted the PBM as one of the means by which the research team could gain useful theoretical and practical insights about formative assessment and the effects of different strategies and practices on students' attitudes to learning, as well as developing teachers' own insights and expertise.

Seven researchers, working in pairs, used the PBM with a total of 49 teachers from 10 institutions (see Table 10.1).

2. The problem-based methodology

Rationale

The version of the PBM used in the project draws on theoretical and empirical work by Joanna Swann and colleagues (see Swann 2003, see Note 5

Table 10.1 Scale of the professional development programmes

Pseudonym for institution	Type of institution – school (sixth form), further education (FE) college, adult and community learning centre (ACL), adult education (AE) college, adult education service (AES)	Number of teachers who completed professional development programme*	Whether teacher participants or teacher researchers (teachers in the latter category were involved in writing reports)
Moorview Community College	comprehensive school	5	4 teacher researchers 1 teacher participant
Southern Counties College	FE college	12	12 teacher researchers
City College, Oldminster	FE college	7	6 teacher researchers 1 teacher participant
Mid-Counties College	FE college	7	4 teacher researchers 3 teacher participants
Westhampton College Bradwell Centre	FE college ACL (college-based)	3	3 teacher researchers
Westhampton College St Marks Centre	FE college ACL (community-based)	3	2 teacher researchers 1 teacher participant
Marketside College	AE/FE college	3	3 teacher researchers
Woodside Adult Learning Centre	ACL	3	3 teacher researchers
Lowfield Adult Education College	ACL	3	3 teacher researchers
Larkshire Education Authority	local authority AES	3	3 teacher researchers

*Includes attendance at a minimum of two workshops, involvement in systematic modifications to professional practice and reflections thereon. For some of the workshops for adult education teachers, the teachers who attended came from more than one institution.

below). We intended it to be a means of encouraging teachers to formulate their own meaningful problems that could potentially be resolved by developing their formative assessment strategies and practices; then to create and adopt practical solutions and evaluate their effects on student learning. In this process, we have been mindful not only of the

British Educational Research Association's (BERA) ethical guidelines for educational research (BERA 2004) but also of the more demanding guidelines for the conduct of action research set out in Kemmis and McTaggart (1988: 106–8).[6]

The PBM is based on three key ideas which are embedded into its design and the rationale, summarized here:

1. *Practical problems require practical trial and error*: The development of educational practice requires practitioners to engage in a trial and error approach to practical problems. Practical problems – such as 'How can I/we improve my/our formative assessment practices?' – are qualitatively different from theoretical problems and, as such, they require qualitatively different kinds of solution. A solution to a practical problem takes the form of an action (or a decision not to act) and the test of an action involves addressing 'What happened?' A rigorous response to this question requires that evidence be sought about the extent to which the original problem has been solved, and, drawing on the ideas of Karl Popper, due consideration must also be given to potential unintended consequences, desirable and undesirable.[7]

2. *Empower the practitioner*: The power to create social policy and practice brings with it a responsibility to critically evaluate the consequences of what has been created. In a society in which there is a plethora of top-down initiatives, practitioners can lose a sense of themselves as creative agents in the workplace. Instead, they may see their role largely in terms of responding to the initiatives of others. Responsibility for policy and outcome is diffuse. When things go wrong, policy-makers blame practitioners for not implementing the policy correctly; practitioners blame policy-makers for instigating the policy or students for not being amenable to the approach being used, while researchers often blame policy-makers and their various implementers such as inspectors, institutional managers and policy officials. There is much blame and complaint but often little progress. For progress, action and responsibility for action need conceptually to be closely linked. Empowering practitioners means helping them to identify which aspects of their situation they can affect, and encouraging them to formulate problems and create and test solutions (as described above).

3. *Feelings matter*: Despite the popularity of constructivist theories about learning and formative assessment among many education researchers, behaviourist ideas still dominate the way that social policy is conceived, implemented and evaluated.[8] A key feature of behaviourist thinking is the idea that an individual's internal states or processes are either to be regarded as irrelevant or,

more radically, non-existent. Instead, behaviours can be defined, trained and assessed, with high levels of transparency and accuracy: this is a fundamental premise of competence and outcome-based assessment.[9] It then follows that social endeavour need not be complicated by reference to intentions and emotions, either conscious or unconscious. This viewpoint is embedded in the target-driven, outcome-based assessment and accountability systems that teachers in post-compulsory education are obliged to use.

Yet, the fact that a phenomenon is not recognized or acknowledged does not mean that it does not exist or that, if it does exist, it is unimportant. In practice, intentions and feelings exist and they, and their underlying values, matter. If we aspire to social progress, rather than mere change, we must acknowledge that how people feel and behave is strongly influenced by values, even if these are not explicit, and we need to consider how what we do affects how we ourselves and other people feel. In short, in order to develop and improve social practice, we need methodologies that are not only rigorous but also humane. Derived from the work of Popper, such methodologies will treat people not as cogs in a machine or as bees in a hive, but as autonomous agents who are capable of engaging in imaginative criticism.[10]

In the context of almost constant change in further and adult education, where many teachers feel beleaguered and disempowered, the PBM is an explicit, albeit small attempt to redress the balance in CPD back towards the imaginative criticism of autonomous professionals. As we show below, requiring teachers to identify practical questions that are genuinely meaningful to them (as opposed to being told what problems or questions to address in the latest policy initiative) (see Box 10.2 and Box 10.3), to identify barriers to change and then to select which of these they can influence, seems to have a powerful effect.

Box 10.2   Stages in the problem-based approach

The basic stages of the PBM are derived directly from these three key ideas. The first seven can be addressed within a single three-hour session. The eighth requires a period of time – usually at least six months – after which the ninth stage is undertaken. When the PBM is being used within an action research project, this is followed by the tenth stage.

1. Address the question, 'What is going well in the present situation and what do I/we anticipate will go well in the future?' (in other words, 'What do we want to defend, maintain and develop?').

    Accentuating the positive in this way may increase our confidence to act, and can guard against the unintended consequence that a seemingly welcome development has involved the loss of desirable features that were taken for granted before the development took place.

2. Address the questions: 'What is not going well?' and 'What do I/we anticipate may not go well in the future?' and, in light of this, 'What developments do I/we wish to bring about?'

3. Address the question: 'What might impede the developments I/we desire to bring about?'

4. Address the question: 'Which impediments fall within my/our sphere of influence?'

5. Given your answers to the earlier questions, formulate one or more practical problems using questions of the kind: 'How can I/we . . . ?'

6. Make a list of the strategies you might adopt in order to solve each problem, and select at least one to adopt and test in practice. (Different members of a team may be able to test different solutions.) The cost implications (monetary and otherwise) of proposed solutions should be considered at this stage.

7. Decide how you will test the efficacy and worth of the solution(s) adopted. Be specific – use the following sentence openings: 'My/our solution to this problem will be successful insofar as it results in . . . ', 'My/our solution will be a failure if it results in . . . ' and 'Success and failure will be judged, at least in part, by . . . '.

8. Implement the chosen solutions, being mindful of the potential not only for desirable intended consequences but also for consequences which are unintended and potentially undesirable.

9. For each problem and each adopted solution: after allowing sufficient time for the solution to be tested properly, carry out a review by addressing: 'To what extent, if at all, has the initial problem been solved?', 'What unintended and unexpected consequences (desirable or undesirable) have arisen?', 'With the benefit of hindsight, might another solution have been preferable?' and 'What new problems might now be formulated, and are they such as to require attention?'

10. When the development process is part of a research project: write a formal account of what has taken place, and in particular what has been learned.

Box 10.3   Typical questions formulated by project teams

College team	Problems formulated at Workshop 1 as focus for professional development
BTEC National Diploma Performing Arts Southern Counties	1. How can we promote ownership of individual formative assessment feedback? 2. How can we focus individual aspirations/ motivation for progression?
BTEC National Diploma Public Services, Oldminster	1. How can we check that our formative assessment is working? 2. How can we get students to identify their own learning needs and to self-assess?
Key skills (embedded) (KSE) Southern Counties	1. How can we address the issue of having no map of unit formative assessment for staff/student – three points of year? (Course specific – HCS and Early Years)
GCSE Health and Social Care, Oldminster	How can we get the learners to self-assess what they have learnt and/or how they have progressed during the week?
Entry to employment (E2E) Southern Counties	1. How can we improve weekly feedback to learners? 2. How can we address the problem of lack of learning style awareness?
E2E Oldminster College	1. How can we build students' confidence quickly by getting them to recognize their own progress/improvement?
Larkshire Adult Education Centre	2. How can we get learners to capture progress somewhere (perhaps using their activity plans?) (NB This would be the start of learners recognising that they are progressing as individuals. They can build on this first step in taking responsibility for their own learning)

Evaluating our approach to professional development

As we explained above, our approach from the outset was both intentionally less intensive and also, during year one of the project, less directive in offering neither detailed ideas of what had worked for other teachers nor a strong lead about different meanings of formative assessment. First, we could not provide convincing examples of good practice as there had been no high-quality research on developing teachers' formative assessment practices in post-compulsory education, and no evaluation of claims that effective formative assessment raises achievement and engages students with learning: our project was designed to fill this gap. Simply offering examples from school contexts and subjects was therefore unlikely to have much credibility with teachers in vocational education and ALLN programmes. Second, our PBM advocates a trial and error approach to professional learning, based on action research; hence we wanted teachers to come to a practical and theoretical understanding of formative assessment, by trying to address a problem meaningful to them in their particular context, even if this led to wrong turns and misunderstandings along the way.

To what extent was the PBM successful? In both years of the project, we evaluated the PBM with participating teachers and within the project team. In the first year of the project, all but three of our participating teachers found that the PBM led to deep learning about formative assessment. Initially, many of the participating teachers had very instrumental interpretations of formative assessment. Through the practical initiatives they undertook in our project, they felt empowered to make changes and, crucially, to identify which aspects of their teaching context they were unable and able to influence. Their evaluation of their own and others' practices led them to understand formative assessment and its effects on students' attitudes to learning. They felt that didactic inputs and direction at the outset would not have enabled them to reach this level of understanding. They were more motivated about their professional development. However, it is important to note that we will not be able to evaluate any long-term changes to understanding or practice unless we interview and observe the teachers at some future date.

The three Science teachers at Moorview College did not feel they had learned anything new because, according to them, they 'would have implemented the change [to their formative assessment practice] anyway' and they felt that they had learned all about formative assessment from numerous INSET days and their initial teacher education. They had found the INSET days on 'assessment for learning' somewhat patronising and simplistic and therefore came to the project somewhat sceptical. The project did not, therefore, change or influence their thinking. Particularly significant in their perception, and one with which we agree, was the combination of their high level of subject expertise and confidence, and the fact they had already gained basic understanding of formative assessment: in retrospect, it is evident that, for them, we needed to build on this and encourage them to consider new ways to link subject-knowledge with formative assessment.

Adapting our approach

We adapted the PBM in the second year of the project in light of insights about formative assessment that emerged both from our project's first year and from other research. First, although there are similarities between the distortion of both summative and formative assessment through the constraints of the National Curriculum testing regime in schools and pre-scriptive systems in lifelong learning, the qualification targets and general climate of turmoil and change in the latter contrast with the relatively stable, homogeneous influence of National Curriculum testing.

In addition, research and development activities to improve formative assessment in schools were designed to integrate a sophisticated holistic view of formative assessment, rooted in pedagogy, with students' cognitive development in specific subject disciplines.[11] In contrast, earlier research in post-compulsory education had shown that developments in the policy and practice of formative assessment have been driven much more by concerns about motivation, engagement and inclusion than by an interest in improving cognition within specific subjects.[12] We therefore needed to address this key underlying difference.

Second, as we argued in the first section of this book, there is no water-tight definition of formative assessment. Instead, there are varied under-standings among practitioners and their managers. Our project provided further examples of the widespread misunderstanding that specific activities are 'formative' and others 'summative', alongside a tendency to see formative assessment as a series of teacher-led techniques for feedback, diagnosis and review. Despite an accompanying rhetoric of 'engaging students with learning', the techniques and associated formal paperwork are often solely to 'track' students towards their summative targets.

A more open-ended PBM was appropriate in the first year because we were also learning with the teachers about formative assessment practices in different settings, and about the factors that either helped or hindered it. In the second year, we wanted to direct the project's teachers more ex-plicitly towards understanding the differences between instrumental and deeper forms of formative assessment and to encourage them to develop the latter.

In the second year, we adopted the same systematic, structured ap-proach to the workshops and to teachers' formulation of meaningful prob-lems, but the project researchers had a stronger input at the beginning of the process with regard to the tensions and findings outlined above. Then, in the second and third workshops, we talked more about the findings, and we sought teachers' insights about the implications of endemic in-strumentalism and pushed them to be critical of their own practice and the learning cultures they worked in.

Another crucial difference was that, in the second workshop, we showed them an hour-long DVD of a lecture by Panl Black about effective classroom questioning and feedback, based on a presentation he had made to a project conference[13] (Black 2007). Despite the didactic nature of the input, and despite being completely located in school examples and contexts, the teachers in our project found Black's ideas relevant and insightful, and his contribution was inspiring in developing their formative assessment strategies.[14]

Effects on teachers' understanding and practice

There is clearly scope for discussion on the merits of a more or less open approach to the PBM, not least because there were differences of opinion among the team about how open-ended the trial and error approach should be, and therefore about how directive researchers should be in steering teachers towards implementing insights and ideas from existing research. Notwithstanding differences, its overriding strength is in empowering the teachers in their endeavours, respecting and working with difference rather than trying to establish conformity. And, in resource terms, the approach is cheap.

Through the use of the PBM, 46 of the project's 49 teachers learned a great deal about formative assessment, changed their practices and felt empowered to do so. They learned that, despite the turmoil and pressures of the further and adult education sector, they could develop aspects of their practice and influence learning cultures they saw largely as highly negative. They found that they could be critical of the ways in which targets and resource constraints undermined their practice, while not feeling overwhelmed by them and therefore disempowered by the pressures they were under. Some felt re-motivated to try to engage students with deeper ideas about learning than they, as teachers, had come to feel were possible.

They also liked the status and affirmation the project gave them as professionals. It is also important to note that although the 26 teachers in the project's second year enjoyed and valued the input of a well-known expert in formative assessment at the mid-point of the development programme, they all said it would have fallen flat if it had been offered at the outset. This attests to the validity of our approach.

Yet, while undoubtedly stimulated and motivated, about half our sample of teachers found the constellation of ideas around formative assessment fitted easily into the way they already conceptualized their work. In addition, while all but three said it helped them think more about their teaching in constructive ways, and provided a focus for interesting formal and informal discussions between themselves and others, half the sample thought it did not challenge their practice in any fundamental way.

The learning cultures of most of our case studies meant that changes to formative assessment were less of a true innovation than a means of intensifying the mode and degree of communication towards existing instrumental goals. Lecturers generally exhibited a reluctance to experiment with formative assessment and to change what they considered to be working well: this was much more evident among vocational education teachers than the ALLN teachers in our sample. According to Neil, a lecturer in BTEC NPDS at Oldminster: 'We tend to stick with what works, really, unfortunately, like most people.' As he elaborated,

> I think we're just in a very . . . 'if it ain't broke, don't fix it', type of mode and we do what we think works and we don't seem to have the time to experiment with stuff. So I think we use a limited range of formative assessment and stuff that we feel actually works.

In this light, if the tendency was typically to focus on checking progress bureaucratically towards abstracted curriculum goals (i.e. to serve the purposes of summative assessment) rather than consider more critically the subject content and goals of various assessment processes, our project could only raise alternative possibilities.

Although the PBM did not bring about profound changes to practice for some of our teachers, it did affect the motivation and professional interest of one e2e course leader, a GCSE teacher and eight ALLN tutors to consider new approaches and to think differently about the purposes of assessment. This encompassed attitudinal change in relation to their role with students, the difference between formative and summative assessment, the effects of instrumentalism and the potential for their own meaningful professional learning.

In ALLN and some of the teams at Southern Counties, teachers were keen to share what they had learnt, for example, by photocopying articles and extracts from papers and books used in the project, to pass on to other colleagues, one of whom has chosen to focus on formative assessment as part of her Adult Literacy Teacher Training assignment. Others have since run staff development sessions and one used the experience of the project to apply for, and secure, a new post in teacher education.

All but three teachers found the activities useful, particularly the workshops. Although some admitted they initially found it all very daunting and wanted stronger guidance at the beginning, they equally felt that they wouldn't have got so much out of it if they had not been able to go through that thinking process for themselves:

> At the beginning when we had that workshop . . . I thought what have I let myself in for! It just sounded so . . . I'd never done anything like that. I thought we were going to be told, here you are,

go and try that, go away and try that. So I was a bit wary and worried and I did find it difficult to start with. I thought what am I doing, it's all vague, I don't know, what I was doing. But when I decided to keep my diary I could just pick out what was important to me . . . just keep that as my focus and I think that really, really helped because otherwise I think that I wasn't getting a handle on it really . . . I don't know if we had got more direction whether I would have got so much out of it.

(Clarissa, literacy teacher, Woodside Adult Learning Centre)

For all but three of the participating teachers, the project made them want more information, more training, 'a list of strategies', 'a resource bank of ideas', 'more workshops', 'books that would help make to make it clearer or make suggestions, pinpoint areas that could be used in learning'.

It is fair to say that in comparison with the outcomes of the intensive work undertaken with school teachers, cited above, we did not transform the teachers' understanding and practice in ways that might be sustained over the long term, especially given the pressure of targets and resources in post-compulsory education. There was therefore a sense at the end of the third workshop that we were only just beginning to transform practice, and we did not create the formative assessment experts that other projects fostered.

Despite this critical evaluation, it is important to reiterate that our intention from the outset was to use an inexpensive, short-term approach that tested a particular theory of professional learning while also illuminating both instrumental and deeper formative assessment practices, and the barriers to the latter, in rich and meaningful ways. This has given us a good basis to create authentic examples of educationally worthwhile formative assessment practices that we could show other teachers, through visual materials such as DVDs.

Box 10.4 Principles and features of the PBM

- Expert input in terms of content and ideas about formative assessment is initially much less of a priority than eliciting teachers' own ideas about what it is, and how they might change their practice to address particular educational problems.
- Teachers may misunderstand formative assessment or adopt very instrumental meanings of it; this is highly predictable given the learning cultures they come from and their initial training in assessment.

- Trial and error, and evaluation with other teachers and an expert lead often but not always to changes in thinking, attitude and insight.
- The simple step in the problem-formulating sequence of questions, outlined above, of being made to move on from barriers to practice to identifying what can be changed, however small or insignificant, is seen almost universally by teachers in this process as extremely motivating and empowering.
- The ability to be critical while identifying positive changes seems also to be empowering.
- Some teachers will extend their insight and skills; others will not.
- Trial and error, and structured discussion, seem often to lead to receptivity for new ideas, if not to immediate practical change.

Conclusion

Our problem-based approach to professional development to improve understanding and practice in formative assessment goes some way to confirming the power of focused, high-quality professional development rooted in research and led by enthusiastic experts. Unlike many ITE and CPD experiences, research-led PBM can change teachers' understanding of what they can and cannot influence in their learning cultures, highlight to institutional managers and staff developers how they can influence both positively and negatively those learning cultures, and thereby enable teachers to change their practice for the better.

Our participation in the learning cultures we studied, including those we could not include in this book, highlights the luxury and privilege afforded to researchers. We can identify factors affecting practice and make connections between these factors and their educational effects without having to experience the learning cultures that these factors both emerge from and shape. Being able to do this, and to explore these with teachers, is a necessary part of continuing professional development.

Yet, sadly, for us both as researchers and practitioners in ITE and CPD, our experience also shows that the state of continuing professional development in post-compulsory education is so poor that almost any intervention that respects teachers, takes them seriously and offers some new ideas from enthusiastic experts, can be effective in re-energizing and re-motivating them.

The depressing scale of the challenge of being able to offer teachers in a beleaguered sector genuinely useful, interesting and educational forms of professional development cannot be underestimated. It is reflected in a widespread misunderstanding throughout the education system that 'simple' advice can be disseminated, illustrated here. Having sat in on all the workshop sessions, and heard our rationale for the PBM teachers' positive evaluations that they had learnt 'properly' about formative assessment through the process they had been through in the project, and despite being highly supportive and understanding of pressures in the college, a college manager said to the project director after the last session had finished:

> Can we just distil the lessons for good practice and you come back next year to tell all the staff in the college how to do formative assessment, and save all that 'learning journey stuff' that these have been on?

Sadly, then, for us both as researchers and practitioners in ITE and CPD, our experience shows that the state of CPD in post-compulsory education is extremely poor. Nevertheless, our project shows that an intervention that respects teachers, recognizes constraints and hindrances on practice yet offers some new ideas from enthusiastic experts, can be effective in re-energizing a sense of professionalism.

Notes

1. See www.tlrp.org.
2. See Black et al. (2003); James et al. (2007); Gardner (2005); Gardner et al. (2010).
3. See Biesta (2007) and Coffield et al. (2008) for critiques of these aims and the role of research in realizing them.
4. See James et al. (2007).
5. See Swann and Ecclestone (1999), and Swann and Arthurs (1999).
6. Researchers had no commitment to report back to institutional managers (and did not do so). Only managers involved in the project, that is, as workshop participants, have had access to teacher plans and reports.
7. Popper (1961 [1957], 1992 [1962], Chapter 5).
8. See Torrance and Pryor (1998), James (2005), for discussion.
9. See Jessup (1991), and Chapter 1 of this book.
10. Popper (1979 [1972]: 148).
11. Black et al. (2003); Gardner (2005); James et al. (2007).
12. See Chapter 1 of this book, and Ecclestone (2002); Torrance et al. (2005).
13. The ideas in Paul Black's DVD for our project have since been published (Black and Wiliam 2009).

14. It is perhaps salutary to note that very few of the teachers had experienced an hour-long lecture of this sort in their own training, and there were disagreements in the project team about whether they would tolerate it, or find it useful (an interesting parallel to low expectations in our case studies among some of the vocational teachers about their own students' motivation!). In the project run by Black and colleagues, teachers came to ask for inputs on theory about learning and methods, reflecting their growing interest in formative assessment as the project progressed (Black et al. 2003).

11 Transforming formative assessment

Introduction

When it comes to offering ideas about improving formative assessment, researchers lucky enough to have extended time to observe and evaluate practice face profound tensions. It seems trite to advise teachers, many of whom are on casual contracts and trying to encourage students, some of whom are often demotivated and have negative experiences of formal education, that coaching to the criteria is neither formative assessment or educationally worthwhile. Declining experience of curriculum development, superficial subject development, and very few opportunities for genuinely useful professional development make it unrealistic to advocate opportunities for teachers to identify problems that they want to solve (rather than being told what to address) to analyse and come to their own understanding of what formative assessment is, and to evaluate what they can and cannot influence.

A climate of disempowerment and intense pressure creates other tensions. Only a tiny number in our sample of teachers felt they could influence the prescriptive assessment systems they had to work with, and their positive responses to the small opportunity the project offered to take part in funded research, led by enthusiastic experts, and to be taken seriously as professionals was humbling to say the least. It therefore seems negative and demotivating of us to draw attention to instrumental and impoverished approaches.

It also seems negative to raise questions about what counts as 'educationally worthwhile' content and processes in the courses we studied. While instrumentalism and, for some teachers in our project, fatalism and cynicism, affect teaching, subject content and assessment adversely, and limit educational aspirations to the mechanistic achievement of targets, many students enjoyed much of what they did and achieved their various targets and qualifications. Indeed, as our case studies also show, some students were able to develop more positive attitudes than they had previously. It therefore seems churlish to question the value of what they achieved and the processes they engaged in, a point that policy-makers repeat every year to counter criticism of falling educational standards.

In the face of such tensions, is tempting for researchers who do not experience the day-to-day pressures that lead to the problems they observe to confine themselves to a view that instrumentalism and low expectations of what students will and will not put up with, are somehow 'inevitable'. These tensions also make it easy to criticize government agencies and awarding bodies for the pressures they have created or to depict reasons for instrumentalism as, in a term much favoured by social scientists, 'complex', thereby offering little in the way of practical alternatives.

Rather than accepting that educationally impoverished practices are inevitable, we adopt the more optimistic view expressed by Karl Marx: that the only things 'inevitable' in life are taxation and death! In this chapter, we acknowledge pressures towards practices and conditions that seem 'inevitable' while drawing out insights from our research and other relevant studies that suggest ways to improve formative assessment practices. We surround our insights with strong caveats, reinforced by our initial theoretical framework of 'learning cultures', namely that advice about how to improve any assessment or teaching method has to be interpreted locally, tailored to the conditions of each learning culture and focused on the things that teachers can realistically influence. Our problem-based approach to professional development, discussed in Chapter 10, shows that this translation has to be done by teachers working with colleagues to go beyond the confines of prescriptive and, in some cases, misconceived specifications. Essential for this translation is scope for teachers to challenge things they and colleagues might take for granted as 'obvious' or 'the way we do things' or 'what our students will and won't tolerate'.

In this chapter, we highlight some pros and cons of the ways in which teachers in our project practised three aspects of formative assessment: (1) tutorials and reviews of progress; (2) questioning and feedback; and (3) self- and peer assessment. All of them, in different ways, have problems in common and corresponding potential for making them less instrumental. We then evaluate how teachers might use the more nuanced meanings of motivation and autonomy, outlined in the first section of this book, to counter the negative effects on activities and their purposes of stereotypes and expectations of students. Then we challenge the ubiquitous and misleading mantras of 'learning' and 'student autonomy' which pervade discussion about teaching and learning and yet often conceal impoverished practice. Finally, we argue that unless government agencies and other interested parties take seriously long-running problems with subject knowledge and expertise, and lack of clear purposes for 'vocational' education and some areas of ALLN, the prognosis for transforming formative assessment is not positive.

1. Enhancing formative assessment

Individual tutorials and reviews of progress

Diverse goals

> After their introductions we never really get to sit and talk to them about what they want to learn, it is an odd minute or two grabbed here and there, so it is very different – gives us an actual chance to talk to them and a chance for them to raise concerns.
>
> (Sarah Robinson, Larkshire Adult Education Centre literacy tutor, 2007)

Teachers in our case studies of e2e, adult literacy and numeracy and GCSE Health and Social Care either introduced tutorials or changed the way they already used them. In different ways, their goals were to diagnose or identify 'needs', to review progress towards targets, evaluate students' progress and particular areas of difficulty and to help students 'take more ownership of their learning'.

In reality, however, the focus was solely on targets and, as we observed in the three examples of tutorial that made up the case study of Larkshire Adult Education Centre, wholly on topics which would appear in the SfL test. In these ALLN classes, tutorials or reviews of progress checked coverage of the curriculum and that the topics covered were the ones needed by the student, they checked the individual's comfort levels with meeting the targets and doing the work, and increased understanding by both parties of what contributes to this or diminishes it. Tutorials sometimes included a check on the student's ambitions and purposes in studying. In e2e, the focus was on behavioural and attitudinal targets that drew down funding, and in GCSE, on moving students up a grade level.

The pressures of the learning cultures meant that although teachers hoped for a qualitatively different kind of exchange to take place, this did not happen. In e2e and ALLN, there were intense pressures on time, a very diverse student body with very different attitudes and beliefs about learning, assessment and the respective roles of the teacher and students. There were also expectations from students that even when working on their own, the tutor would be available and not carrying out a tutorial with someone else.

Diverse goals were both fuelled and exacerbated by what we called a 'modular mindset', something we also observed among GCSE Business and Health and Social Care students. This is built overtly into the summative assessment requirements of both SfL and the GCSE assignments. For example, in this exchange at Larkshire, Sarah, one of the numeracy teachers gave information to a student about how the qualification was structured in modules to help individuals achieve in stages:

> [T]hey do it in modules so you will be working towards the first module for November. So, really, you have only got to retain that information in that block, work through to November, you can't completely forget it obviously, because being Maths, you use it in everything. But then you start on another module and then take the exam for that in March, put that aside, start another one and do the exam in June, so I think that will work very well for you.

In the Larkshire tutorial, there was little actual teaching or feedback on learning taking place. Instead, these were seen by both parties as classroom work and the tutorial was more of an aid to the teacher's planning and to identify any contextual problems that might affect learning, rather than clarifying and exploring particular aspects of literacy or numeracy in any depth.

Despite these limitations, discussion in ALLN and e2e tutorials did encourage self-reflection in the students, helping them think of themselves as a 'learner' and what that might mean. In the example cited here, the student displayed a mix of nervousness and determination. She was visibly going through a process of re-assessing herself, following a bad experience of school, and constructing a new sense of herself as someone with potential and ability to learn and achieve, and to become a professional, either a nurse or a teacher. She had come to enjoy maths since joining this class, and she might have been using this as a springboard for shifting or even transforming her sense of identity.

Encouraging a divergent mindset

In order to challenge a narrow focus on checking and target-tracking, the very positive relationships between teachers and students in ALLN and e2e learning cultures that used tutorials, and the process of reflection (which, for many adults and young people, might be the first time they had thought about themselves as a learner), could encourage a more divergent mindset on both 'sides'. In other words, these factors are a powerful springboard to something more worthwhile.

As we show in our discussion below of questioning and feedback, this requires teachers to regard apparently diversionary or irrelevant questions or students' expressions of interest, either as a way of engaging deeper interest in a topic or as a way of working out what is missing or lacking in a student's understanding of something.

Again, the example of the tutorial with Summer at Larkshire, discussed in Chapter 8, illuminates the potential for this. Instead of seeing her animated interest in her son's experience of assessment in GCSE Maths at school as an opportunity to talk about her own learning of Maths, Sarah noted that 'She does tend to talk quite a lot and went off on a tangent about herself; although it is relevant really ... but it is nothing I could comment on, so I felt that probably did waste time.'

In e2e, the fleeting, often sudden and precarious, glimpses of intrinsic motivation, such as Charles Lambert's discovery of interest in learning about animals, was at risk of being side-tracked by his tutor's concern to use his new-found motivation to reflect on his 'learning to learn' skills because these formed part of the attitudinal changes e2e is designed to bring about. Again, targets that focused on him and his respones threatened to shut out new ideas and topics that might have been intrinsically motivating in their own right, especially, for a young person who had long forgotten the joy of this in a formal educational setting.

Discouraging a mechanistic approach

The ALLN tutors in our sample who used ILPs as the basis for tutorials were divided between those who saw the requirement to complete Individual Learning Plans as a bureaucratic and onerous distraction, and those who managed to use them creatively. A question raised by some adult education teachers in our project and numerous other teachers we carried out staff development sessions with, based on the findings of the project, was how recording progress is linked to formative assessment practices, particularly the use of ILPs.

At Woodside Adult Learning Centre, Ikemna made full use of the ILP with her adult literacy students, all of whom have learning disabilities and difficulties, in order to keep separate detailed progress reviews:

[O]n the ILPs, everybody has their individual goals, and it's really useful to know when things have changed for the ILP, and so the ILP is a constant review of their progress as well, but it doesn't stay the same, it's not set in stone ... It is time-consuming, but, you know what? I really do like it ... when I'm writing my lesson plan and I'm setting work, it's very useful. I just take the progress review and say, 'Oh well, she's done that ... he's done that ... but she hasn't so I still have to do this for this person and set something different, because it's going to be monotonous and not challenging for them any more, because they've achieved that.' So we have to set more challenging goals for them, obviously with their consent as well ... it gives you direction ... so I think it makes it easier to do my lesson plans using that.

Although the mechanistic prescriptions of ILPs can dominate teachers' practices, this example shows that it is the learning culture and the central role of the teacher's expertise and beliefs within it that make potentially bureaucratic tools or processes either educationally worthwhile or merely an exercise in tedious bureaucratic compliance. Other teachers in our ALLN programmes also addressed this tension, aiming consciously to make ILPs the former.

Resisting individual support

The e2e and GCSE learning cultures simultaneously encouraged and responded to expectations of intensive support. In e2e, the combination of intensely personalized and emotionally focused support was central to participants' perceptions that e2e was different from school. In GCSE, as one of the students pointed out, there was a sense from teachers and students that they could not and would not get through without one-to-one support:

> A lot of people obviously like one-on-one help, and I think that the people that haven't done it, that aren't enjoying the course, do need a bit of help to just want to do it ... Plus most people don't do it at home, so if they get it done in the lesson then it's done then, and they don't take it home because they probably won't do it ... So ... really I think that everybody should have the tutorials.
> (Hannah, GCSE HSC student, Oldminster)

In growing numbers of institutions, mentoring, learning support and tutoring are leading to a big increase in individual rather than group working, and to the corresponding decline of teacher-centred inputs.[1] In our case studies, antipathy to group and teacher-led activity was strongest in e2e, but it was also influential in ALLN classes where teachers and students expected to work individually, and dominated the GCSE courses.

A growing emphasis on individual work is highly problematic for creative and effective approaches to formative assessment since questioning, feedback and peer assessment require teachers to engineer joint understandings and to build knowledge collectively. These are far less effective with a predominantly individual focus and in many contexts, virtually pointless. Yet, an expectation appears to be taking hold in the two areas we studied that group teaching and teacher-led input are demotivating and that students cannot get through without intensive individual support.

Questioning and feedback

Challenging the dominance of summative assessment

> [A]s they are going through the assessment, which is being marked all the time, I'm ... trying to guide them, so if they make a mistake,

I won't knock the grade off, I'll go up to them, stop the practical and say to them 'Right, what did you do wrong then?' ... and then I'll say 'think about this' and give them a scenario where this went wrong or that went wrong and hopefully they come across with the answer and then I can grade them ... If it doesn't work, we get into groups, discuss it: 'Why don't you know the answer, why don't you understand what I'm saying?' We try and find out what the stumbling block is and I try and work another way around teaching it.

(Frank, course leader NDPS, Mid-Counties)

The case studies of vocational education show that the merger of teaching and formative and summative assessment, noted in studies of the late 1990s and mid-2000s, has intensified. With varying degrees of reluctance, 43 teachers in our sample have merged their teaching and assessment roles to act as a translator of the prescriptive official criteria and specifications which comprise a so-called 'curriculum'. Planning, questioning and providing oral and written feedback mean breaking up the assignment briefs provided by the specifications into sequential tasks to meet each criterion. In the case of the NDPS at Mid-Counties, students were grouped according to the levels offered by the criteria, sometimes task by task.

Formative or summative purposes have merged to a great extent, driven to some extent by the strong emphasis from awarding bodies on standardization of summative judgements between different centres. In the case of Mid-Counties as we noted in our chapter on 'learning cultures', fear of management sanctions for poor achievement rates led to an excessively instrumental approach. Yet, in many settings, summative assessment, achievement and learning have become to a large extent synonymous, something observed in an earlier study:

The clearer the task of how to achieve a grade or award becomes, and the more detailed the assistance given by tutors, supervisors and assessors, the more likely the candidates are to succeed; but succeed at what? Transparency of objectives, coupled with extensive use of coaching and practice to help learners met them, is in danger of removing the challenge of learning and reducing the quality and validity of outcomes achieved ... assessment procedures and practices come completely to dominate the learning experience, and 'criteria compliance' comes to replace 'learning'.

(Torrance et al. 2005: 46)

Drafting, questioning around the targets, followed either by coaching and constant feedback, and sometimes both, are core features of pedagogy, with large amounts of lesson or contact time used to introduce students to each assignment but also to talk through the outcomes of draft assignments, and to allow students to work on assignments. In GCSE Health and Social Care, some students receive one-to-one mentoring as well as target-setting tutorials. In this context, students expect, and depend upon, written advice to 'plug' and 'cover' gaps in the criteria, cross-referenced to the assessment specifications:

> I'm coming from a place of "This is what you need to know, this is how we're going to do it, this *is* how we're going to get you through. Jump, jump, jump, jump" and I don't think they like that.
>
> (Deborah, teacher, HSC GCSE, Oldminster)

In strict technical terms, it is very significant that grading criteria in all the vocational courses we studied are not criteria at all but merely descriptions of tasks: instead of assignments set on broad teaching of an area, designed to test knowledge, understanding and skills, the assignments are set on these tasks.

Self- and peer assessment

Avoiding the merger of 'evaluation' of teaching and self-assessment of learning

Teachers in e2e, GCSE Business, ESOL and BTEC National Diploma in Public Services used self-assessment, and Business and ESOL teachers combined it with peer assessment. With the exception of the ESOL classes, discussed in Chapter 9, the goals and activities of self- and peer assessment were dominated either by grade achievement or 'owning the targets'.

Crucially, in their questions to students, teachers confused *evaluation of teaching* with self-assessment of learning. In e2e, this enabled young people who were already disaffected from formal education and who had very strong views about teaching, learning and what they would and would not put up with, to off-load difficulties onto 'boring' teaching, or difficult topics.

Similarly, while far from being as difficult to motivate as the e2e participants, BTEC students also had strong beliefs about 'acceptable' teaching and about their own learning styles so that the self-assessment process introduced by their teachers encouraged evaluation of these aspects of what teachers referred to as 'learning'. In the latter case, a hazy emphasis on 'learning' which elided motivation, enjoyment and achievement, led teachers to become more insecure about topics that students might resist, or find tedious or difficult, and to adopt a somewhat apologetic tone for them, thereby undermining their own expertise and confidence.

Reducing the emphasis on the 'skills' of self- and peer assessment

Two depictions of the skills needed for students to be good at self-assessment were apparent. In e2e and BTEC, teachers and some of the students saw it as a lifeskill, something they would need at work, as well as a more general ability to be reflective, to set targets and to monitor progress, and to be 'independent lifelong learners'. In GCSE, the 'skill' was developed solely to help teachers raise levels of grade achievement which, in turn, motivated students. In e2e, the process of filling out the progress sheets triggered the much-valued individual tutorial and its combination of strong emotional support, cajoling and discipline from a well-liked tutor.

Emphasizing the skill of self-assessment as a rationale detracted further from the potential to use it to explore the learning of specific topics, and to identify possible topics of genuine interest, thereby making it more mechanistic and instrumental (Box 11.1).

Box 11.1   Resisting simplistic advice

When I trained to be a teacher I was told don't ever ask students 'Do you understand?' because they will all be nervous and say 'Yes, I understand.'

(Allan, ESOL teacher, Westhampton)

Much advice for teachers in further and adult education takes the form of 'tips' or 'do's and don'ts'. Some of them are inimical to good formative assessment, others simply disguise the fact that they can either be used instrumentally or in more worthwhile ways, or focus on quite different goals. They include:

- make sure learners know what they are aiming for;
- share the grade criteria;
- carry out regular reviews of progress;
- make sure you start with praise, then provide clear, unambiguous advice for improvement and end with a positive comment (the highly popular and unquestioned 'praise sandwich' taught to all students on most if not all teacher education courses for further and adult education);
- give clear advice about exactly what students must do to improve their work;
- never write on students' work;
- never use a red pen;
- only provide 'constructive' advice;
- never criticize.

2. Challenging stereotypes and expectations

Understanding motivation and autonomy

> Even if we knew precisely how to describe and to identify types
> of motivation, what would we do with this information?
> (Alice, literacy teacher, Larkshire Adult Education Centre)

'Improving' the motivation of students and developing their independence or their 'ownership of their own learning' was seen by all of the
teachers in our project, as one of their objectives. With the exception
of Derek in AVCE Science, Ben in BTEC Public Services, and Ruth and
Allan in the ESOL classes, this seemed to mean simply increasing their
self-confidence and positive motivation to take part in processes and activities. The exceptions among our sample had a clear sense of trying to
get students to think for themselves, to take control of procedures and to
use technical language as a springboard for deeper learning.

Generally, there was very little overt attention to encouraging students
to both expect and develop cognitive autonomy or intrinsic motivation
for subjects or topics. This was much more marked in vocational education
than in ALLN classes, reflected in an overwhelming view that students
were, by and large, difficult to motivate intrinsically and that few topics
and subjects might be potentially interesting in their own right. This is
not to say that teachers in our project were negative about students or
their own subject areas: many enjoyed teaching their students, and liked
their positive attitude. Nevertheless, motivation and a good relationship
between teachers and students in vocational education classes seemed to
be highly conditional on constant, detailed feedback, on playing down
the difficult or onerous demands of the course and on presenting some
topics defensively in advance, as intrinsically 'boring' or something to be
tolerated in the pursuit of better grades.

Like all categories encapsulated in a typology, Prenzel's categories of
motivation and our own categories of autonomy are not clearly delin-
eated and they cannot, on their own, capture the subtleties and idiosyn-
crasies of either motivation or autonomy. Yet, to our knowledge, Prenzel's
typology, developed through numerous studies in the German vocational
system, is the only one that takes us beyond old psychometric notions
found still in most educational texts that students are generally either
'extrinsic' or 'intrinsic' learners. We believe it to be useful and therefore
worth using more widely with teachers. Not least, in a highly instrumental context, it reasserts the expectation that more is possible with
more students than teachers seem to think, than extrinsic or introjected
motivation.

In the learning cultures of vocational education and ALLN, the typology of autonomy enables us to discern which goals and practices lie behind the much-vaunted goal of independent learning. The categories show how procedural and personal autonomy could be a springboard for subject-based critical autonomy: for example, Allan, in our case study of ESOL, consciously used the technical mastery of basic English to enable his students to develop some personal autonomy as the basis for cognitive autonomy. All too often in other contexts, procedural autonomy restricted students to a comfortable straitjacket of independence with the specifications but little else.

Within individual course-based learning cultures, both typologies also revealed how students are socialized to develop particular dispositions and expectations. For example, in our case studies of vocational GCSEs, students' expectations were already formed for assessment in courses at the next level. When applied to the learning cultures of vocational education case studies, they expose the dominance of highly instrumental goals for achievement, and the ways in which these were underpinned by certain expectations (or stereotypes) of a 'type' of young person who will choose (or, as is increasingly likely, be selected by the school) to do a vocational instead of an 'academic' general course. In ALLN, the typologies revealed the much stronger potential for intrinsic and interested motivation than existed in the vocational learning cultures. In other courses, they show that teachers seemed to underestimate examples, albeit fleeting and precarious, of intrinsic and interested motivation.

Box 11.2   Enhancing motivation and autonomy

There is fine balance between unhelpful and limiting stereotypes and realistic, experienced insights about 'typical' participants in courses. Some researchers advocate better knowledge among teachers of their individual students' dispositions and learning identities.[2] Yet not only is this highly time-consuming and potentially intrusive if done in-depth, but teachers and students are not immune from the ways in which stereotypes and a culture of instrumentalism reinforce each other and become a self-fulfilling prophecy; the more students are socialized into instrumentalism, the more they come to expect it. This suggests a need to do the following:

- evaluate the images and expectations of motivation and autonomy embedded in the official specifications and held by teachers and students in a particular course;
- identify different forms of autonomy reflected in the grade criteria or targets; to what extent is one form emphasized over another?;

- look for examples of students' interested and intrinsic motivation, however fleeting;
- expect and encourage intrinsic motivation for all topics, however difficult, boring or tedious they might seem!;
- discuss types of motivation and autonomy with students;
- make professional value judgements about the pros and cons of encouraging different types of motivation and autonomy.

3. Changing the subject

Degrading meanings of 'vocational'

One of the strongest themes to emerge in our project is that it is too easy to take for granted that there is a subject-base in which to root a formative assessment method or approach. In the research which, in part, our project built upon, work on formative assessment with school teachers was undertaken in clear, well-known and long established subject domains, with teachers who were well-qualified to teach them and also highly enthusiastic.[3] Teachers' participation in this earlier research led to numerous, highly popular 'Black Box' publications offering advice for improving specific techniques of formative assessment in areas such as English, Maths, Geography and Science.[4]

In almost total contrast, our project offered virtually no specific subject-based insights that we can draw on for advice. Outside ESOL, and AVCE Science, and to a lesser extent, literacy and numeracy for adults, any meaningful sense of a 'subject curriculum' was conspicuous by its absence. In the case of vocational science, the AVCE students had learnt science from Year 7, and built up a conceptual framework over time and, although their course was termed 'vocational', it was rooted in accepted academic disciplines.

In strong contrast to the case study in this book of another Level 3 course, BTEC National Public Services, neither Science students nor teachers equated 'vocational' with 'practical' activities as opposed to didactic teaching or written work although there was a practical, laboratory experiments element to each of the three science subjects on the AVCE. Instead, students attributed a greater ratio of coursework to exams than the single-subject A-levels, and valued the way teachers linked scientific knowledge to real life situations and to careers. The simplistic associations of 'vocational' with less written work, no exams, 'active learning' and freedom from didactic inputs are especially problematic.

Creating a curriculum of the 'self'

Although we recognize that Science is in some ways a special case, we do not agree with a view that we cannot use this example to argue for a more coherent sense of what vocational subjects are trying to achieve. Nor do we agree that singling Derek out is unrealistic because his confidence, enthusiasm and his strong sense of the importance of his expertise to his students' motivation and achievement make him 'untypical' of vocational education teachers.

It is, however, undoubtedly the case that growing numbers of teachers of vocational subjects do not have strong subject expertise, nor authentic experience in the occupational areas they teach. This is especially true in schools. Our research suggests that this tendency will increase, the more that 'vocational' comes to mean attitudes, dispositions, positive behaviours and psychological responses as social, life and work 'skills'.

A 'subject curriculum' of the self does not require specialists: in a list of 'values' that all good teachers hold, the General Teaching Council identifies a list of personal attributes and dispositions that include respect, empathy and communication, and the willingness to update one's professional skills but nothing whatsoever about love of a subject or a commitment to developing expertise in it. As Frank Furedi observes in his analysis of a crisis of adult authority in education, this list could apply to any professional from doctors to lawyers and is therefore highly symbolic in its generalism.[5]

In our study, e2e was the most stark example of a 'curriculum of the self', requiring professionals trained in tutoring, counselling, study skills, coaching and mentoring. One of the colleges in our case studies was reviewing teachers' roles across all courses, in the light of e2e. A shift to welfare and more emotionally-focused roles was also evident in other studies of similar courses.[6]

Although an overtly emotional and welfare role was not evident in our case studies of vocational education, a slow but inexorable shift towards the self, its positive attitudes and its ability to discipline itself while seeking and receiving coaching and 'support', was emerging. Part of this was a desire to prepare students for work. Formative and summative assessment processes were seen by students and teachers as valuable in themselves because they mirror the same competence-based assessments used in workplace appraisal, coaching and mentoring and performance review, and which teachers themselves also experience. Emphasis on the self was also a response to assumptions of vulnerability. A focus on the self has, become another association of 'vocational' education.

4. Going beyond the mantra of 'learning'

Removing 'students'

Absence of a clear purpose for the subject of vocational education goes hand in hand with what Michael Young argues has become a disdain for subject knowledge across education generally, but especially in vocational education.[7] This has created a vacuum into which a growing focus on attitudes, dispositions and behaviours is both reflected in, and reinforced by the ubiquitous mantras of 'learning' and 'autonomy'. This removes 'studying' a subject from educational expectations.

None of our teachers, apart from Derek, referred to participants in their courses as 'students'. The disappearance of students from the education system is reflected in the widespread orthodoxy that we should call young people and adults 'learners,' in preference to 'students', 'trainees' or 'group members':

> This is not an arbitrary decision . . . it describes what we are aiming for. It reminds us every time we see it that our prime person as professionals is to help people to learn, and, if possible, to help them learn how to keep learning. At the very least we want to motivate them to become sufficiently proficient learners that they are able to proceed to the next step of their choice . . . Regarding them as learners and being seen to regard them as learners is one of the first positive steps we can take towards motivating them to be exactly that.
>
> (Wallace 2007: 4)

This is a significant but overlooked problem: once the subject of learning is the self and its dispositions, it becomes rare to refer to 'Business studies students' or 'literacy students'. Instead, we have general learners whose 'learning' increasingly floats free of subjects and becomes focused on them, their lives, their social skills, work and learning to learn 'skills'. For some critics of policy and practice, a focus on learners and learning, together with policy claims to put 'learning and teaching at the heart' of FE, require a coherent theory of learning. This would also counter the technocratic language of delivery, targets and performance management that creates an impoverished view of 'learning'.[8]

Re-thinking 'learning'

Calls to focus on 'learning' cannot counter instrumentalism. Nor do they compensate for the lack of proper debate and agreement about curriculum content and the knowledge and skills that, in the words of the Nuffield Review of Education, 'an educated 14–19 year old needs', and on which there is no agreement.[9] Indeed, repeated amendments that have added more and more personal, social and learning-related, and work-related 'skills' to vocational education mean that we cannot take the misnamed 'curriculum' for granted. Without a robust subject to learn, meanings of learning and autonomy are degraded.

We advocate a different focus, drawing on a critique of the mantra of 'lifelong learning' which drew on Wittginstein's injunction that sometimes a term has to be sent for cleaning before it can be put back into circulation.[10] The case studies here show that 'learning' is a prime candidate for this cleaning: so too are 'vocational', 'curriculum', 'studying', 'autonomy' and 'subject'. We return to the significance of the findings of the Nuffield Review and its links to our own conclusions, in the closing section of this chapter.

Box 11.3   Promoting a holistic view of formative assessment

Our case studies illuminate some common characteristics that hinder a more holistic, educational approach to formative assessment. These require robust challenges.

Clarifying purposes

The purposes of formative assessment are frequently confused to include: evaluation of teaching and the relevance and interest of topics; getting students to reflect on their 'learning'; monitoring and disciplining individuals to meet their targets; diagnosing problems or misunderstandings with specific topics. Without a clear subject focus, tutorials and self-assessment in particular run the risk of being tedious, ritualistic and devoid of any intrinsic interest. They also risk intersifying a focus on the self.

There are important questions about what students are really qualified to comment on and an associated danger of over-emphasizing students' views at the expense of teachers' expertise and professional judgement; without careful consideration of this, students gain unrealistic influence over processes, content, outcomes and purposes.

Resisting the demand for more and more clarity

The inexorable drive for transparency and attempts to make criteria more precise, easier to understand, and therefore easier for students to use, leads to unrealistic expectations on both sides and to a growing unwillingness to take risks, to teach topics outside the criteria, and to emphasize constant external motivation.

Challenging expectations for more and more individual support

Coaching to the criteria has moved to a new level of intensity in some courses, where mentoring and support seem to be the only things to get students through. This can lead to a paucity of aspirations that students can manage without it.

Locating practices in a subject domain

The growing array of generic life, work and personal attributes, dispositions and behaviours (aka 'skills') added over the past 30 years to vocational education, and an emphasis in vocational education and ALLN on encouraging a positive attitude to 'engagement' in processes (aka 'inclusion') detract from a serious focus on cognitive progression and development of concepts, knowledge and skills in subject domains.

Conclusion

Advice to teachers in further and adult education typically comprises bullet-point checklists: indeed, we have a couple in this chapter! While sometimes useful, they do not help teachers take account of the factors that will make them take very different forms depending on the learning culture.

Instead, we have aimed to highlight factors crucial to all formative assessment approaches that are genuinely educationally worthwhile. These include:

- strong and confident expectations of motivation from well-qualified subject teachers who are confident, expert and enthusiastic;
- clarity of purpose and subject focus of any formative assessment;
- positive images of potential, intrinsic motivation, achievement and ability;
- a clear subject focus, whether practical, theoretical or both, on which to develop a clear sense of cognitive progression in understanding and skill.

Although there are significant pressures in the learning cultures of ALLN and vocational education militating against these factors, it is hard to escape the fact that they counter negative images of demotivation, a view that students will not like or tolerate particular processes, the supposedly fixed nature of 'learning styles' and other negative images common in many courses, including 'vulnerable', 'fragile' 'learners'. Without attention to these pressures, teachers surrender more of their expertise and authority.

We saw glimpses in our research of learning cultures that resist these trends. Teachers with a clear sense of purpose and expertise were central to that resistance. We believe that a need to rethink subject content and stereotypes of students, both within vocational education domains, but also more broadly, is key to resisting instrumentalism. Here, the recommendations of the extensive Nuffield Review of 14–19 Education are highly relevant and important, both endorsing and confirming our own findings.

First, it calls for a radical and far-reaching exploration of teaching, assessment and general and vocational subjects for 14–19-year-olds. In our study, it seemed that radical ideas were needed for young people such as those on e2e programmes. In this case, imaginative community and arts projects offer a much broader view of both learning and subject content, where young people deemed to be beyond education benefit hugely from liberal and arts subjects, including classical music and dance. Of course, this is just one example: it signals the need to rethink completely the content and purpose of general and vocational education.

Second, we need to challenge and resist the endemic language of targets, delivery and the associated practices of teaching to the test. Yet, as we have argued, this is not the only damaging language: learning and learners, and all the associated mantras we have highlighted throughout the book also need to be questioned.

Finally, we agree with the views of Richard Pring, the Nuffield Review's director, writing in the Education Guardian in 2009, that inserting self-related personal skills, and related notions such as thinking skills is no compensation for sound subject-based teaching:

> If you're teaching literature, maths or history well, you are teaching young people to think for themselves. Teaching 'thinking skills' as an abstract subject makes no sense and it is uninteresting. Young people switch off.

> Teachers need to be seen to be experts in the subject, whether that is history, science or crafts. They have to have the motivation to share their passion for their subject.

This means asserting much more clearly and strongly a need to resist teaching to the assessment criteria and to resist the shaping of teaching and assessment methods, and subject content, around personal attributes and dispositions and 'transferable skills', and to encourage a return to topic-based teaching.

Of course, it is stating the obvious that there are profound structural constraints to all these ideas, alongside severe constraints on conditions of service and opportunities for professional development: unemployment, uncertain job and educational opportunities for young people and adults after their courses have finished and constraints on time and resources. And, of course, some students will never be drawn to do more than take part with minimal engagement or get through without close coaching and support, while SfL tests, prescriptive and limiting assessment specifications, punitive targets and lack of professional development militate against the spirit of formative assessment.

As we acknowledged at the start of this chapter, it is all too easy for researchers to observe practice, and the factors that make it take one form or another, and then to come up with what they see as good advice. Nevertheless, this should not stop us arguing that structural constraints, pernicious instrumentalism, and low expectations that we can motivate students beyond targets that focus or themselves raise intractable questions about what knowledge and skills young people need, and what subject content, coherent curricula and professional expertise might support them.

To address these problems, developing a theory of learning is much less pressing than developing a coherent theory of education, resisting the dominance of assessment on teaching, and creating an alternative to the subject of the self. Unless we put the subject back into the learning cultures of vocational education and ALNN, we cannot transform formative assessment.

Notes

1. See also Atkins (2009) for a detailed study of young people on Level 1 courses in an FE college.
2. See for example James and Biesta (2007).
3. Black et al. (2003); James et al. (2007).
4. These popular booklets are published by NFER, see www.nfer-nelson. co.uk.
5. Furedi (2009).
6. James and Biesta (2007); Ecclestone and Bailey (2009); Atkins (2009).
7. Young (2007); see also Furedi (2009); Ecclestone and Hayes (2009).
8. See James and Biesta (2007); Coffield et al. (2008); Coffield (2008).
9. Hayward et al. (2005, 2009).
10. Coffield (1999).

Bibliography

Ainley, P. and Corney, M. (1990) *Training for the Future: The Rise and Fall of the Manpower Services Commission*. London: Cassell.

Alexander, R. (2001) *Culture and Pedagogy: International Comparisons in Primary Education*. Oxford: Blackwell.

Assessment Reform Group (2002) *10 Principles of Assessment for Learning*. Cambridge: University of Cambridge Press.

Atkins, E. (2009) *Invisible Students, Impossible Dreams: Experiencing Vocational Education 14–19*. Stoke-on-Trent: Trentham Books.

Avis, J. (2009) *Education, Policy and Social Justice: Learning and Skills*, 2nd edn. London: Continuum.

Baird, J., Cresswell, M. and Newton, P. (2000) Would the real gold standard please step forward?, *Research Papers in Education*, 15(2): 213–19.

Ball, S.J., David, M. and Reay, D. (2005) *Degrees of Difference*. London: RoutledgeFalmer.

Ball, S.J., Maguire, M. and Macrae, S. (2000) *Choices, Pathways and Transitions Post-16: New Youth, New Economies in the Global City*. London: RoutledgeFalmer.

Barnett, R. (1994) *The Limits of Competence*. Buckingham: Open University Press.

Bates, I. (1998a) The empowerment dimension in GNVQs: a critical exploration of discourse, pedagogic apparatus and school implementation, *Evaluation and Research in Education*, 12(1): 7–22.

Bates, I. (1998b) Resisting 'empowerment' and realising power: an exploration of aspects of the GNVQ, *Journal of Education and Work*, 11(2): 187–205.

Bathmaker, A-M. (2002) Wanting to be somebody: post-16 students' and teachers' constructions of full-time GNVQs in a college of further education, PhD thesis, University of Warwick.

Bathmaker, A.M (2005) Hanging in or shaping a future? Defining a role for vocationally related learning in a 'knowledge' society, *Journal of Education Policy*, 20(1): 81–100.

BERA (British Educational Research Association) (2004) *Revised Ethical Guidelines for Educational Research*. www.bera-ac.uk/publications/guidelines

Biesta, G.J.J. (2007) Why 'what works' won't work: evidence-based practice and the democratic deficit of educational research, *Educational Theory*, 57(1): 1–22.

Black, P. (2000) Research and the development of educational assessment, *Oxford Review of Education*, 26(3 & 4): 407–19.

Black, P. (2007) The importance of feedback in formative assessment, keynote presentation to Improving Formative Assessment Project conference, National College of School Leadership, Nottingham, February.

Black, P., Harrison, C., Lee, C., Marshall, M. and Wiliam, D. (2003) *Assessment for Learning: Putting It into Practice*. Buckingham: Open University Press.

Black, P., McCormick, R., James, M. and Pedder, D. (2006) Learning how to learn and assessment for learning: a theoretical inquiry, *Research Papers in Education*, 18(4): 119–32.

Black, P. and Wiliam, D. (1998) Assessment and classroom learning, *Assessment in Education*, 18: 1–73.

Black, P. and Wiliam, D. (2009) Developing the theory of formative assessment, *Educational Assessment, Evaluation and Accountability*, 2(1): 5–31.

Bloomer, M. and Hodkinson, P. (2000) Learning careers: continuity and change in young people's dispositions to learning, *British Educational Research Journal*, 26(5): 583–98.

Bloxham, S. and West, A. (2006) Tell me so that I can understand, paper presented at European Association for Learning and Instruction Assessment Special Interest Group Bi-annual Conference, Darlington, 30 August–1 September.

Broadfoot, P. and Pollard, A. (2000) The changing discourse of assessment policy: the case of English primary education, in A. Filer (ed.) *Assessment: Social Process, Social Product*. London: Falmer Press.

Brookes, B., Derrick, J. and Lavender, P. (2004) *Testing, Testing, Testing: Assessment in Adult Literacy, Language and Numeracy*, a NIACE policy discussion paper, Leicester: National Institute for Adult and Continuing Education.

Boud, D. and Falichov, N. (eds) (2007) *Re-thinking Assessment in Higher Education: Learning for the Long Term*. London: RoutledgeFalmer.

Burgess, T. and Swann, J. (2003) The rejectability of Karl Popper: why Popper's ideas have had so little influence on social practice, *Higher Education Review*, 35(2): 57–65.

Coffield, F. (1999) Breaking the consensus: lifelong learning as social control, *British Education Research Journal*, 25(4): 479–99.

Coffield, F. (2008) *Just Suppose Teaching and Learning Became the First Priority*, paper for the Learning and Skills Development Agency. London: Learning and Skills Network.

Coffield, F., Edward, S., Finlay, I., Hodgson, A., Spours, K. and Steer, R. (2008) *Improving Learning, Skills and Inclusion: The Impact of Policy on Post-Compulsory Education*. London: Routledge.

Colley, H. (2003) *Mentoring for Social Inclusion: A Critical Approach to Nurturing Mentoring Relationships*. London: Routledge.

Colley, H. (2006) Learning how to labour with feeling: class, gender and emotion in childcare, education and training, *Contemporary Issues in Early Childhood*, 7: 15–29.

Colley, H. and Hodkinson, P. (2001) The problem with 'Bridging the Gap': the reversal of structure and agency in addressing social exclusion, *Critical Social Policy*, 21(3): 335–59.

Dale, R., Harris, D., Loveys, M., et al. (1989) *The TVEI Story: Policy, Practice and Preparation for the Workforce*. Buckingham: Open University Press.

Davies, J. (2007) Tentative futures: exploring the formation and transformation of young people's vocational aspirations, PhD thesis, University of Exeter.

Davies, J. and Biesta, G. (2006) Going to college: aspirations and experiences of vocational education students, *Research Papers in Education*, 22(1): 32–41.

Derrick, J., Ecclestone, K. and Merrifield, J. (2007) A balancing act? The English and Welsh model of assessment in adult basic education, in P. Campbell (ed.) *Measures of Success: Assessment and Accountability in Adult Basic Education*. Toronto: Grassroots Press.

DfES (2003) *Every Child Matters*. London: Department for Education and Skills.

Ecclestone, K. (2002) *Learning Autonomy in Post-Compulsory Education: The Politics and Practice of Formative Assessment*. London: RoutledgeFalmer.

Ecclestone, K. (2004) Learning in a comfort zone: cultural and social capital in outcome-based assessment regimes, *Assessment in Education*, 11(1): 30–47.

Ecclestone, K. (2006) *Assessment in Post-14 Education: The Implications of Politics, Principles and Practices for Learning and Achievement*, report for the Nuffield Review of 14–19 Education. Oxford: University of Oxford Press.

Ecclestone, K. (2010) Changing the subject?: interdisciplinary perspectives on emotional well-being and social justice, End of Award Report, ESRC Seminar Series. Swindon: Economic and Social Reserach Council.

Ecclestone, K. and Bailey, J. (2009) Developing students' emotional well-being in a further education college, Final Research Report for Centre for Excellence in Teacher Training, Oxford, Oxford Brookes University.

Ecclestone, K., Biesta, G. and Hughes, M. (eds) (2010) *Transitions and Learning through the Lifecourse*. London: Routledge.

Ecclestone, K. and Daugherty, R. (2005) The politics of formative assessment in the four countries of the UK, in J. Gardner (ed.) *Assessment and Learning*. London: Sage.

Ecclestone, K. and Hayes, D. (2008) *The Dangerous Rise of Therapeutic Education*. London: Routledge.

Ecclestone, K. and Hayes, D. (2009) Changing the subject: the educational implications of emotional well-being, *Oxford Review of Education*, 35(3): 371–89.

Ecclestone, K. and Pryor, J. (2003) 'Learning careers' or 'assessment careers'?: the impact of assessment systems on learning, *British Educational Research Journal*, 29: 471–88.

Edwards, R. and Usher, R. (1994) Disciplining the subject: the power of competence, *Studies in Education of Adults*, 26(1): 1–15.

Eruat, M. (1994) *Developing Professional Knowledge and Competence*. London: Routledge/Falmer.

European Association for Learning and Instruction (2006) Assessment Special Interest Group Bi-annual Conference, Darlington, 30 August–1 September.

Field, J. (2006) *Lifelong Learning and the New Educational Order*, 2nd edn. Stoke-on-Trent: Trentham Books.

Filer, A. (2000) *Assessment: Social Process and Social Product*. London: RoutledgeFalmer.

Further Education Unit (1979) A Basis for Choice. London: FEU.

Furedi, F. (2009) *Wasted: Why Education Isn't Educating*. London: Continuum.

Gardner, J. (ed.) (2005) *Assessment and Learning*. London: Sage.

Gardner, J., Harlen, W., Hayward, L. and Stobart, G. with Montgomery, M. (2010) *Developing Teacher Assessment*. Maidenhead: McGraw-Hill/Open University Press.

Goldstein, H. and Heath, A. (eds) (2000) *Educational Standards*. London: British Academy.

Hall, K., Murphy, P. and Soler, J. (2008) *Pedagogy and Practice: Culture and Identities*. Buckingham: Open University Press.

Hamilton, M. (2009) Managing transitions in skills for life, in K. Ecclestone, G. Biesta and M. Hughes (eds) *Transitions and Learning Through the Lifecourse*. London: Routledge.

Hamilton, M. and Hillier, Y. (2006) *The Changing Face of Adult Literacy: Language and Numeracy 1970–2000: A Critical History*. Stoke-on-Trent: Trentham Books.

Hargreaves, A. (1989) *Curriculum and Assessment Reform*. Buckingham: Open University Press.

Hargreaves, E. (2005) Assessment for learning: thinking outside the black box, *Cambridge Journal of Education*, 35(2): 213–24.

Hayward, G., Hodgson, A., Johnson, J., et al. (2005) *Nuffield 14–19 Review Annual Report*. Oxford: Oxford University Department of Educational Studies.

Hayward, G., Hodgson, A., Johnson, J., et al. (2009) *Nuffield 14–19 Review Final Report*. Oxford: Oxford University Department of Educational Studies.

Hodgson, A. and Spours, K. (2003) *Beyond A-levels: Curriculum 2000 and the Reform of 14–19 Qualifications*. London: Kogan Page.

Hodgson, A. and Spours, K. (2008) *Education and Training 14–19: Curriculum, Qualifications and Organization*. London: Sage.

Hodkinson, P. and Issitt, M. (eds) (1995) *The Challenge of Competence*. London: Cassell.

Hodkinson, P., Sparkes, A.C. and Hodkinson, H. (1996) *Triumphs and Tears: Young People, Markets and the Transition from School to Work*. London: David Fulton.

Hyland, T. (1994) *Competence, Education and NVQs*. London: Cassell.

Ivanic, R., Edwards, R., Barton, D. et al. (2009) *Improving Learning in College: Rethinking Literacies across the Curriculum*. London: Routledge.

James, D. and Biesta, G. (2007) *Improving Learning Cultures in Further Education*. London: Routledge.

James, M. (2005) Assessment, teaching and theories of learning, in J. Gardner (ed.) *Assessment and Learning*. London: Sage.

James, M., McCormick, R., Black, P. et al. (2007) *Improving Learning: How to Learn, in Classrooms, Schools and Networks*. London: Routledge.

Jessup, G. (1991) *Outcomes: NVQs and the Emerging Model of Education and Training*. London: Falmer.

Journal of Vocational Education and Training (2004) Special edition *Transforming Learning Cultures in Further Education*, 55(4): 389–518.

Kemmis, S. and McTaggart, R. (eds) (1988) *The Action Research Planner*. Victoria, Australia: Deakin University Press.

Lawy, R., Quinn, J. and Diment, K. (2009) Listening to 'the thick bunch': (mis)understanding and (mis)interpretation of young people in jobs without training in the South West of England, *British Journal of Sociology of Education*, 30(6): 741–55.

Marshall, B. and Drummond, M.J. (2006) How teachers engage with assessment for learning: lessons from the classroom, *Research Papers in Education*, 18(4): 119–32.

McNair, S. (1995) Outcomes and autonomy, in J. Burke (ed.) *Outcomes, Learning and the Curriculum: Implications for NVQS, GNVQS and Other Qualifications*. London: Falmer Press.

Otter, S. (1989) *Understanding Learning Outcomes*. Leicester: Unit for the Development of Adult and Continuing Education.

Otter, S. (1995) Assessing competence: the experience of the Enterprise in Higher Education initiative, in P. Knight, and A. Edwards (eds) *Assessing Competence in Higher Education*. London: Kogan Page.

Pollard, A. and Filer, A. (1999) *The Social World of Pupil Career: Strategic Biographies Through Primary School*. London: Cassell.

Popper, K. (1961 [1957]) *The Poverty of Historicism*. London: Routlege and Kegan Paul.

Popper, K. (1979 [1972]) *Objective Knowledge: An Evolutionary Approach*. Oxford: Oxford University Press.

Popper, K. (1992 [1962]) *Unended Quest: An Intellectual Autobiography*. London: Routledge.

Prenzel, M., Kramer, K. and Dreschel, B. (2001) Self-interested and interested learning in vocational education, in K. Beck (ed.) *Teaching-Learning Processes in Business Education*. Boston: Kluwer.

Pring, R., Hayward, G., Hodgson, A. et al. (2009a) *The Nuffield Review of 14–19 Education and Training in England and Wales*. London: Nuffield Foundation.

Pring, R., Hayward, G., Hodgson, A. et al. (2009b) *Education for All: The Future of Education and Training for 14–19 Year Olds*. London: Routledge.

Radnor, H., Ball, S. and Burrell, R. (1989) The CPVE, in A. Hargreaves and D. Reynolds (eds) *Education Controversies and Critiques*. London: Falmer Press.

Raggatt, P. and Williams, S. (1999) *Government, Markets and Vocational Qualifications: An Anatomy of Policy*. London: Falmer Press.

Reay, D. and Wiliam, D. (1999) 'I'll be a nothing': structure, agency and the construction of identity through assessment, *British Educational Research Journal*, 25: 343–54.

Sadler, R. (1989) Formative assessment and the design of instructional systems, *Instructional Science*, 18: 119–44.

Social Exclusion Unit (1999) *Bridging the Gap: New Opportunities for 16–18 Year Olds Not In Education, Employment or Training*. London: Cabinet Office.

Social Exclusion Unit (2005) *Transitions: Young Adults with Complex Needs*. London: Cabinet Office.

Stanton, G. (1998) Patterns in development, in S. Tomlinson (ed.) *Education 14–19: Critical Perspectives*. London: Athlone Press.

Stobart, G. (2008) *Testing Times: Uses and Abuses of Assessment*. London: Routledge.

Swann, J. and Arthurs, J. (1999) Empowering lecturers: a problem-based approach to improve assessment practice, *Higher Education Review*, 31(2): 50–74.

Swann, J. and Ecclestone, K. (1999) Empowering lecturers to improve assessment practice in higher education, in J. Swann and J. Pratt. (eds)

Improving Education: Realist Approaches to Method and Research. London: Cassell.

Tomlinson Working Group (2005) *Reform of the 14–19 Curriculum*. London: Department for Education and Skills.

Torrance, H., Colley, H., Garratt, D. et al. (2005) The impact of different modes of assessment on achievement and progress in the learning and skills sector, Learning and Skills Development Agency, available at https://www.lsda.org.uk/cims/order.aspx?code=052284&src=XOWEB.

Torrance, H. and Pryor, J. (1998) *Investigating Formative Assessment: Teaching, Learning and Assessment in the Classroom*. Buckingham: Open University Press.

Turner, P. (2007) The transition to work and adulthood, in D. Hayes, T. Marshall and A. Turner (eds) *A Lecturer's Guide to Teaching in Further Education*. Buckingham: Open University Press.

Unit for the Development of Adult and Continuing Education (1994) *Learning Outcomes in Higher Education*. London: Further Education Unit/UDACE.

Usher, R. and Edwards, R. (1994) *Postmodernism and Education: Different Voices, Different Worlds*. London: Routledge.

Wallace, S. (2007) *Getting the Buggers Motivated in FE*, FE Toolkit Series. London: Kogan Page.

Williams, J. (2009) Social inclusion, education and New Labour, PhD thesis, Canterbury, Canterbury Christ Church University.

Winter, R. and Maisch, R. (1996) *Professional Competence in Higher Education*. London: Falmer Press.

Wolf, A. (1995) *Competence-based Assessment*. Buckingham: Open University Press.

Young, M. (2007) *Bringing Knowledge Back In: From Social Constructivism to Social Realism in the Sociology of Education*. London: Routledge.

Index